Trust in Regulatory Regimes

Trust in Regulatory Regimes

Edited by

Frédérique Six

Associate Professor of Public Governance, Vrije Universiteit Amsterdam, the Netherlands

Koen Verhoest

Research Professor in Public Administration, University of Antwerp, Belgium

Edward Elgar
PUBLISHING

Cheltenham, UK • Northampton, MA, USA

Published by
Edward Elgar Publishing Limited
The Lypiatts
15 Lansdown Road
Cheltenham
Glos GL50 2JA
UK

Edward Elgar Publishing, Inc.
William Pratt House
9 Dewey Court
Northampton
Massachusetts 01060
USA

A catalogue record for this book
is available from the British Library

Library of Congress Control Number: 2016949976

This book is available electronically in the **Elgar**online
Business subject collection
DOI 10.4337/9781785365577

MIX
Paper from
responsible sources
FSC® C013604

ISBN 978 1 78536 556 0 (cased)
ISBN 978 1 78536 557 7 (eBook)

Typeset by Servis Filmsetting Ltd, Stockport, Cheshire
Printed and bound by CPI Group (UK) Ltd, Croydon, CR0 4YY

Contents

Contributors

Erik Baekkeskov is Lecturer of Public Policy and Political Science at The University of Melbourne's School of Social and Political Sciences. He has previously held research and teaching positions in the United States and Denmark. His work investigates factors that shape public decision- and policy-making. His empirical interests include public health events and public sector reforms. His work has appeared in various edited volumes and in journals including *Administration & Society, Disaster Prevention & Management, Governance, Journal of European Public Policy, Policy Sciences* and *Public Administration*.

Geert Bouckaert is full Professor at the KU Leuven Public Governance Institute. He is currently President of the International Institute of Administrative Sciences (IIAS), and is former President of the European Group for Public Administration (EGPA). His main fields of research are (comparative) public management reform, performance management and financial management in public administration.

Betsy Carter is Assistant Professor of Political Science at the University of New Hampshire. She recently spent two years as a researcher at the Max Planck Institute for the Study of Societies in Cologne, Germany, and one year as a lecturer in comparative politics at the University of California Irvine. She earned her PhD in political science at the University of California Berkeley and her MPA from the University of Washington. Her research combines politics with sociology, economics and history to explore the dynamics between politics, producer organization, the construction of taste, and market prices in high value-added sectors. Her current research investigates the political construction of taste and value in the fashion, food, and music sectors, building on her past research on wine markets. Carter's past professional experience includes consulting for the World Bank and researching as a Visiting Scholar at Collegio Carlo Alberto (University of Turin).

Russell W. Mills is Associate Professor in the Department of Political Science at Bowling Green State University. His research is focused on improving governance, accountability and performance in regulation and crisis management networks. He has received two grants from the

IBM Center for the Business of Government to explore the use of voluntary reporting programs by the Federal Aviation Administration. His work has appeared in outlets including *Regulation and Governance*, *The Journal of Public Policy*, *The Journal of Benefit–Cost Analysis*, and *Public Administration Review*, where his 2012 article on the response to Hurricane Katrina won the Marshall Dimock Award for best lead article in the journal.

Lovisa Näslund is Assistant Professor at Stockholm Business School at Stockholm University and researcher at the Stockholm Centre for Organizational Research (Score). She received her PhD in business administration in 2012 from Stockholm School of Economics. In her research, she has studied the creation of trust in systems and inter-personal relations on markets and across organizational boundaries in professional services and in the agri-food sector. Her research interests also include organizational storytelling, and its impact on organizational change and sensemaking. Her research has been published in journals such as *Human Relations*, and has been highlighted in *The Economist*.

Peter Oomsels is Researcher at the KU Leuven Public Governance Institute. He obtained his PhD in Social Sciences with a dissertation on interorganizational trust in the Flemish administration. His fields of research are interorganizational trust, public administration and public management reform. He holds master's degrees in Public Management and in Policy Economics.

Dorit Rubinstein Reiss is Professor of law at UC Hastings College of the Law. She has researched and published in the areas of comparative and domestic administrative law and regulation, with a focus on agency accountability, and teaches administrative law.

Frédérique Six is Associate Professor of Public Governance at the Vrije Universiteit Amsterdam. Her research focuses on public governance issues and in particular the relation between trust and control. She applies this to regulation and to how (public) professionals are governed. She has published in journals such as *Public Management Review*, *Journal of Management Studies*, *International Review of Administrative Sciences* and *Journal of Comparative Policy Analysis*, and co-edited *The Trust Process* (with Bart Nooteboom, Edward Elgar, 2003) and *Local Integrity Systems* (with Leo Huberts and Frank Anechiarico, Boom, 2008). She is associate editor of the *Journal of Trust Research* and member of the strategic advisory board of the Netherlands Food and Consumer Product Safety Authority.

Kristina Tamm Hallström is Associate Professor in Management at the Stockholm School of Economics and Director of Research at the Stockholm Centre for Organizational Research (Score). She has conducted research on the construction of legitimacy and authority within transnational standard setting and certification and accreditation as auditing practices. Tamm Hallström is the author of *Organizing International Standardization* (2004, Edward Elgar) and has published articles in journals such as *Organization, Global Environmental Politics* and *Nature+Culture*.

Haiko Van der Voort is Assistant Professor at Delft University of Technology, Faculty of Technology, Policy, and Management. His research focuses on regulation and governance in varying institutional environments, such as organizations, markets, nations, and supranational communities. For this he uses theory of both organizations and regulation. He earned his PhD with an extensive study on co-regulation, focusing on operational interaction between public and private regulators. Other topics of study include supranational co-regulation and risk management dialogue between organizations and regulators. He teaches public administration, organization theory, and institutional design for undergraduate students, graduate students and professionals.

Hans Van Ees is founding dean of the University College Groningen and Professor of corporate governance and institutions at the Faculty of Economics and Business of the University of Groningen (the Netherlands). His research deals with corporate governance, theory of business groups, board of directors and sustainable corporate performance. He is associate editor of *Corporate Governance: An International Review*, and as director of the *Corporate Governance Insights Centre* of the University of Groningen, involved in executive teaching, consultancy and research for private companies and the Dutch government on the principles of good governance.

Koen Verhoest is Research Professor (BOF/ZAP Hoogleraar) at the Research Group on Public Administration and Management, Department of Political Science at the University of Antwerp, Belgium. His main research interest is on the organizational aspects of public tasks and their (regulatory) governance in multi-level and multi-actor contexts, including the autonomy, control and coordination of (regulatory and other) agencies, the governance of liberalized markets, and the governance of public private partnerships. He has published in journals like *Governance, Organization Studies, Review of Public Personnel Administration, Public Management Review, International Public Management Journal, International Review of Administrative Sciences, Public Performance and Management Review,*

International Public Management Journal and *Transport Reviews*. Recent international books include *Multi-level regulation in the telecommunications sector*; *Autonomy and control of state agencies – comparing states and agencies*; *The coordination of public sector organizations*; as well as *Government Agencies: Practices and lessons from 30 countries* (with others). Since July 2012 he has been co-chair of the ECPR Standing Group on Regulatory Governance together with assoc. Prof. Anne Meuwese (University of Tilburg).

1. Trust in regulatory regimes: scoping the field

Frédérique Six and Koen Verhoest

This edited volume is the first endeavour to systematically investigate the role of trust in the different relations within regulatory regimes. Academics as far back as John Locke have argued that trust is the bond of society or a lubricant for social relations. So it would seem logical to assume that it also plays this role within regulatory regimes. But within public administration and political science in general, trust is a concept whose role is contested. Authors such as Rosanvallon (2008) argue that a democracy involves mechanisms grown from distrust for those in power, while others show the beneficial effects of trust in government. The role of trust between regulator and regulated actor is also contested, with some authors showing empirically how trust improves public safety (e.g., Gunningham and Sinclair, 2009b), while others focus on the detrimental societal effects of regulatory capture. The aim of this book is to scope the field, with a review of the literature and a selected set of more detailed contributions; and to set the agenda for further research.

In this introductory chapter we map the different relations within regulatory regimes and review empirical research into the role of trust within these different relations. Our literature review reveals several themes that we address either in the different empirical chapters or in the research agenda formulated in the concluding chapter. The chapter is structured as follows: first we provide a brief overview of the two central concepts regulation and trust. Then we map the different trust relations within regulatory regimes. Next we present the results of a semi-systematic literature review of empirical research into regulation and trust. We conclude by introducing the contributions to this edited volume.

REGULATION AND TRUST

Conceptualizing Regulation

Regulation is a concept that has many different meanings in the English language and definitions of regulation vary widely (see Black, 2002, for an overview). This variation seems to centre on the actors involved and their mandates (Black, 2002; Grabosky, 2013; Hood et al., 2001). Traditionally, regulation was a state activity performed in a strictly hierarchical relation with only one actor involved as the regulator: the state. The limits of this approach have been recognized for many decades, which led to the study of the role of non-state actors, such as public interest groups and market actors (e.g., Ayres & Braithwaite, 1992; Black, 2008; Braithwaite, 2008; Grabosky, 2013; Hood et al., 2001).There is less variation in the activities that regulation consists of: standard-setting, information-gathering, judging whether standards have been met and, where necessary, behaviour-modification through sanctions (e.g., Black, 2002; Braithwaite, 2008; Hood et al., 2001). This approach comes from the cybernetics literature where no attention is paid to the role of rewards in stimulating and reinforcing desired behaviour. However, in social systems rewards are relevant in regulating behaviour. This expands the last activity of behaviour-modification to behaviour-influencing.

In this edited volume we focus on what the OECD has defined as "regulatory enforcement", "covering all activities of state structures (or structures delegated by the state) aimed at promoting compliance and reaching regulations' outcomes" (OECD, 2014, p. 11), but extend the analysis to include private regulation as well. There is an important difference between public and private regulation, which is relevant for trust. Normally, regulation by public actors is nonvoluntary, while private regulation is voluntary. And where certification (a form of private regulation) is obligatory, for example in the Dutch asbestos removal sector, the regulated actor has a choice which certifying institution to hire. In other words, regulated actors may select the regulator that they trust most.[1]

In terms of actors involved, traditionally the state was in the central command and control role. It was assumed that the state had the capacity to command and control and was the only controller (Black, 2002). Over time, as the central role of government receded, other actors are acknowledged to also perform roles in regulatory regimes. Sometimes non-state actors only play a role in information gathering or participate in standard setting and states still have the central role in judgment and enforcement. But increasingly non-state actors are seen to also participate in forming the judgment and have a role in the enforcement of rules through their capacity to impose sanctions on perpetrators (e.g., Grabosky, 2013). But to play an effective role, the actor involved in information gathering has to have a mandate to collect relevant information, while the regulated actor is often not keen to provide that information, either because it is sensitive information for its reputation or competitive position, or because it is expensive to collect the information. The actor involved in behaviour influencing often, but not always, needs a mandate to punish a regulated actor who is found to be in violation. An interesting development in this context is the role of activist groups towards business firms: without such an official mandate activist groups have devised many tactics to influence the behaviour of firms whom they believe are not operating in a socially responsible way; these tactics include, for example, demonstrations, shareholder activism, negative publicity, boycotts and buycotts (e.g., Den Hond et al., 2010).

Conceptualizing Trust

Trust has been studied in many different academic disciplines and this has resulted in many different definitions. Dietz (2011) provides a useful overview of the trust process distinguishing between (1) trustworthiness: the beliefs, (2) trust decision and (3) trust-informed actions (see also Dietz & Den Hartog, 2006). "[T]here is *always* an assessment (however thorough) of the other party's trustworthiness which informs a preparedness to be vulnerable that, in genuine cases of trust, leads to a risk-taking act" (Dietz, 2011, p. 215). Authors place different emphasis on different phases of the universal trust process depending on whether they define trust as an attitude or belief, or as an action. A definition that is widely accepted only focuses on one step of the trust process, "trust is a psychological state comprising the intention to accept vulnerability based upon the positive expectations of the intentions or behavior of another" (Rousseau et al., 1998, p. 395). Trust implies that there is uncertainty about the trustee's future behaviour. Möllering's key point regarding trust is that none of the three bases that he identifies – reasons, routines/roles or reflexivity – can ever provide certainty about the trusted party's future actions and therefore, trust inevitably involves a leap of faith in which the "irreducible social vulnerability and uncertainty [are suspended] *as if* they were favourably resolved" (Möllering, 2006b, p. 111).

Trust is a relational concept: an actor trusts another actor with respect to a certain future behaviour (Hardin, 2002; Nooteboom, 2002). The relatively simple trust relationship is that between two persons: John trusts Beth. Usually there is a reverse relationship as well: Beth may also trust John. But usually what the trust is about differs in a relationship. The uncertainty an inspector faces when inspecting a regulated actor is different from the uncertainty the director of the regulated actor faces because of that inspection. So inspector John may trust director Beth if she provides all the information he needs for his inspection, while director Beth trusts inspector John if he is fair and procedurally just in his judgement (cf Murphy et al., 2009).

Important in trust is that it is not simply the more trust the better it is. Trust is not always justified. But at the same time, generic distrust is also not justified (Hardin, 1993). The key question is: how well do I know the other so that I can trust the other to do what I need her to do (Gabarro, 1978)? Trust and distrust are both selective: how well can the trustworthy be distinguished from the not trustworthy? How much tolerance for errors in the judgment is acceptable? The answer to the last question will depend on the risks involved in making errors. This may be different in regulating hospital operating rooms compared with regulating higher education or tax.

In this volume we focus on regulated actors that are organizations, and since regulators are also organizations operating within regulatory regimes, we are not only interested in trust in organizations but also in trust in systems.

Trust in Organizations and Systems

Both trust in organizations and trust in systems are multilevel constructs (cf Kroeger, 2012; Kroeger & Bachmann, 2013; Möllering, 2006a; Sydow, 2006): trust exists at the interpersonal level, where the "face work" (cf Giddens, 1990) takes place and at the organizational or system level that is independent of specific individuals. How these two levels – interpersonal and organizational/system level – connect and interact is still an outstanding issue.

As Möllering (2006a) notes in his review of the literature on trust in institutions, both Simmel and Luhmann suggest that trust in systems is not much more than an assumption that a system is functioning, and a willingness to place trust in that system without placing trust in people. Luhmann (1979) adds that system trust includes the assumption that everybody else also trusts the system. In his conceptualization experts play the role of controlling the system to ensure its proper functioning. Giddens (1990) also gives experts a central role to play in system trust, but in his conceptualization they are the representatives of the system at the "access points" where the trustor experiences the system. It is not clear, however, how exactly trust in these experts and trust in the abstract system connect and interact.

Kroeger (2012; Kroeger & Bachmann 2013) has begun to formulate a theory about possible institutionalization processes to explain this interaction for trust in organizations. Trusting organizations occurs when "an actor who trusts an organization makes themselves vulnerable to the actions of others who are guided by the organization, based on what the actor knows about the regularities of organizational behaviour and about the behavioural incentives and norms as set by the organization" (Kroeger, 2012, p. 747). Effective face work by the boundary spanner, i.e. the person interacting on behalf of the organization with the outside world (cf Williams, 2002), leads to trust in that individual, but as they represent the organization, it is also role-based trust: "a transference from interpersonal to organizational trust can occur if the representative's conduct is viewed as typical of the organization" (Kroeger, 2012, p. 747). And the other way around, organizational characteristics will help facilitate the trust in the individual representative when that individual is not yet known to the outside world.

For the first phase in the trust process (cf Dietz, 2011), trustworthiness judgements, many different categorizations for dimensions of trustworthiness have been proposed, with Mayer et al.'s (1995) Ability, Benevolence and Integrity (ABI) model as possibly the most often cited. A common distinction appears to be two dimensions of trustworthiness: competence, which concerns expectations of the abilities of the organization, and goodwill, which relates to expectations of integrity and non-harmful behaviour (Dekker, 2004; Sako, 1998; Searle et al., 2011). Benevolence and integrity are taken together in this second categorization, as empirically there is often not a clear distinction between these two dimensions, especially in organizational or system trust. Dietz (2011) argues that in almost all situations people use multiple sources of evidence for their assessment of the other party's trustworthiness, the most common sources being institutional and interactional. In interpersonal trust relations the interactional source is most directly relevant, with the institutional source operating more in the background. When assessing an organization's trustworthiness, however, both may be equally relevant but this remains an underexplored area. Giddens (1990, p. 34) relates trust in organizations to "reliability and faith in the correctness of abstract principles", while Maguire and Phillips (2008: 372) define organizational trust as "an individual's expectation that some organized system will act with predictability and goodwill".

Individuals trust, but is it possible for organizations to trust as well? Researchers have different views on that. Janowicz-Panjaitan and Krishnan (2009) argue that only individuals can trust and not organizations. Kroeger (2012) used institutionalization theory to propose that individuals' trusting behaviours may be institutionalized within their organization as they get replicated and habitualized "due to the economy of effort this affords the actors" (p. 751), which would in turn make it more likely that other individuals that are guided by the organization, i.e. work there, will trust as well.

Trust between organizations in a collaboration has been studied extensively in business research and relatively more recently in public administration research. Much of the literature on public collaboration points at trust as a key success factor, but does not delve deeply into processes of trust building, maintenance or repair (e.g., Ansell & Gash, 2008; Isett et al., 2011; Klijn et al., 2010; Klijn et al., 2016; Klijn & Eshuis 2013; McGuire, 2006; Thomson & Perry, 2006; Vangen & Huxham, 2003; Weber & Khademian, 2008; Weber et al., 2007; Williams, 2002). In the business literature inter-organizational collaborations are assumed to occur between two (or more) organizations that choose to collaborate. In most public collaborations this assumption does not hold. Most public collaborations are geographically determined. The Dutch tax office cannot choose to collaborate with the German Food Authority, because the relationship is better; it has to collaborate with the Dutch Food Authority. How this obligatory relationship affects trust building and cooperation is as yet unclear.

Trust and Related Concepts

When researching trust in regulatory regimes, the relations between trust and distrust, confidence and control need to be reviewed.

Trust and distrust

In the public debate and some academic literature it is often assumed that low trust equals distrust, but that is incorrect; trust and distrust are best conceptualized as distinct concepts (Lewicki et al., 1998; Oomsels, 2016; Van de Walle & Six, 2014). Also, many trust researchers focus on the positive side of trust, assuming that the higher the trust the better it is, and they see distrust as dysfunctional, assuming that broken trust always needs to be repaired. But as Luhmann (1979, 1988) argues conceptually, trust and distrust are functional equivalents. Oomsels, Callens, Vanschoenwinkel & Bouckaert (2016) empirically investigate the functional and dysfunctional aspects of both trust and distrust in interorganizational relations in the public sector, and find that distrust can be functional in such relations.

However, even though distrust can be functional when the context warrants it, in the long run functional trust has more benefits in a democracy, or possibly more precisely absence of active distrust. Hardin (2004) argues that active trust in government involves knowledge about how government operates that goes beyond what can be expected of normal citizens. He introduces the concept of active distrust as he argues that we should not strive for citizen trust but work towards avoiding that citizens actively distrust government. For citizens to actively distrust, they need to have enough information to form such an informed judgement, which is often lacking.

Trust and confidence

Luhmann (1988) distinguishes trust from confidence, a distinction that many trust researchers nowadays seem to disregard. Confidence is the normal everyday situation: "you are confident that your expectations will not be disappointed" (p. 97). You not only disregard the possibility of disappointment because you think it is unlikely, but also "because you do not know what else to do", i.e., you experience a situation where you cannot see an alternative. Trust, on the other hand, "presupposes a situation of risk" (p. 97) and you can avoid taking this risk. Luhmann adds an interesting requirement for trust: "trust is only required if a bad outcome would make you regret your action" (1988, p. 98), because you had a choice between alternatives and would with hindsight choose another alternative. This would imply that much of what we now call trust in institutions or systems is really confidence.

A distinction between trust and confidence is also made by Earle et al. (2007) in their Trust, Confidence and Cooperation (TCC) model, which sees two principal pathways to cooperation. One path is via social trust and is based on morality information, while the second path is via confidence and is based on performance information, *"trust* is social and relational; *confidence* is instrumental and calculative" (Earle, 2009, p. 786). Earle et al. (2007) see the two concepts as connected. The bases for confidence "are justified and accepted only within the group or community of trust that generated them. Also, any judgment of trust presupposes judgements of confidence" (Earle et al., 2007, p. 4). And "loss of confidence makes trust necessary for establishing a new record of experience or past performance, allowing the replacement of trust by confidence" (p. 5). The implications are, they claim, that in times of low social uncertainty, when morality information is not relevant, social trust does not play the dominant role in cooperation. Social trust becomes more important in times of uncertainty, when morality information is relevant. They refer to a long list of often cited sources to claim the "ubiquity of [their] two core concepts: trust [. . .] and confidence" (p. 11), even though these sources do not use the concept of confidence, but only trust (e.g., Das & Teng, 1998; Kramer, 1999; Lewicki & Bunker, 1995; Rousseau et al., 1998; Sitkin & Roth, 1993; Zucker, 1986).

Our position is that Earle et al. (2007) push Luhmann's distinction between trust and confidence too far by making all competence-related bases about confidence and all system- and institution-based trust to them is really about confidence. We call for a proper comparative study into these different conceptualizations in our agenda for future research in the concluding chapter. For clarity's sake, we choose to talk only of trust unless in our review of the literature authors make the distinction between trust and confidence when they apply the TCC model.

Trust and control

The different perspectives found in both the academic literature and the public debate about the relationship between trust and control are relevant to regulation, since regulation may be viewed as a form of control. After all, regulation is about setting standards, gathering information, judging and intervening (Black, 2002) and so is control (e.g., Weibel, 2007). The dominant perspective on the relation between trust and control is that they are substitutes (for an overview of perspectives see Das & Teng, 2001; Weibel, 2007); the dominant regulation theory, responsive regulation theory fits in that perspective (Ayres & Braithwaite, 1992). More generally in the literature on democracy (e.g., Rosanvallon, 2008) this is also the dominant perspective; when you trust, you cannot control and when you control, you do not trust, as control is done from distrust. This makes trust blind. In this perspective, it is almost impossible to get the regulatory relationship between regulator and regulatee to be a trusting relationship.

The other perspective on the relationship between trust and control is that they can complement each other. Control may strengthen trust and vice versa, if certain conditions are met. These conditions have been studied in manager-subordinate relationship and in business alliances and supplier-customer relationships (e.g., Das & Teng, 2001; Weibel, 2007). Six (2013) proposed that the same underlying theory appears to be applicable to regulatory relations and thus proposes that trust and control may also strengthen each other in regulatory relationships. This underlying theory is Self Determination Theory (Deci & Ryan, 2000; Ryan & Deci, 2000). Six identifies empirical studies that support her propositions. When the standards are set in dialogue between regulator and regulatee and when interpretation of information collected is done with input from regulatees, regulation is more likely to generate trust. Also the more regulatees experience procedural justice and restorative justice, the more likely it is that regulation generates trust. And finally, competence on the part of the regulatee to understand the regulations and comply with them is important (Six, 2013).

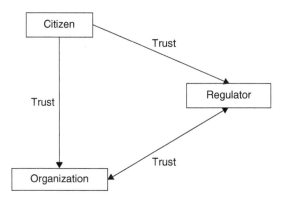

Figure 1.1   The regulatory trust triangle

MAPPING TRUST RELATIONS IN REGULATORY REGIMES

At the heart of a regulatory regime is the regulatory trust triangle (Figure 1.1) based on third-party trust.

Third-party Trust

Regulation exists because organizations who are providers of goods and services, or employers, may create social, economic or health risks for citizens or risks to the environment (Sparrow, 2000). This makes citizens vulnerable to the actions of those organizations. In principal–agent theory, citizens would be conceptualized as principals with the organization their agents and high vulnerability and risk would be acknowledged in this relationship. Principal–agent theory, however, then comes with several instrumental remedies to reduce the vulnerability. As Möllering (2006b) argued these will never be sufficient to create certainty and reduce all vulnerability. Trust helps to overcome situations of vulnerability as trust is based on positive expectations and then requires a leap of faith which the trustor is more likely to take when risks and vulnerability are deemed small enough and positive expectations high enough (cf Möllering, 2006b).

This creates the first relation in Figure 1.1: between citizens, in whatever role, and regulated organizations. To what degree may citizens trust organizations? Because individual citizens do not have the competencies or access to the information needed to make good judgements about the trustworthiness of these organizations to manage these risks appropriately, regulators are created to provide assurance. Thus, regulators act as third-party providers of trust (cf Nooteboom, 1999) in the relationship between citizens and organizations. Third-party trust works as follows: A is not in a position to make a good judgment about the trustworthiness of B, but C is; and because A trusts C that makes it possible for A to trust C's judgment about B's trustworthiness. So, when C trusts B, A will also trust B. Also, when two actors (A and B) are connected by a mutual third party (C), this third party may exert sanctions that restrain the two actors in the dyad from behaving opportunistically or counter-normatively toward each other (Coleman, 1990). This is what regulators aim to do with regulated organizations. Yet, as Shapiro (1987, p. 648) rightly asks, "who guards the guardians [of trust]?" In most countries there are legal and democratic institutions accessible to both citizens and regulated organizations to challenge regulator actions (or inaction), although this may be costly.

In regulatory regimes, the provision of third-party trust by regulators is only useful as long as citizens trust regulators. "We trust that regulatory judgements are being made honestly by appropriately knowledgeable, motivated and qualified people, who are credibly representing the public for whom they act as proxies" (Downer, 2010, p. 94). When regulators have been "captured" by the regulated sector or organization, they may not be trusted by citizens anymore (Levine & Forrence, 1990).

On the other hand, some authors argue that for regulators to be trusted by citizens, the regulators should distrust the regulated organizations or regulatees (van Montfort, 2010). After all, the argument goes, if regulatees could be trusted, regulatory enforcement is not needed. And after each serious incident where citizens are put at risk, the call for more and stricter regulatory enforcement and more repression (distrust) is strong.

To explain these apparently contradictory perspectives we argue that the latter perspective – that regulators should distrust regulated organizations – is flawed. If indeed *all* regulatees could be trusted *all the time*, regulation would not be needed. When this is not the case, as it often is, this does not imply that *all* regulatees should now be distrusted *all the time*. It is therefore important for regulators to be responsive in their regulatory style to the regulatee's compliance ability and motivation. If regulators distrust regulatees, they should act upon that distrust until regulatees can be trusted to comply with regulation again or stop their activity (Braithwaite, 2008).

Regulators cannot supervise every regulated activity 24/7, so regulation cannot provide 100 per cent certainty; it encompasses irreducible uncertainty and risk. This is regardless of whether regulators trust or distrust regulatees. Below we present empirical evidence from prior research that suggests that trust in the relation between regulators and regulatees has a positive effect on regulatee compliance and therefore helps safeguard public interests and control public risks, provided each performs their role. Interestingly, Näslund and Tamm Hallström (this volume) use a different line of reasoning when they argue that private regulators should communicate to customers that they distrust the businesses that they monitor and certify. We pick this up in the concluding chapter in our agenda for further research.

Polycentric Regulatory Regimes

These three relations form the basic trust triangle for regulation between citizen, regulated organization and regulator. However, this basic trust triangle needs to be further developed to properly encompass all the complexities of regulatory regimes. First, regulated organizations may be private/third sector or public. This distinction is relevant since public organizations are (ultimately) accountable to elected officials, such as members of parliament or local councillors; whereas private organizations are accountable to shareholders and third sector organizations are accountable to those who support them, financially or otherwise. Also, citizens often do not have a choice in which public organization to interact with, while they usually have a choice with which private or third sector organizations they want to be a client. This difference may be relevant for trust. This is why a distinction is made between citizen trust in private/third sector organizations (relation 1) and public organizations (relation 2) in Figure 1.2.

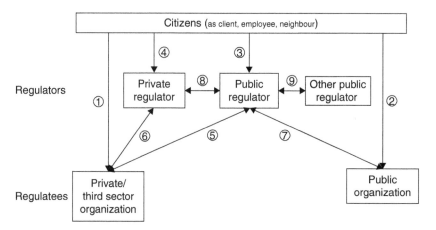

Figure 1.2   Role of trust in different relationships within regulatory regimes

Second, regulators may be public or private. In many situations private regulation is voluntary while public regulation is obligatory. Private regulation often works through private certification that regulates how a provider should interact with customers to take account of customers' interests (e.g., for e-commerce eTrust and Verisign; Bart et al., 2005) or it provides assurance to the consumer that products have the quality that sellers claim, for example sustainable products (see Näslund & Hallström, this volume). Providers pay to be allowed to use that certificate and the certifying company regularly audits the provider. If the provider fails to meet the conditions of the certificate, the provider should not be allowed to use the certificate. This third party trust mechanism works as long as customers trust the certifying company to withhold the certificate if the provider fails to meet the standards; which may be difficult given the commercial relation between private regulator and regulated organization. Hence the distinction between citizen trust in public regulators (relation 3) and citizen trust in private regulators (relation 4) in Figure 1.2.

The relation between regulator and regulated organization is also different when the regulator is public versus private. A public regulator is generally given for a regulated organization; in other words, the regulatee has no choice in the matter. A recent initiative in England, the Primary Authority, gives regulated organizations a choice which local regulator is its primary contact when it operates in many different locations with different local regulators.[2] Often, organizations have a choice between different private certificates or labels, each with their own distinctive criteria. And for each label or certificate there is often a choice among different certifying institutions. In sum, there is usually a choice in private regulator for regulated organizations seeking private regulation, while such a choice is generally lacking in public regulation. This choice is relevant for trust. Hence the distinction in Figure 1.2 between trust between private/third sector organizations and public regulators (relation 5) on the one hand, and trust between private/third sector organizations and private regulators (relation 6) on the other hand. Often, public organizations are also regulated, in particular when they provide public services or when they operate locally with national regulation (relation 7). It is relevant to distinguish this from private/third sector organizations, because the relation between public regulator and public regulatee is embedded within a wider network where the relationship is not necessarily hierarchical but horizontal (see for example, Six and Van Ees, this volume).

The third direction in which the basic regulatory trust triangle needs further development is to acknowledge the different collaborative relations between regulators. Increasingly, regulatory regimes are characterized by multiple regulators. The first is the collaboration between public and private regulators (relation 8). In some instances this is done when regulatory regimes are designed with roles for both private and public regulator (co-regulation) as Van der Voort's study (this volume) shows. In other situations public regulators acknowledge the presence of private regulation and take this into account in their own regulatory strategy, in particular in their risk analyses. In today's increasingly complex society, organizations are often regulated by more than one public regulator, sometimes even at multiple levels of government (e.g. tax, food safety, labour conditions, smoking ban, fire safety for restaurants and bars; or telecom, media and general competition regulators regulating telecom companies active in broadcasting) leading to calls for these regulators to collaborate in order to reduce the administrative burden for the regulated organizations (Jordana & Sancho Royo, 2004; Doern & Johnson, 2006; Aubin & Verhoest, 2014). Furthermore, regulators in different geographic regions need to collaborate when organizations cross jurisdictions (relation 9); examples are tax, food safety or shipping.

A final complication is the role of organizations that represent public interests within regulatory regimes. For example, Abbot (2012) concludes that

> when designing a regulatory framework for new technology, special attention must be paid to the need to ensure that public trusts both technology being regulated and mode of regulation. Whilst a degree of government oversight can promote public trust in several ways, it can also diminish it. To counter this, regulatory controls must provide non-state actors with the tools necessary to hold industry and government to account. (Abbot, 2012, p. 357)

This resonates with Ayres and Braithwaite's (1992) proposal for tripartite regulation. Tripartism, according to Ayres and Braithwaite, gives Public Interest Groups (PIGs) three roles in the regulatory process. PIGs are groups that represent one or more public interests relevant to the regulated organizations, such as consumer interests, environmental interests, worker interests.

> First, it grants the PIG and all its members access to all the information that is available to the regulator. Second, it gives the PIG a seat at the negotiating table with the firm and the agency when deals are done. Third, the policy grants the PIG the same standing to sue or prosecute under the regulatory statute as the regulator. (Ayres & Braithwaite, 1992, pp. 57–8)

The public interest group acts as a guardian to the regulatory arrangement, or as Ayres and Braithwaite call it "contestable guardianship", i.e., the performance of the regulator as the primary guardian may be contested by the public interest group, who represents the vulnerable citizens, in whatever role as consumer, labourer or neighbour to a hazardous plant, that the regulation is meant to protect. We have not included this relation in Figure 1.2 for practical reasons only and will pick this up in our agenda for future research in the concluding chapter. We did not find any empirical studies that included public interest groups as formal actors in regulatory regimes in our semi-systematic search.

EMPIRICAL RESEARCH INTO TRUST IN REGULATORY REGIMES

In this section we report the results from a semi-systematic literature review for empirical research into the relation between trust and regulation in the different relationships that we have identified within regulatory regimes.

Empirical research into regulation and trust within regulatory relations is scattered across many different academic fields and, as a consequence, across many publication outlets. Core fields are law, political science, public administration and sociology, but sector-specific journals also publish research on regulation, for example in health care, environmental management, food, financial services, nano- or biotechnology. This makes it very difficult to do a proper systematic review of the literature, so we cannot and do not claim to be complete or exhaustive. We searched within the Web of Science database in the Social Science Citation Index between 2000 and 2015 on the search terms Trust* *and* Regulat*; and focused on English language journal articles. This generated more than 1000 hits. Next, we selected research areas: law, public administration, sociology, health care, food/agriculture, environment/resource management, education, risky technologies. This generated 500–600 sources that were scanned by title and abstracts; when in doubt they were saved for the next step. The selection was based on whether the article was empirical and whether trust and regulation were the topic of the research or whether the words were just mentioned in passing. Also, the term trust was sometimes used in its legal form such as NHS trust. This selection step generated a list of 125 sources for which the pdfs were downloaded and searched in full on what was said about trust and regulation. When reference was made to another relevant article not captured in our search this article was added to our list. Some conceptual publications found in the search were used to strengthen the previous, conceptual section and the empirical findings.

LITERATURE REVIEW RESULTS

In total 33 empirical studies were found in the literature review. Table 1.1 provides a descriptive overview in terms of which trust relationships are covered, which method was used, and the industry/sector and region of the study. The results of the literature review fall into three main categories: research that focuses on (1) public regulatory trust triangles; (2) private regulatory trust triangles; and (3) collaboration between regulators. These main categories are sometimes further subdivided.

Public Regulatory Trust Triangle

Most studies fall within the public regulatory trust triangle. We first discuss studies that focus on regulator-regulatee relation, then studies that cover the whole triangle, and finally studies that focus on citizen trust in regulator or regulated organization.

Regulator–regulatee relations (relations 5, 6 and 7)

Trust between a public regulator and regulatees has received a fair amount of attention in research, especially with respect to its impact on compliance (e.g., Braithwaite & Makkai, 1994; Gunningham & Sinclair, 2009b; Heimer & Gazley, 2012; Murphy, 2004). These studies focus on the interaction between the individual inspector representing the regulator and the individual representing the regulated organization in the regulatory encounter, distinguishing inspector trust in the regulatee from regulatee trust in the inspector, and how these two trust relations interact. Overall, these studies suggest that regulator trust in regulatees and regulatee trust in the regulator have a positive effect on compliance and thus help safeguard public interests.

According to Heimer and Gazley (2012, p. 853), who study regulatory encounters between health inspectors and HIV clinics,

> as regulatory encounters unfold, clinics' carefully prepared performances sometimes change into more cooperative interactions where inspectors and regulatees hash out details about how rules will be applied and even work together on reports for the regulators' supervisors. By "performing together," regulatory inspectors gain access to the clinic's backstage where they can assess clinic workers' deeper conformity to ethical and scientific norms. But such joint performances are less likely where cultural divides and material scarcity make it difficult for clinic staff to gain inspectors' trust.

Braithwaite and Makkai's (1994) research shows that inspector trust has a positive effect on compliance. More precisely, they find that the more care

Table 1.1 Semi-systematic literature review: description of empirical studies found

Source	Trust relationship(s)	Method	Industry/sector	Region
Braithwaite & Makkai (1994)	Regulator–regulatee	Longitudinal survey	Care homes	Australia
Downer (2010)	Regulator–regulatee	Documents	Aviation	US
Heimer & Gazley (2012)	Regulator–regulatee	Ethnography	Health care	US, Thailand, Uganda, South Africa
Murphy (2004)	Regulator–regulatee	Survey	Tax	Australia
Murphy et al. (2009)	Regulator–regulatee	Survey	Taxation, social security and law enforcement	Australia
Gouldson (2004)	Whole public triangle	Interviews	Environmental regulation	UK
Gunningham & Sinclair (2009a)	Whole public triangle	Interviews	Occupational health and safety	Australian mines
Gunningham & Sinclair (2009b)	Whole public triangle	Interviews	Occupational health and safety	Australian mines
Holm & Halkier (2009)	Whole public triangle	Interviews, documents	Food	Europe
Thiers (2002)	Whole public triangle	Documents, interviews	Organic food	China
Gillespie & Hurley (2013)	Public–private triangle	Document study	Financial system	US
Nienaber et al. (2014)	Citizen–regulated company-regulation	Meta-analysis	Banking	Worldwide
Axelsson & Schroeder (2009)	Citizen–public regulation	Interviews, documents	Data sharing for research: eResearch, eScience	Sweden
Brabers et al. (2013)	Citizen–public regulator	Citizen survey	Health care	The Netherlands
Brown & Kuzma (2013)	Citizen–public regulator/ regulation	Focus groups	Nanotechnology in food products	US

Study	Regulation type	Method	Topic	Location
Chou (2008)	Citizen–public regulator/regulation	Documents, citizen survey	Food safety	Taiwan
Chou & Liou (2010)	Citizen–public regulator/regulation	Survey	Food safety	EU, UK, Germany, Taiwan
Farrell (2012)	Citizen–public regulator/regulation	Documents	Risk innovation and regulation in health technologies	EU
Harmon et al. (2013)	Citizen–public regulator/regulation		Biobanks	
Phillimore et al. (2007)	Citizen–public regulator	Interviews	External safety, chemical plants	Scotland, Germany
Satterfield et al. (2013)	Citizen–public regulator/regulation	Telephone survey	Nanotechnology	US
Sylvester et al. (2009)	Citizen–public regulator/regulation	Essay	Nanotechnology	Worldwide
Walls et al. (2004)	Citizen–public regulator	Focus groups	Health and safety, and Railways Inspectorate	UK
Bart et al. (2005)	Private regulatory triangle	Survey	eCommerce	Worldwide?
King & Lenox (2000)	Private regulatory triangle		Chemical industry	
Coslovsky & Locke (2013)	Co-regulation	Audits and interviews	Sugar plants	Brazil
Delmas (2002)	Co-regulation	Survey	Business firms	Compares US and Europe
Fernandez et al. (2010)	Co-regulation	Interviews	EU environmental policy	Spain, Portugal, Greece
Garcia Martinez et al. (2013)	Co-regulation		Food	
Larsson (2005)	Co-regulation		External auditor	Sweden
Liu (2011)	Co-regulation		Organic food certificates	US
Rommel & Verhoest (2014); Rommel (2012)	Public collaboration	Documents, interviews	Energy regulators	Flanders (Belgium)
Schmidt (2009)	Public collaboration	Essay	Single market for services in EU	EU

home directors perceive that inspectors trust them, the better their compliance at the next inspection. Inspector trust in regulatees has another effect as well, since "as long as [inspectors] believe a clinic is adhering to the spirit of the regulations, regulatory inspectors will join clinic staff in working around 'inconsequential' technical mistakes" (Heimer & Gazley, 2012, p. 882). This does not necessarily imply regulatory capture, because "a good monitor knows when and how to join the performance and therefore how to get backstage to see what is really happening" (Heimer & Gazley, 2012, p. 882).

Regulatee trust in inspectors is equally important and "an opportunity to correct mistakes only occurs when there is trust on both sides—when regulators believe the clinic staff is competent and good-willed and the staff in turn are willing to acknowledge errors because they expect to be treated fairly" (Heimer & Gazley, 2012, p. 882). Procedural justice, fair treatment, is a key antecedent to regulatee trust in inspectors and an important driver of regulatees' intention to comply (Murphy, 2004, 2016; Murphy et al, 2009).

The studies reviewed here are all related to public regulators regulating private organizations. We found no empirical research on trust in relations where public regulators regulated public organizations. We present two such studies in this volume by Van Ees and Six, and Oomsels and Bouckaert.

Whole triangle
We found four studies in different sectors and on different continents that use all three parties in the public regulatory trust triangle as data sources (relations 1, 3 and 5) (Gouldson, 2004; Gunningham & Sinclair, 2009b; Holm & Halkier, 2009; Thiers, 2002) and one covering both public and private regulatory actors, but not gathering data directly from all actors (Gillespie & Hurley, 2013). In these studies the regulator's challenge of being the go-between or trusted third-party between citizens' interests on the one hand and the regulated business' interests on the other hand is highlighted. Citizen perceptions of the regulator are very sensitive to whether the regulator is seen as independent to business or as too cosy with business. In all four studies regulators are seen by citizens, at least at some point in time, as being captured by the businesses they are supposed to inspect and as not paying enough attention to citizen concerns. For example, in Thiers' (2002) study of organic agriculture in China, there is a structural problem since the Chinese government tries to be both the regulator and producer of organic foods. As a result, the Chinese government is not trusted in the role of regulator who safeguards citizen concerns.

Two empirical studies are longitudinal and show that, over time, a collaborative regulatory style, seeking to build trust, is more effective in safeguarding citizen and employee interests than a repressive style, based on distrust. Gouldson's (2004) study of the UK's Environment Agency's regulatory strategy shows that giving the Environment Agency the discretion to be responsive in its approach of business firms had a positive effect on overall compliance and the willingness of regulated firms to provide the information that regulators need. But regulators are not always given this kind of discretion, since citizens do not always trust regulators enough, especially after a period where regulators have (appeared to have) been captured by business. Gunningham and Sinclair's research into Australian mine safety regulation looks simultaneously at the employees' and trade unions' perspective, the employers' and firm owners' perspective and the role of the regulator. They find that regulation and "instructions" change under successive governments, depending on the relative power and influence of unions versus mining companies. They conclude that a more collaborative regulatory strategy and style leads to safer working conditions than a more repressive strategy and style (Gunningham & Sinclair, 2009a, 2009b).

As we showed in the section on the role of trust in the regulator-regulatee relation, there is ample empirical evidence to suggest that a critical cooperative relation between regulator and regulatee has positive effects on compliance levels and the reduction of citizen vulnerabilities. However, such cooperation does not occur in isolation. The regulator also needs to take into account the position of the citizen. There are two possibilities here: either citizens trust the regulatory agency enough to allow it to exercise discretion in the regulatory relationship; or as Gouldson puts it, alternatively, "[stakeholders] have such limited influence that they are unable to disrupt cooperative approaches when they emerge" (Gouldson, 2004, p. 589). The latter option, the exclusion of citizens, we suggest, is not a viable long-term option in many (developed) countries today, and is not compliant with the OECD's best practice principles for regulation (OECD, 2014).

Gillespie and Hurley (2013) examine the breakdown of trust in the US financial system including the regulatory regime after the global financial crisis. They observe that trust failures occurred at multiple levels and by multiple agents, both public and private. They distinguish three groups of actors: financial institutions, the rating agencies – who may be seen as private regulators – as well as the government and its regulatory agencies. This analysis is valuable as it looks at the whole financial system, but stays rather superficial for our purposes: there is no empirical data gathering directly from actors involved, but rather from published reports and media stories. They conclude that increased (regulatory) control is central to rebuilding stakeholder – read mainly citizen – trust in financial organizations and institutions.

Citizen trust (relations 1, 2 and 3)

Empirical research into citizen trust in private and third sector organizations (relation 1) is scattered across many academic disciplines and journals and practice-oriented publications; and therefore difficult to find. Also, only some of this research is related to regulation. For example, Nienaber et al. (2014) perform a meta-analysis of factors that impacted on customer trust in business organizations and one of the factors was "regulation and control mechanisms". They find a moderately high impact of this factor on citizen trust in all organizations (r = 0.330) and an even higher impact for financial organizations (r = 0.638). It remains, however, unclear to what degree the items in this factor refer entirely to public regulation, as they speak of "mechanisms such as binding contracts, web site security or privacy regulations" (Nienaber et al., 2014, p. 382). In this research regulation is seen as an institution in the background that influences citizen trust in the regulated business corporation (cf Zucker, 1986).

In our semi-systematic search we found only one study into citizen trust in public organizations that are regulated (relation 2): in Sweden a lot of personal data is stored by public organizations for research and science and citizens trust the privacy regulation that is involved with privacy concerns (Axelsson & Schroeder, 2009).

The empirical research focusing on citizen trust in specific regulators or a regulatory regime (relation 3) relies on various methods of data collection, such as interviews, document analyses, focus groups or surveys. Some studies focus on citizen trust in regulators or regulatory regimes in general (Brabers et al., 2013; Walls et al., 2004), while other studies focus on citizen trust in regulators or regulatory regimes after an incident (Chou, 2008; Chou & Liou, 2010) and still others focus on citizen trust for regulating new risks (Brown & Kuzma, 2013; Farrell, 2012; Harmon et al., 2013; Satterfield et al., 2013; Sylvester et al., 2009) or risks more generally (Pollak, 1996). They identify factors that influence the degree of trust citizens have in regulators or regulatory regimes. Some may easily be addressed by regulators while others are more challenging.

Citizen trust in regulators in general In 2007 the Dutch Health Care Inspectorate introduced its mission statement "for a justified trust in responsible health care", in which it acknowledged relation 1, citizen trust in health care providers, as its *raison d'être* and also acknowledged the need for citizen trust in the inspectorate (Paauw-Fikkert et al., 2014). It has since commissioned research into how much citizens trust the Inspectorate (Brabers et al., 2013), but these data are difficult to interpret and analyse without further context, such as either longitudinal or comparative scores of citizen trust in regulators.

Walls et al.'s (2004) study, however, compares two regulators and combines focus group discussions with a short questionnaire among focus group participants (n = 201) about their trust ratings in specific public regulators. With this combination of methods they are able to probe into how ratings of citizen trust in particular regulatory agencies were formed; in other words how citizens assess a regulator's trustworthiness, the first phase in Dietz's (2011) trust process. Participants used different modes of reasoning to come to their judgments, largely because only a few actually had had direct experience with the regulator. Walls et al. (2004, p. 133) conclude that "views of participants are the outcome of a reconciliation of diverse perceptions concerning the role of the organisation, structural factors and the nature of the regulated risks". The Health and Safety Executive (HSE) received higher trust ratings (m = 2.5; SD = 0.78) than the Railways Inspectorate (m = 1.7; SD = 0.70), even though the latter is formally part of the former. Participants more often knew of HSE and "it was perceived to be independent of the legislature and seen to be acting in the public interest, although some concerns were expressed [about adequate funding]" (p. 138). The Railways Inspectorate was almost completely invisible to the public and the negative public debates about rail safety had a negative impact on the trust ratings: "a negative perception of the UK rail system as a whole emerged . . . Perceptions of the regulator thus seemed to suffer by association" (p. 144).

Citizen trust in regulators or regulatory regimes after incidents   The impact of incidents, such as dioxins found in food, on citizen trust in regulators and regulatory regimes is studied by Chou in two studies (Chou, 2008; Chou & Liou, 2010). In both cases governments used technical performance information to address citizen concerns after an incident (e.g., when dioxins were found in food), but this did not help citizens to trust the technology or organizations. If anything the use of technical performance information led to lower trust in government as the regulating actor. As Chou (2008, p. 181) concludes, the impact of a technocratic approach to risk assessment as the basis for risk regulation has "systematically destroy[ed] public trust in regulators". He critically investigates how a newly industrialized country like Taiwan has responded to dioxin in food crises and compares it with how EU countries have dealt with them. He observes that in both cases the first response had been one where communication to the public was delayed due to "technocrats risk assessments in terms of positivistic regulatory science, which hides and delays risk and ignores risk communication" (Chou, 2008, p. 181), because of the need for accuracy. He goes on to show how the delayed and hidden risk governance structure alters public perception and systematically destroys public trust in regulators' risk governance. EU countries then moved to a new risk governance paradigm (Chou & Liou, 2010), while he wonders whether this will also happen in newly industrialized countries like Taiwan. Taiwan's tradition and culture of authoritarian technological decision-making and positivistic risk assessment makes it harder to move towards more open risk governance and risk communication to the public (Chou, 2008). More generally, Pollak (1996, p. 25) concludes that "inadequacy of scientific knowledge, coupled with lack of public trust in government make risk assessment based on experts inadequate".

Citizen trust in regulating emerging risks   Similar observations are made in empirical studies into how regulatory regimes may take into account citizen concerns about emerging risks due to new technologies, such as nanotechnology or biotechnology. In their study of the GMO regulation debate, Sylvester et al. (2009, p. 172) observe that, whereas the US government did not take strong regulatory action, leading to declining public trust in the regulatory agencies, the UK government did react in support of GMO's benefits and safety. However, this behaviour of the UK government also led to declining public trust as the public "viewed government and industry to be in cahoots." They furthermore observe that at the heart of the GMO "debacle" was the public perception of risks, not of scientific facts. This suggests that moral information was dominant and the scientific technical information was not accepted, because it did not come from trusted experts with shared values (cf Earle, 2010).

Satterfield et al. (2013, p. 254) point to the dramatic effects on public opinion whenever regulators and scientists presume that new technologies are safe and are then not found to be so. They conclude that, from a policy point of view, "it is best to foresee unexpected harm to human and environmental health, or at least to recognize that unfounded promises of safety are unwise", because "trust in regulation, once lost, is difficult to recover". What is needed are

> governance frameworks that are capable of simultaneously managing risk, coping with uncertainty, combatting ambivalence, and building trust, all the while encouraging the delivery of those instrumental outputs that we value/demand (better health, new technologies, commercial reward). This multi-dimensional task makes the design and delivery of good governance frameworks (ones that are effective, efficient, responsive, and proportionate) extremely difficult. (Harmon et al., 2013, p. 31)

Farrell (2012, p. 473) comes to a similar observation when she concludes that the political context brings complexity to EU regulatory processes, which in turn may lead to messiness and unpredictability in relation to managing the relationship between risk and innovation. This may be particularly apparent in politically sensitive areas of EU governance where public trust may be at issue, such as those involving health technologies.

Public engagement exercises are important in helping to shape public risk perceptions in a responsible way, but Harmon et al. (2013, p. 31) also argue that the challenge facing regulators and policy makers is "how to push public engagement results up into a policy framework paralleled with a need to make regulation more socially receptive and reflexive". In conclusion, policy makers and regulators are continuously looking for approaches that allow for the public to have trust in regulators' ability in keeping them safe and protected while at the same time facilitating innovation by businesses.

Private Regulatory Trust Triangle (Relations 1, 4 and 6)

Empirical research into private regulation is relatively new, especially in regulation literature. In the business literature, trust in private certificates and labels has received more attention, because a certificate will only be effective if it is trusted by its consumers (e.g., for e-commerce eTrust and Verisign; Bart et al., 2005). Our semi-systematic search, using the search terms trust and regulation, did not find most of these sources, probably because they do not use the term regulation. Our chapter on private regulation covers more of this literature (Näslund & Hallström, this volume).

Proponents of industry self-regulation in environmental protection argue that the establishment of self-regulatory structures may institutionalize environmental improvement, and critics suggest that without explicit sanctions, such structures will fall victim to opportunistic behaviour. King and Lenox's (2000, p. 698) study of the Chemical Manufacturers Association's Responsible Care Program finds that opportunistic tendencies were strong and that "effective industry self-regulation is difficult to maintain without explicit sanctions". Hence the need for regulatory regimes with roles for both state and non-state actors and co-regulation (see relation 8 below).

Regulatory Collaboration

Regulatory collaboration may occur between private and public regulators in a mixed regulatory regime (co-regulation; relation 8), or between public regulators (relation 9).

Co-regulation (relation 8)

As regulatory regimes are increasingly (re)designed in negotiations between industry and government with attention to reducing industry's regulatory burden, more and more examples of co-regulation emerge. In co-regulation both private and public regulators play a role in the regulatory regime. Sometimes private regulation is obligatory, for example in the Dutch asbestos removal sector, while in other situations private regulation is voluntary. Recently empirical research into this relation is emerging (Coslovsky & Locke, 2013; Fernandez et al., 2010; Garcia Martinez et al., 2013; Larsson, 2005). Coslovsky and Locke (2013) study the Brazilian sugar sector's regulatory regime with both private and public regulators. They find that "although private and public agents rarely communicate, let alone coordinate with one another, they nevertheless reinforce each other's actions" (Coslovsky & Locke, 2013, p. 497).

In their comparative study of EU regulatory influence on southern European member states, Fernandez et al. (2010) observe the critical role of trust between state and non-state actors in their collaboration within regulatory regimes. EU environmental policy stimulates the involvement of non-state actors such as private certification institutes, while in some Southern European member states (Spain, Portugal and Greece) such involvement is not commonplace. In Greece they find high distrust between public and private actors in general (all of society), which makes cooperation in environmental regulation more difficult than in Spain, where overall there was more trust and as a consequence better collaboration in environmental regulation, with clear regional variations. In their study of co-regulation in the European food industry, Garcia Martinez et al. (2013, p. 1117) conclude that "co-regulation is thus most likely to appear where related public and private objectives and interests are aligned and compatible with each other".

Liu's (2011) study into the trustworthiness of the US Department of Agriculture organic certification process shows the importance of correctly understanding how system trust works. He concludes "that the current regulatory framework is not only inadequate to the task of regulating domestic organics, but also incapable of ensuring the integrity of imported organics. Thus, the 'USDA Organic' seal misleads customers" (Liu, 2011, p. 333). The certification is performed by private certifying agents and the USDA officials do not have enough capacity to supervise these agents, according to Liu. According to Luhmann (1988) people have system trust if they believe the system is functioning and assume others also trust the system. Liu's conclusion that the USDA is not able to perform enough inspections to ensure the integrity of the products and therefore should not be trusted is in Luhmann's conceptualization irrelevant. Only when citizens hear about the number of USDA inspections *and* judge that to be inadequate for a judgment that the system is functioning, may citizens' trust in the USDA Organic system disappear.

In sum, the results of co-regulation research have so far shown that co-regulation is facing challenges in terms of achieving improved compliance or higher trust. The jury is still out whether the basic idea of co-regulation is flawed, because interests vary too widely; or whether it is just very difficult to get the collaboration to work effectively and we have not yet figured out how to achieve this.

Public collaboration (relation 9)
In general, research into public collaborations emphasizes the importance of trust (e.g., Ansell & Gash, 2008; Isett et al., 2011; Thomson & Perry, 2006; Weber & Khademian, 2008), but we found only a few studies that specifically focus on trust in the collaboration between different regulators within one jurisdiction, or on trust in the international collaboration between regulators. One more recent phenomenon is that regulatory agencies increasingly collaborate across national borders, e.g. through European regulatory networks (Levi-Faur, 2011; Maggetti, 2014), or across sectors (e.g. collaboration between telecom and media regulators, see Aubin and Verhoest, 2014). Schmidt (2009) investigates trust of European Union member states in each other's regulatory systems with regards to the implementation and enforcement of the Service Directive from 2004. She observes that mutual recognition was much more controversial in developing a single market for services than it was for goods. "Old" member states distrusted whether "new" member states (from Eastern Europe) would abide by the rules given the high levels of unemployment in many of the latter countries. Her analysis shows why a single market for services generated distrust while a single market for goods did not:

> For goods, in general, governments only have to trust each other to maintain sufficient regulation and control of product standards. This is supported by the interest of governments in the well-being of their own populations, and the interest of manufacturers in their reputation, which extends to exported goods. In the case of services, however, process standards have to be controlled which only in part affect the quality of services. Where services are being exported using the competitive advantage of lower wages, this requires a higher degree of trust. Governments have to trust that their counterparts behave altruistically and [that these latter actors] control service providers simply for the sake of other member states. (pp. 855–6)

Rommel and Verhoest (2014) call for a "relational perspective" on regulatory agency autonomy as they find that "de facto discretion of regulators can be increased or reduced by other public regulators besides the parent minister", with whom they need to coordinate. They assert that trust is a key variable in the relationship between public regulators (Rommel & Verhoest, 2014, p. 298). First, regulatory agencies can increase their de facto autonomy towards the responsible minister by using reputation as a trust building mechanism. One important way in which regulatory agencies can build reputation towards their minister is by accumulating technical expertise and reputational power through the interaction with other regulatory agencies in the context of European regulatory networks or cross-sectoral collaborations (Rommel, 2012; Verhoest et al., 2015). Second, Rommel (2012) shows in case studies of labour and social inspections as well as energy regulation in the multi-level context of federal Belgium that the emergence of deeper forms of collaboration between regulators within and between levels of government depends upon trust between them and the extent to which one regulator can signal its trustworthiness to other regulators.

CONCLUSIONS AND INTRODUCTION TO CHAPTERS

Our scoping of the field in terms of the different trust relations within regulatory regimes and our semi-systematic literature review show the current state of knowledge. We identify five themes, the first four of which are gaps in the literature. First, not all relations are studied to the same extent in the context of trust in regulatory regimes. In particular relation 7, the relation between a public regulator and a public regulated organization, is heavily understudied. This is why we have two chapters in this volume that explicitly address relation 7 (Six & Van Ees, and Oomsels & Bouckaert).

Second, even though a fair amount of studies look at the interactions between trust relations within regulatory regimes, few studies collect data from different actors involved in the different relations so that different perspectives are included and several trust relations may be studied in relation to one another. Many chapters in this volume collect data from more than one actor and some look at the interaction between several relations.

The third gap we identify is that little attention is paid to the dynamics of processes of trust building and repair and the role of distrust in such processes. For example, Responsive Regulation theory (Ayres & Braithwaite, 1992), a dominant theory in regulation research, has cooperation and trust at its heart. Braithwaite and Makkai recommend "a dynamic regulatory strategy of dialogue and trust as a first choice followed by escalation to more punitive regulation when trust is abused"

(Braithwaite & Makkai, 1994, p. 1). They do, however, underplay the importance of processes of trust building and repair. We have two chapters that focus on trust processes and interactions in detail (Six & Van Ees, and Oomsels & Bouckaert).

Fourth, there are still outstanding conceptual issues around trust and related concepts that need further study: trust and confidence, trust and distrust and trust and control; all in the context of trust in regulatory regimes. The chapters in this volume sometimes address these issues but do not resolve them, if they can actually be resolved.

A final, fifth, theme is that the methods used to date vary widely, with an emphasis on exploratory qualitative research (see Table 1.1). There is relatively little systematic theory building or hypothesis testing research and little comparative or integrative research. This makes sense given the phase in the development of research in this field, but we feel that it is time to start more theory building and hypothesis testing research, given the amount of knowledge we have gathered in all these rather dispersed studies. In the concluding chapter to this volume we elaborate on these conclusions, together with the contributions that the chapters in this volume make.

Contributions in this Volume

The chapters in this volume make a substantial contribution in addressing the gaps identified and also highlight the dilemmas regulators face as they work to perform their role in regulatory regimes: gaining and maintaining the trust of citizens while at the same time keeping regulatory burdens on responsible regulatees within reasonable limits; yet being firm on irresponsible regulatees. Further research, however, is needed to formalize and validate the emerging theoretical insights.

Russell W. Mills and Dorit Rubinstein Reiss, in their chapter *The role of trust in the regulation of complex and high-risk industries: the case of the U.S. Federal Aviation Administration's voluntary disclosure programs*, study relationship 5 between aviation companies and the public regulator. They examine the evolution of the role of trust in the Federal Aviation Administration's Voluntary Disclosure Programs by developing case studies of two voluntary disclosure programs: the Aviation Safety Action Program (ASAP) and the Voluntary Disclosure Reporting Program (VDRP). Using interview, document and observational data from both parties, they examine how the level of trust between the FAA and air carriers varies across regions and how the level of trust is often contingent upon the enforcement style of the regulator and on institutional arrangements to enhance trustworthiness and confidentiality.

In Chapter 3, *When the going gets tough: exploring processes of trust building and repair in regulatory relations*, Six and Van Ees focus on the dynamics of processes for trust building and repair that are underplayed in current regulation theory. They reconstruct and analyse the interaction process between a public regulator (water board in charge of licensing and enforcement for water management) and a public regulatee (local authority developing new housing district) in the Netherlands; in other words relation 7. Even though (dis)trust was not often explicitly mentioned, processes of trust building and repair provide a fruitful conceptual lens through which they could understand and explain what happened. Their micro-level study shows how trust is built and what happens after trouble occurs and conflict erupts. They tentatively formulate propositions on processes of trust building and repair at individual and organizational level.

In Chapter 4, *Interorganizational trust in Flemish public administration: comparing trusted and distrusted interactions between public regulatees and public regulators*, Peter Oomsels and Geert Bouckaert study in detail the interactions between the boundary spanners from public regulators and public regulatees (relation 7). They include in their analysis how system-level (in their terminology macro-level) characteristics impact on the interaction and the resulting trust perceptions. Findings from a nested mixed-method analysis of trusted and distrusted interorganizational interactions with horizontal departments in Flemish public administration show that macro- and meso-level interaction aspects affect the trust process through various direct and indirect mechanisms, that both extent and form of these interaction aspects are important to understand how they affect the trust process, and that macro- and meso-level interaction aspects shape each other in neo-institutional structuration processes. On the basis of these findings, they suggest that any due understanding of interorganizational trust must acknowledge that no single group of institutional, rational, or social exchange theories can provide a full understanding of interorganizational trust. They conclude that a model that allows interdependent macro- and meso-level interaction characteristics to affect the trust process may be required to achieve a comprehensive understanding of interorganizational trust.

In Chapter 5, *In vino veritas? The development of producer trust and its market effects in regulated French and Italian quality wine markets*, Betsy Carter uses extensive interviews with many actors in the regulatory regime to study the challenge of building trust in luxury markets and the role of public regulation to facilitate that trust. She studies the consumer trust in the government mark (certificate) in the luxury wine market in France and Italy, and finds that this trust as well as the prices obtained differ substantially despite similar volumes of wine available. France manages to obtain higher prices as well as higher consumer trust than Italy. She finds that the differences in price premium obtained and in consumer trust may be explained by the administrative heritage, business/citizen trust in government, the market structure and trust among supply chain actors. This in turn leads to differences in business trust in the government mark (certificate) and citizen trust in the government mark and this results in different price premiums that may be obtained. In France, trust of citizens in public regulation (relation 3) clearly evokes trust of citizens in producers (relation 1) and fosters producers' trust in the public regulator (relation 5); while in Italy, lack of citizen trust in public regulation leads to lack of citizen trust in producers and leads to lack of producers' trust in the public regulator. Hence this chapter sheds light on the positive reinforcing mutual influence from trust relations between citizens (consumers), organizations (producers) and the public regulator.

Lovisa Näslund and Kristina Tamm Hallström study the position of private regulators and how they operate in relations 4 and 6; and what that implies for relation 1. In the chapter *Being everybody's accomplice: trust and control in eco-labelling*, they study the emergence of ecolabels, that promise to control the means of production of the goods marked with their labels, thus increasing these products' trustworthiness in the eyes of the consumers. These labelling organizations act as guardians of trust, creating a chain of trust that enables consumers to trust the products, even if they are not in a position to trust the producers. On closer inspection, however, it would seem that this solution gives rise to new problems, as the labelling organization is unlikely to get the desired compliance of the producer solely by means of control and distrust – especially since adhering to these standards is voluntary. The relationship between labelling organizations and producers thus has to be able to harbour contradictory notions of trust and distrust, of control and customer relations and of independence and dependence. Empirically, the study is based on case studies of three eco-labels available on the Swedish market: Bra Miljöval (Good Environmental Choice), Svanen (Svan) and KRAV ("Requirement"). They show that the labelling organization is able to combine independent control and trusting collaboration by separating the different tasks necessary to create an eco-label, namely the writing of criteria, the monitoring and the communication of the worth of the label to consumers and producers. The study also demonstrates how processes of trust creation may run parallel to and separate to each other. The chapter does so by combining interviews with document analysis.

In his chapter *Trust and cooperation over the public–private divide: an empirical study on trust evolving in co-regulation*, Haiko Van der Voort studies two examples of co-regulation in the Netherlands, using interviews with all parties involved in the co-regulation regimes and document analysis. The focus is on relation 8, with attention also paid to relations 5 and 6. Both examples of co-regulation start by announcing trust among collaborators, yet in only one case is the trust actually built and maintained, while in the other case trust among collaborators collapsed – if it ever truly existed. The cases confirm that on an operational level, trust is both an enabler and a result of cooperation. However, this mutual reinforcement process of trust and cooperation needs to be supported by actors on a political level. This support includes emphasizing the importance of cooperation, but also allowing for problem solving on an operational level. The latter is of significant importance, because co-regulation provides incentives to government to over-organize the cooperation process by organizing institutional arrangements upfront. This blocks trust to grow within cooperation and vice versa. Cooperation and trust prove to be dependent on the way they are embedded in institutional arrangements of co-regulation. At the same time, these institutional arrangements may also be artefacts of distrust.

In the final empirical chapter Erik Baekkeskov empirically investigates the trust building efforts that an expert agency, charged with monitoring, engages in with other agencies in the regulatory regime (relationship 9). In *Deliberate trust-building by autonomous government agencies: evidence from responses to the 2009 H1N1 swine flu pandemic* the research question is, do independent agencies tasked with expert regulatory roles act deliberately to gain and maintain trust among policy stakeholders? Baekkeskov explores the question through a study of influenza pandemic response processes in an anonymized European public health agency (EPHA). In particular, he asks whether seeking a reputation for trustworthiness could shape the agency's 2009 "swine" flu pandemic responses. In doing so, the analysis shows whether reputation-seeking behaviours discovered in US federal agencies are useful in discovering trust building by agencies in Europe. The chapter also breaks new methodological ground: where previous analyses of agencies' reputation-seeking have relied on retrospective studies, this analysis uses a unique, first-hand participant-observer record and interviews collected within EPHA.

In the concluding chapter Six and Verhoest present *An agenda for further research into the role of trust in regulatory regimes*. This agenda follows the five themes identified in the introductory chapter: 1) there are outstanding issues for most trust relations within regulatory regimes that need further research; 2) the interactional dynamics between the different trust relationships within regulatory regimes needs more systematic research; 3) the dynamics of processes of trust building and repair within regulatory relationships are understudied; 4) there are still unresolved conceptual issues around trust and related concepts that need further study; and 5) the field is ready to move to more theory building and hypothesis testing research.

NOTES

1. Strictly speaking citizens and companies can choose their public regulator by choosing their residence, but this is a more invasive choice than choosing your private regulator.
2. https://primaryauthorityregister.info/par/index.php/home.

REFERENCES

Abbot, C. (2012), 'Bridging the gap – non-state actors and the challenges of regulating new technology', *Journal of Law and Society*, **39**(3), 329–358.

Ansell, C. and A. Gash (2008), 'Collaborative governance in theory and practice', *Journal of Public Administration Research and Theory*, **18**(4), 543–571.

Axelsson, A.S. and R. Schroeder (2009), 'Making it open and keeping it safe e-enabled data-sharing in Sweden', *Acta Sociologica*, **52**(3), 213–226.

Aubin, D. and K. Verhoest (2014), *Multilevel regulation in telecommunications: adaptive regulatory arrangements in Belgium, Ireland, the Netherlands, and Switzerland*, Basingstoke: Palgrave Macmillan.

Ayres, I. and J. Braithwaite (1992), *Responsive regulation, transcending the deregulation debate*, New York: Oxford University Press.

Bart, Y., V. Shankar, F. Sultan and G.L. Urban (2005), 'Are the drivers and role of online trust the same for all web sites and consumers? A large-scale exploratory empirical study', *Journal of Marketing*, **69**(4), 133–152.

Black, J. (2002), *Critical reflections on regulation*, London: Centre for Analysis of Risk and Regulation, LSE.

Black, J. (2008), 'Constructing and contesting legitimacy and accountability in polycentric regulatory regimes', *Regulation & Governance*, **2**, 137–164.

Brabers, A., M. Reitsma and R. Friele (2013), *Het beeld van zorggebruikers over de Inspectie voor de Gezondheidszorg* [perceptions of care users about the Healthcare Inspectorate], Utrecht: NIVEL.

Braithwaite, J. (2008), *Regulatory capitalism, how it works, ideas for making it work better*, Cheltenham, UK and Northampton, MA, USA: Edward Elgar Publishing.

Braithwaite, J. and T. Makkai (1994), 'Trust and compliance', *Policing and Society*, **4**, 1–12.

Brown, J. and J. Kuzma (2013), 'Hungry for information: Public attitudes toward food nanotechnology and labeling', *Review of Policy Research*, **30**(5), 512–548.

Chou, K.T. (2008), 'Glocalized dioxin – regulatory science and public trust in a double risk society', *Soziale Welt-Zeitschrift Fur Sozialwissenschaftliche Forschung Und Praxis*, **59**(2), 181–197.

Chou, K.T. and H.M. Liou (2010), 'System destroys trust? Regulatory institutions and public perceptions of food risks in Taiwan', *Social Indicators Research*, **96**(1), 41–57.

Coleman, J.S. (1990), *Foundations of social theory*, Cambridge: Harvard University Press.

Coslovsky, S.V. and R. Locke (2013), 'Enforcement: private compliance, public regulation, and labor standards in the Brazilian sugar sector', *Politics & Society*, **41**(4), 497–526.

Das, T.K. and B. Teng (1998), 'Between trust and control: developing confidence in partner cooperation in alliances', *Academy of Management Review*, **23**(3), 491–512.

Das, T.K. and B. Teng (2001), 'Trust, control and risk in strategic alliances: an integrated framework', *Organization Studies*, **22**(2), 251–284.

Deci, E.L. and R.M. Ryan (2000), 'The "what" and "why" of goal pursuits: human needs and the self-determination of behavior', *Psychological Inquiry*, **11**(4), 227–268.

Dekker, H.C. (2004), 'Control of inter-organizatonal relationships: evidence on appropriation concerns and coordination requirements', *Accounting, Organizations and Society*, **29**(1), 27–49.

Delmas, M.A. (2002), 'The diffusion of environmental management standards in Europe and in the United States: An institutional perspective', *Policy Sciences*, **35**(1), 91–119.

Den Hond, F., F.G.A. De Bakker and P. De Haan (2010), 'The sequential patterning of tactics: institutional activism in the global sports apparel industry, 1988–2002', *International Journal of Sociology and Social Policy*, **30**(11/12), 648–665.

Dietz, G. (2011), 'Going back to the source: why do people trust each other?', *Journal of Trust Research*, **1**(2), 215–222.

Dietz, G. and D.N. Den Hartog (2006), 'Measuring trust inside organisations', *Personnel Review*, **35**(5), 557–588.

Doern, B. and R. Johnson (eds) (2006), *Rules, rules, rules, rules: multi-level regulatory governance*, Toronto: University of Toronto Press.

Downer, J. (2010), 'Trust and technology: the social foundations of aviation regulation', *British Journal of Sociology*, **61**(1), 83–106.

Earle, T.C. (2009), 'Trust, confidence, and the 2008 global financial crisis', *Risk Analysis*, **29**(6), 785–792.

Earle, T.C. (2010), 'Trust in risk management: A model-based review of empirical research', *Risk Analysis*, **30**(4), 541–574.

Earle, T.C., M. Siegrist and H. Gutscher (2007), 'Trust, risk perception, and the TCC model of cooperation', in M. Siegrist, T.C. Earle and H. Gutscher (eds), *Trust in cooperative risk management*, London: Earthscan, pp. 1–49.

Farrell, A.M. (2012), 'Risk, innovation and the regulation of health technologies: examining EU governance of blood and plasma products', *Innovation – The European Journal of Social Science Research*, **25**(4), 461–477.

Fernandez, A.M., N. Font and C. Koutalakis (2010), 'Environmental governance in Southern Europe: the domestic filters of Europeanisation', *Environmental Politics*, **19**(4), 557–577.

Gabarro, J.J. (1978), 'The development of trust, influence and expectations', in A.G. Athos and J.J. Gabarro (eds), *Interpersonal behavior, communication and understanding in relationships*, Englewood Cliffs, NY: Prentice Hall, pp. 290–303.

Garcia Martinez, M., P. Verbruggenand and A. Fearne (2013), 'Risk-based approaches to food safety regulation: what role for co-regulation?', *Journal of Risk Research*, **16**(9), 1101–1121.

Giddens, A. (1990), *The consequences of modernity*, Stanford: Polity.

Gillespie, N. and R. Hurley (2013), 'Trust and the global financial crisis', in R. Bachmann and A. Zaheer (eds), *Handbook of advances in trust research*, Cheltenham, UK and Northampton, MA, USA: Edward Elgar Publishing, pp. 177–203.

Gouldson, A. (2004), 'Cooperation and the capacity for control: regulatory styles and the evolving influence of environmental regulations in the UK', *Environment and Planning C-Government and Policy*, **22**(4), 583–603.

Grabosky, P.N. (2013), 'Beyond *Responsive Regulation*: the expanding role of non-state actors in the regulatory process', *Regulation & Governance*, 7, 114–123.

Gunningham, N. and D. Sinclair (2009a), 'Organizational trust and the limits of management-based regulation', *Law & Society Review*, **43**(4), 865–899.

Gunningham, N. and D. Sinclair (2009b), 'Regulation and the role of trust: Reflections from the mining industry', *Journal of Law and Society*, **36**(2), 167–194.

Hardin, R. (1993), 'The street-level epistemology of trust', *Analyse & Kritik*, **14**, 152–176.

Hardin, R. (2002), *Trust and trustworthiness*, New York: Russell Sage Foundation.

Hardin, R. (2004), *Distrust*, New York: Russell Sage Foundation.

Harmon, S.H.E., G. Laurie and G. Haddow (2013), 'Governing risk, engaging publics and engendering trust: New horizons for law and social science?', *Science and Public Policy*, **40**(1), 25–33.

Heimer, C.A. and J.L. Gazley (2012), 'Performing regulation: Transcending regulatory ritualism in HIV clinics', *Law & Society Review*, **46**(4), 853–887.

Holm, L. and B. Halkier (2009), 'EU food safety policy. Localising contested governance', *European Societies*, **11**(4), 473–493.

Hood, C., H. Rothstein and R. Baldwin (2001), *The government of risk, understanding risk regulation regimes*, Oxford: Oxford University Press.

Isett, K.R., I.A. Mergel, K. LeRoux, P.A. Mischen and R.K. Rethemeyer (2011), 'Networks in public administration scholarship: Understanding where we are and where we need to go', *Journal of Public Administration Research and Theory*, **21**, I157–I173.

Janowicz-Panjaitan, M.K. and R. Krishnan (2009), 'Measures for dealing with competence and integrity violations of interorganizational trust at the corporate and operating levels of organizational hierarchy', *Journal of Management Studies*, **46**(2), 245–268.

Jordana, J. and D. Sancho Royo (2004), 'Institutional constellations and regulatory policy', in J. Jordana and D. Levi-Faur (eds), *The politics of regulation: Institutions and regulatory reforms for the age of governance*, Cheltenham, UK and Northampton, MA, USA: Edward Elgar Publishing, p. 296.

King, A.A. and M.J. Lenox (2000), 'Industry self-regulation without sanctions: The chemical industry's Responsible Care Program', *Academy of Management Journal*, **43**(4), 698–716.

Klijn, E.H., V. Sierra, T. Ysa, E. Berman, J.Edelenbos and D. Chen (2016), 'The influence of trust on network performance in Taiwan, Spain and the Netherlands: a cross country comparison', *International Public Management Journal*, **19**(1), 111–139.

Klijn, E.H. and J. Eshuis (2013), 'Trust in networks', in S. Llewellyn, S. Brookes and A. Mahon (eds), *Trust and confidence in government and public services*, New York: Routledge, pp. 46–61.

Klijn, E.H., J. Edelenbos and A.J. Steijn (2010), 'Trust in governance networks; its impact and outcomes', *Administration and Society*, **42** (2), 193–221.

Kramer, R.M. (1999), 'Trust and distrust in organizations: emerging perspectives, enduring questions', *Annual Review of Psychology*, **50**, 569–598.

Kroeger, F. (2012), 'Trusting organizations: the institutionalization of trust in inter-organizational relationships', *Organization*, **19**(6), 743–763.

Kroeger, F. and R. Bachmann (2013), 'Trusting across boundaries', in J. Langan-Fox and C.L. Cooper (eds), *The Routledge companion to boundary spanning in organizations*, London: Routledge, pp. 253–284.

Larsson, B. (2005), 'Patrolling the corporation – the auditors' duty to report crime in Sweden', *International Journal of the Sociology of Law*, **33**(1), 53–70.

Levi-Faur, D. (2011), 'Regulatory networks and regulatory agencification: towards a single European regulatory space', *Journal of European Public Policy*, **18**(6), 810–829.

Levine, M.E., and J.L. Forrence (1990), 'Regulatory capture, public interest, and the public agenda. Toward a synthesis', *Journal of Law Economics & Organization*, **6**, 167–198.

Lewicki, R.J. and B.B. Bunker (1995), 'Trust in relationships, a model of development and decline', in B.B. Bunker and J.Z. Rubin (eds), *Conflict, cooperation and justice*, San Francisco: Jossey-Bass, pp. 113–173.

Lewicki, R.J., D.J. McAllister and R.J. Bies (1998), 'Trust and distrust: new relationships and realities', *Academy of Management Review*, **23**(3), 438–458.

Liu, C.L. (2011), 'Is "USDA organic" a seal of deceit?: The pitfalls of USDA certified organics produced in the United States, China and beyond', *Stanford Journal of International Law*, **47**(2), 333–378.

Luhmann, N. (1979), *Trust and power*, Chicester: John Wiley & Sons.

Luhmann, N. (1988), 'Familiarity, confidence and trust: problems and alternatives', in D. Gambetta (ed.), *Trust, making and breaking cooperative relations*, New York, NY: Basil Blackwell, pp. 94–108.

Maggetti, M. (2014), 'The rewards of cooperation: The effects of membership in European regulatory networks', *European Journal of Political Research*, **53**(3), 480–499.

Maguire, S. and N. Phillips (2008), '"Citibankers" at citigroup: A study of the loss of institutional trust after a merger', *Journal of Management Studies*, **45**(2), 372–401.

Mayer, R.C., J.H. Davis and F.D. Schoorman (1995), 'An integrative model of organizational trust', *Academy of Management Review*, **20**(3), 703–734.

McGuire, M. (2006), 'Collaborative public management: Assessing what we know and how we know it', *Public Administration Review*, **66**, 33–43.

Möllering, G. (2006a), 'Trust, institutions, agency: towards a neoinstitutional theory of trust', in R. Bachmann and A. Zaheer (eds), *Handbook of trust research*, Cheltenham, UK and Northampton, MA, USA: Edward Elgar Publishing, pp. 355–376.

Möllering, G. (2006b), *Trust: reason, routine, reflexivity*, Amsterdam: Elsevier.

Murphy, K. (2004), 'The role of trust in nurturing compliance: A study of accused tax avoiders', *Law and Human Behavior*, **28**(2), 187–209.

Murphy, K. (2016). 'Turning defiance into compliance with procedural justice: Understanding reactions to regulatory encounters through motivational posturing', *Regulation & Governance*, **10**(1), 93–109.

Murphy, K., T.R. Tyler and A. Curtis (2009), 'Nurturing regulatory compliance:

is procedural justice effective when people question the legitimacy of the law?', *Regulation & Governance*, **3**, 1–26.

Nienaber, A.-M., M. Hofeditz and R.H. Searle (2014), 'Do we bank on regulation or reputation? A meta-analysis and meta-regression of organizational trust in the financial services sector', *International Journal of Bank Marketing*, **32**(5), 367–407.

Nooteboom, B. (1999). 'The triangle: roles of the go-between', in R.T.A.J. Leenders and S.M. Gabay (eds), *Corporate social capital and liability*, Boston: Kluwer Academic Publishers, pp. 341–355.

Nooteboom, B. (2002), *Trust: forms, foundations, functions, failures and figures*, Cheltenham, UK and Northampton, MA, USA: Edward Elgar Publishing.

OECD (2014), *Regulatory enforcement and inspections, OECD best practice principles for regulatory policy*, Paris: OECD.

Oomsels, P. (2016), *Administrational trust: an empirical examiniation of interorganisational trust and distrust in the Flemish administration*, PhD Thesis, Leuven: KU Leuven.

Oomsels, P., M. Callens, J Vanschoenwinkel and G. Bouckaert (2016). 'Functions and dysfunctions of interorganizational trust and distrust in the public sector', *Administration & Society*. Prepublished September 8, 2016.

Paauw-Fikkert, L.A.V., F.E. Six and P.B.M. Robben (2014), 'Vertrouwen in toezichtbeleid' [trust in regulation policy], *Beleid & Maatschappij*, **41**(3), 185–204.

Phillimore, P., A. Schluter and T. Pless-Mulloli (2007). 'Residents, regulators, and risk in two industrial towns', *Environment and Planning C-Government and Policy*, **25**(1), 73–89.

Pollak, R.A. (1996), 'Government risk regulation', *Annals of the American Academy of Political and Social Science*, **545**, 25–34.

Rommel, J. (2012), *Organisation and management of regulation. Autonomy and coordination in a multi-actor setting*, PhD Thesis, Leuven: KULeuven.

Rommel, J. and K. Verhoest (2014), 'Exploring effects of coordination on the autonomy of regulators: energy regulators in Belgium', *International Review of Administrative Sciences*, **80**(2), 298–317.

Rosanvallon, P. (2008), *Counter-democracy, politics in an age of distrust*, Cambridge: Cambridge University Press.

Rousseau, D.M., S.B. Sitkin, R.S. Burt and C. Camerer (1998), 'Not so different after all: a cross-discipline view of trust', *Academy of Management Review*, **23**(3), 393–404.

Ryan, R.M. and E.L. Deci (2000), 'Self-determination theory and the facilitation of intrinsic motivation, social development, and well-being', *American Psychologist*, **55**(1), 68–78.

Sako, M. (1998), 'Does trust improve business performance?', in C. Lane and R. Bachmann (eds), *Trust within and between organizations*, Oxford: Oxford University Press, pp. 88–117.

Satterfield, T., J. Conti, B.H. Harthorn, N. Pidgeon and A. Pitts (2013), 'Understanding shifting perceptions of nanotechnologies and their implications for policy dialogues about emerging technologies', *Science and Public Policy*, **40**(2), 247–260.

Schmidt, S.K. (2009), 'When efficiency results in redistribution: The conflict over the single services market', *West European Politics*, **32**(4), 847–865.

Searle, R., D.N. Den Hartog, A. Weibel, N. Gillespie, F.E. Six, T. Hatzakis and D. Skinner (2011), 'Trust in the employer: the role of high-involvement work practices and procedural justice in European organizations', *International Journal of Human Resource Management*, **22**(8), 1823–1823.

Shapiro, S.P. (1987), 'The social control of impersonal trust', *American Journal of Sociology*, **93**(3), 623–658.

Sitkin, S.B. and N.L. Roth (1993), 'Explaining the limited effectiveness of legalistic remedies for trust/distrust', *Organization Science*, **4**(3), 367–392.

Six, F.E. (2013), 'Trust in regulatory relations: how new insights from trust research improve regulation theory', *Public Management Review*, **15**(2), 163–185.

Sparrow, M.K. (2000), *The regulatory craft, controlling risks, solving problems and managing compliance*, Washington: Brookings Institution Press.

Sydow, J. (2006), 'How can systems trust systems? A structuration perspective on trust-building in inter-organizational relations', in R. Bachmann and A. Zaheer (eds), *Handbook of trust research*, Cheltenham, UK and Northampton, MA, USA: Edward Elgar Publishing, pp. 377–392.

Sylvester, D.J., K.W. Abbott and G.E. Marchant (2009), 'Not again! Public perception, regulation, and nanotechnology', *Regulation & Governance*, **3**(2), 165–185.

Thiers, P. (2002), 'From grassroots movement to state-coordinated market strategy: the transformation of organic agriculture in China', *Environment and Planning C-Government and Policy*, **20**(3), 357–373.

Thomson, A.M. and J.L. Perry (2006), 'Collaboration processes: Inside the black box', *Public Administration Review*, **66**(s1), 20–32.

Van de Walle, S. and F.E. Six (2014), 'Trust and distrust as distinct concepts: why studying distrust in institutions is important', *Journal of Comparative Policy Analysis*, **16**(2), 158–174.

Van Montfort, C. (2010), 'Ontwikkelingen in toezicht en verantwoording bij instellingen op afstand. Een terugblik en een blik in de toekomst', *Tijdschrift voor Toezicht*, **1**(1), 6–20.

Vangen, S. and C. Huxham (2003), 'Nurturing collaborative relations: Building trust in interorganizational collaboration', *Journal of Applied Behavioral Science*, **39**(1), 5–31.

Verhoest, K., J. Rommel and J. Boon (2015), 'How organizational reputation and trust may affect autonomy of independent regulators? The case of the Flemish energy regulator', in A. Waeraas and M. Maor (eds), *Organizational Reputation in the Public Sector*, London: Routledge, pp. 118–138.

Walls, J., N. Pidgeon, A. Weyman and T. Horlick-Jones (2004), 'Critical trust: understanding lay perceptions of health and safety risk regulation', *Health, Risk & Society*, **6**(2), 133–150.

Weber, E. and A.M. Khademian (2008), 'Managing collaborative processes: Common practices, uncommon circumstances', *Administration Society*, **40**(5), 431–464.

Weber, E.P., N.P. Lovrich and M.J. Gaffney (2007), 'Assessing collaborative capacity in a multidimensional world', *Administration Society*, **39**(2), 194–220.

Weibel, A. (2007), 'Formal control and trustworthiness: Shall the twain never meet?', *Group & Organization Management*, **32**(4), 500–517.

Williams, P. (2002), 'The competent boundary spanner', *Public Administration*, **80**(1), 103–124.

Zucker, L.G. (1986), 'Production of trust: institutional sources of economic structure, 1840 – 1920', *Research in Organizational Behavior*, **8**, 53–111.

2. The role of trust in the regulation of complex and high-risk industries: the case of the U.S. Federal Aviation Administration's voluntary disclosure programs

Russell W. Mills and Dorit Rubinstein Reiss

As part of the shift from command and control to process oriented regulatory regimes (Gilad, 2010), building trust between regulators and the regulated firms has grown in importance. Collaborative mechanisms often rely on a free-flow of information and communication, which requires the building and maintenance of trust. This exchange of information and trust building is even more vital in complex and high-risk industries where potential information asymmetries and prevailing motivations could lend themselves to the hiding of information (Gormley, 1986; May, 2005). In this chapter, we examine the evolution of the role of trust in the U.S. Federal Aviation Administration's Voluntary Disclosure Programs by developing case studies of three voluntary disclosure programs: the Aviation Safety Reporting System (ASRS), the Aviation Safety Action Program (ASAP) and the Voluntary Disclosure Reporting Program (VDRP). Using extensive interview and observational data, we demonstrate how trust is essential to the operation of the problems. We show how the FAA used institutional mechanisms to create trust at the national level, but at the local level, personal relationships had to be built to foster trust. The need for relationship-based trust building meant that the level of trust between the FAA and air carriers varied across regions and was often contingent upon the enforcement style of the regulator. While trust is necessary for the programs we describe and can provide substantial benefits to the public, it can also lead regulators to ignore warning signs and miss problems. We explore this darker side of trust using the Southwest Airlines incident.

As regulators move away from command and control models and towards more process oriented models (Gilad, 2010), the relationship between regulator and industry needs to be re-examined. A part of this re-examination is considering the role of trust in regulatory monitoring and enforcement activities. Fostering trust in cooperative regulatory mechanisms requires a delicate balance. On one hand, quite a few process-oriented mechanisms require a high-degree of trust to operate effectively, including voluntary disclosure programs. Voluntary disclosure programs offer industry reduced enforcement and sanctions in exchange for voluntary reporting of violations of regulations and problems. Participating firms also gain reputational benefits with the public by being seen as socially responsible or safe (Potoski and Prakash, 2009) and having the reputation with regulators as "good guys" to be trusted more and given more autonomy (Leach and Sabatier, 2005). The benefit of voluntary disclosure programs to regulators is an increase in available information on non-compliance at a lower cost and access to secondary information on the operation of firms that would otherwise be completely inaccessible (Alberini and Segerson, 2002; Mills and Reiss, 2014).

The voluntary disclosure programs we discuss are an excellent example of the necessity of trust in collaborative regulatory arrangements: pilots, mechanics and other workers must have trust in the regulatory agency not to take punitive action based on the disclosures of violations made to the agency while regulators must have trust in individual and firm-level reporters to fully disclose and not omit larger, more serious violations. While the development of trust is often necessary for self-regulatory programs to operate effectively, it can also lead to regulators becoming too cosy with, or "captured" by, the firms they are charged with regulating and can lead regulators to ignore or miss serious problems (Carpenter and Moss, 2014). The Southwest incident described here is, arguably, a good example of excessive trust that led to the ignoring of serious safety problems by the FAA. This chapter uses the FAA's voluntary disclosure programs to examine the following research questions: what is the role of trust in ensuring the success of collaborative regulatory regimes? How can regulators balance the need for trust with the fear of capture?

REGULATORY RELATIONSHIPS, TRUST AND CAPTURE

Part of the reason for the move to collaborative regulatory mechanisms is the desire for better regulatory results. In instances where both regulators and firms have the desire and authority, cooperative enforcement and monitoring can lead to excellent results (Potoski and Prakash, 2004). Extensive literature highlights that trust is essential for these collaborative mechanisms to work effectively (e.g., Ansell and Gash, 2008; Gunningham and Sinclair, 2009; Gunningham and Sinclair, 2012). The importance of trust in cooperative regulatory environments has led scholars to examine more closely the building of relationships between regulators and industry and the factors that lead to the building of trust in regulatory relationships (Black, 2008; Gunningham and Sinclair, 2009; Heimer and Gazley, 2012; Six, 2013).

For our analysis, we use Rousseau et al.'s (1998) definition of trust: "It is a psychological state comprising the intention to accept vulnerability based upon the positive expectations of the intentions or behaviour of another" (p. 395). Trust scholars have conceptualized two perspectives on the relationship between trust and control. The substitution perspective posits an inverse relationship between trust and control – low trust requires formal controls while higher levels of trust allow for more flexible arrangements. The complementary perspective argues that formal controls can build trust by providing objective measures and rules that lead to a track record of compliance to be used in future trust evaluations (Costa and Bijlsma-Frankema, 2007). Importantly, scholars have noted that the trust-control relationship is not stationary, but dynamic. Fryxell et al. (2002) found that the types of mechanisms employed by members of international joint ventures (IJVs) were initially very formal and rigid but evolved to become more flexible overtime as participants developed trust in one another. Finally, as Hedgecoe (2012) notes, the relationship between trust and control often produces spillover effects that influence the level of trust placed in arrangements by outside parties including citizens vis-à-vis regulatory agencies or business consortiums vis-à-vis individual firms.

Building from this literature, regulatory scholars group theories of the interaction of regulatory oversight and trust into two camps. Proponents of responsive regulatory theory (RRT) argue that regulators are responsive in enforcement style to the perceived ability and propensity of regulated firms to comply. RRT is largely based upon a "tit-for-tat strategy" where regulators view enforcement options as a "regulatory pyramid" with more cooperative strategies at the base of the pyramid and more punitive approaches at the top (Nielsen and Parker, 2009). In this model, the level of trust (sometimes referred to as deterrence-based trust) is based upon the willingness of the regulated firm to change their behaviour in response to the threat of moving from cooperative to more punitive enforcement styles (Ayres and Braithwaite, 1992). Empirical tests of RRT have found that the regulated firm's perception of regulatory trust in it increased compliance in future inspections and that higher levels of a regulatee's trust in the regulator also led to higher voluntary compliance (Braithwaite and Makkai, 1994; Murphy, 2004).

Critics of RRT charge that the theory's focus on the role of trust in improving behaviour is misguided. Regulatory arrangements based on deterrence-based trust, critics charge, are not rooted in trust, but rather "low distrust" and must be considered as a separate concept (Six, 2013). Rather than a focus on the effect of trust on behaviour, proponents of Self Determination Theory (SDT) focus on the effect of trust on an individual's motivations and attitudes towards compliance and regulators. Empirical studies of SDT emphasize that trust occurs between regulators and regulated firms when the actors subjected to formal controls internalize and integrate the values of the actors imposing the formal controls (Six, 2013). SDT scholars have identified three needs of regulated firms that, if met, can lead to higher levels of value internalization and trust: autonomy, competence, and relatedness (Deci and Ryan, 2000; Six, 2013). Autonomy refers to the ability of regulated firms to participate in and freely process and endorse transmitted values and regulation. Competence refers to the ability of the regulated firm to be given a chance to understand or grasp the meaning behind a regulation and to offer constructive feedback. Finally, relatedness is the ability of the regulated firm to internalize the values of one's social groups and to understand the positive intentions of the regulator through procedural justice and through communication of the regulator's trust in the regulated firm (Six, 2013).

While it is clear that trust between regulated firms and regulatory agencies can have significant benefits for the successful implementation of cooperative regulatory agreements, several studies have identified possible hazards associated with excessive trust in these environments. Möllering (2008) notes that trust involves a leap of faith that results in the suspension of the belief that a trusted actor would deceive (known as as-if trust). This suspension of belief in deception leads Möllering to claim that actors who trust others are in fact poor at detecting deception because they are overconfident in their ability to detect deception due to their misplaced level of trust in other actors. Möllering's work illustrates the "dark side of trust" – a concept that has important implications for regulatory oversight. For example, regulatory scholars have argued collaborative regulatory mechanisms are less effective when they are not complemented by traditional enforcement mechanisms such as fines or other punitive actions designed to deter deception (May, 2005; Short and Toffel, 2008). Similarly, Raymond (2006) argues that regulators should seek to develop creative positive incentives to reduce the threat of deception by regulated entities. Finally, it is important to note that deception works both ways. Regulated firms often worry that voluntarily submitting data to regulators will result in deception vis-à-vis punitive actions (Mills and Reiss, 2014).

Another example of the dark side of trust is the concept of regulatory capture. Carpenter and Moss (2014) define capture as "process by which regulation . . . is consistently or repeatedly directed away from the public interest and toward the interests of the regulated industry by the intent and action of the industry itself" (p. 13). This traditional view of capture implies that regulators and interest groups engage in purposeful and rational deception to achieve material self-interest. Kwak (2014) identifies another type of capture: cultural capture. Trust leads to cultural capture when regulators internalize the values of the industry they are charged with regulating and then accommodate its interests. Cultural capture is based upon three mechanisms: identity (more likely to adopt positions of folks in their "in-group"), status (more likely to adopt positions of those in higher statuses), and relationships (more likely to adopt positions of those in their social networks). Kwak's conceptualization of cultural capture employs many of the same mechanisms of Möllering's "as-if" trust – because regulators develop trust with those they interact with more, they suspend the belief of deception. This suggests that regulators face a challenge. In order to achieve the benefits of collaborative mechanisms, they need to establish trust. However, misguided trust can lead to overly lax regulation and potential regulatory failures. Our case study explores both sides of the equation.

Examining the role of trust in aviation regulation is particularly interesting given the alignment of interests between industry and regulators. As Perrow (1984, p.167) notes: "The aircraft and airlines industries are uniquely favored to support safety efforts. Profits are tied to safety; the victims are neither hidden, random, nor delayed and can include influential members of the industry and Congress".

In his study of the relationship between FAA officials and its Designated Engineering Representatives, Downer (2010) notes the alignment of interests is pervasive in the aviation industry and reaches far beyond the corporate level to the individual industry–regulator relationship. The complementary nature of the regulated–regulator relationship in the aviation industry coupled with the vital role of trust at a corporate and individual level has led some to claim that the FAA is particularly vulnerable to regulatory capture (Dana and Koniak, 1999; Niles, 2002). In this chapter, we will unpack the role of trust in aviation regulation in the United States while also examining the potential for regulatory capture.

METHODOLOGY

This chapter uses a single-embedded case study design (Yin, 2003) by focusing on three separate voluntary disclosure programs within the same agency (the FAA). This approach allows for comparative analysis of the structure of each voluntary disclosure program operated by the FAA along with an assessment of the role of trust in each program. The authors chose to develop case studies of ASRS, ASAP and VDRP because these voluntary disclosure programs differ in several key areas that can provide theoretical leverage in assessing the degree to which trust shapes the relationship between inspectors and air carrier officials.

The primary data used to develop the ASRS, ASAP and VDRP case studies are a total of 13 interviews and two participant observations (Appendix A). Specifically, the lead author interviewed three FAA headquarters staff responsible for designing and implementing both ASRS, ASAP and VDRP at the national level, four FAA field managers/inspectors responsible for overseeing ASRS, ASAP and VDRP implementation at four different air carriers, four air carrier managers (from four different air carriers) responsible for implementing ASAP and VDRP, one NASA official responsible for analysing ASRS data at the national level, and one aviation trade association official who was responsible for creating VDRP and who has experience in implementing both programs. Additionally, one of the authors was granted access to two confidential ASAP Event Review Committee (ERC) meetings at two separate air carriers. While the number of interviews and observations is fairly limited, the sample of air carriers and their corresponding local FAA offices that was selected by the authors is a representative sample comprising a variety of air carriers including two major legacy air carriers, one low cost carrier, and one regional carrier. This diverse sample of air carriers and local FAA offices also comprised a variety of relationships between the local regulator and regulated entity, ranging from very collaborative to adversarial (see Mills, 2010), which provides additional theoretical leverage for assessing the degree of trust between air carriers and inspectors. Individual interviewees were chosen through a purposive snowball sampling approach. Specifically, following meetings and interviews with FAA headquarters personnel familiar with all ASRS, VDRP and ASAP programs in operation, the authors contacted a sample of FAA local officials and air carrier officials listed by the FAA headquarters staff for interviews based on the type of air carrier (major, regional, low cost) and the type of perceived interaction (collaborative or adversarial) between the local FAA office and the air carrier as identified by FAA headquarter personnel.

Each semi-structured interview was recorded and lasted approximately one to one and a half hours in length. Each participant group (air carrier ASAP representatives, FAA Certificate Management Office principal maintenance inspectors, flight standards voluntary safety branch personnel, etc.) were asked questions from a pre-developed interview protocol, though the interviewer would allow the interviewee to take the conversation in whichever direction they wanted. However, each question on the interview protocol was covered during the course of the interview. The questions covered during the interview focused on the structure of interaction between local FAA and air carrier personnel in implementing the ASRS, ASAP and VDRP programs, how local FAA and air carriers decided which reports would be accepted into each program, how both local FAA officials and air carrier officials worked on corrective actions once a hazard was identified through a voluntary disclosure, and how each viewed their relationship with the other party. Secondary sources of data include scholarly and news accounts of the FAA's voluntary disclosure programs, documentation from Congressional hearings and reports from the U.S. Government Accountability Office (GAO) (a Congressional oversight agency) and Department of Transportation Inspector General (DOT-IG) (an oversight organization specifically for agencies within the Department of Transportation [DOT]). The data collected via the interviews and observations were analysed using an open coding scheme developed to gain insight into the behaviours by regulators and air carrier officials in each program. The researchers triangulated the coded interview data with several other sources of data including GAO and DOT-IG reports, news accounts, and the ERC observations to derive the in-depth examination and analysis of the FAA's voluntary self-disclosure programs.

AIR SAFETY REGULATIONS, THE MOVE TO VOLUNTARY PROGRAMS AND THEIR BENEFITS

The Federal Aviation Administration (FAA) is the primary regulatory agency in charge of air transportation in the United States and is tasked with regulating both commercial and general aviation, promoting and encouraging the development of air service, developing and maintaining a system of air traffic control, and developing programs that mitigate the environmental effects of air transportation. A major task of the FAA is to issue and enforce safety regulations that set minimum standards covering manufacturing, operating, and maintaining aircraft. In order to accomplish this task, the FAA's flight standards service (AFS) uses 14 Certificate Management Offices (CMO) that include dedicated teams of inspectors assigned to certify, oversee, and inspect the operations of a major commercial air carrier. For example, the CMO for US Airways is located in Pittsburgh, Pennsylvania, while the CMO for American Airlines is located in Fort Worth, Texas. Each CMO is organized according to the primary functions of the carrier it is overseeing. Specifically, a CMO will typically have a cadre of operations inspectors, maintenance inspectors, and avionics inspectors who are organized by aircraft type. Through the CMO system, the FAA traditionally conducted inspections of maintenance repairs and check-rides of pilots. However, the FAA's limited inspector resources coupled with the complexity of the aviation industry made effective oversight difficult.

After a series of crashes in the early to mid-1990s, the agency was criticized for the ineffectiveness of its government-centred oversight mechanisms (Gore, 1997). One of the changes the FAA made in response to this criticism was to move towards a more process-oriented approach to safety oversight of air carriers. The FAA developed the Air Transportation Oversight System (ATOS) in 1998. Under ATOS, inspectors develop surveillance plans for each airline, based on data analysis and risk assessment, and adjust the plans periodically based on inspection results (GAO, 2006). The process-oriented approach to oversight inherent in ATOS is dependent upon detailed operational and human factors data to constantly evaluate areas of risk and hazard within a carrier. The FAA's limited inspector resources made collecting this volume of information impossible. To gain access to this valuable safety information, the FAA has developed a suite of voluntary self-disclosure programs that offer a regulatory incentive to both air carriers and employees to voluntarily submit incident reports to the agency.

The FAA uses the data from voluntary self-disclosures and through its close interaction with industry to proactively target its oversight of air carriers while also identifying systemic areas of safety concern across the national air space system. Importantly, the FAA's traditional inspection processes remain a vital part of the agency's approach to regulatory oversight of air carriers. The combination of robust voluntary self-disclosure programs with the FAA's proactive inspection protocols has been given credit for the highest level of safety in the history of the aviation industry (Mouawad and Drew, 2013). Specifically, there has not been a fatal crash of a U.S. based carrier in the U.S. since 2008. However, the success of these programs depends in large part on the level of trust between air carriers and the regulatory agencies responsible for providing oversight. The reason is simple: without trust, airlines and airline employees may not disclose violations or safety problems (for similar reality in the mining context, where the level of trust determined the success of management-based programs, see Gunningham and Sinclair, 2009).

This chapter will investigate three voluntary disclosure programs used to ensure aviation safety: the Aviation Safety Reporting System, the Aviation Safety Action Program, and the Voluntary Disclosure Reporting Program (VDRP). We will demonstrate the building of trust in each and the importance of that trust, and then provide an example where, arguably, excessive trust led to a potentially serious safety problem.

THE FAA'S VOLUNTARY DISCLOSURE PROGRAMS

Aviation Safety Reporting System

Created in 1975, the Aviation Safety Reporting System (ASRS) is a confidential voluntary reporting system that receives, processes, and analyses incident reports from pilots, air traffic controllers, dispatchers, flight attendants, maintenance technicians, and others that describe unsafe occurrences and hazardous situations. In exchange for their submissions, reporters are ensured confidentiality of their reports and a waiver of sanction. Reporters can fill out a paper or electronic form that is submitted to a national-level system. Analysts then review all of the reports submitted from around the country to identify large-scale trends that illuminate potential safety hazards in the national airspace system.

During the initial implementation of the program, the FAA realized that its regulatory and enforcement roles would discourage the aviation community from trusting and using the new program if the FAA were to operate the system. Therefore, the FAA signed a Memorandum of Agreement (MOA) with NASA to operate ASRS for it in 1975. A NASA official described the importance of having NASA rather than the FAA operate ASRS:

> In other setups, it is hard to discover an honest broker. In aviation, we have been very fortunate that NASA has a mission that is research and development. It is not accountability, it is not enforcement, it is not the things that FAA has. It is part of their mandate as an agency from Congress, just as NTSB has a mandate to investigation [sic] aviation accidents and incidents. NASA is a "R&D" mission. It allows us to stand on the side with the white hat and say we have the expertise and we can build the trust, confidence, and credibility with the people in the field to tell us the truth. We will protect you. (NASA Official Interview, 1/4/2010)

NASA and FAA also realized that in order to foster trust and collaboration between the aviation community and the ASRS program, the program would need to guarantee that reporters' confidentiality would be maintained and that if the report met certain conditions, any sanction imposed on the individual would be waived. ASRS program guidance directs NASA to remove all identifying name, air carrier, and third party references from ASRS reports within 72 hours of NASA's receipt of the report if no further information is required. Ensuring the confidentiality of reporters has been crucial to the longevity of the ASRS program. One NASA official noted, "We guard the data and confidentiality of reporters religiously. We are at about 880,000 reports that have been submitted over 34 years and we have had no breach of identity" (NASA Official Interview 1/4/2010). ASRS also provides a regulatory incentive to those who submit a report within the guidelines of the program. A reporter to ASRS will receive a waiver of enforcement action by the FAA if the reported violation was inadvertent, the violation does not involve a criminal act, the person has not been found to have violated a Federal Aviation Regulation (FAR) in the past five years, and the person completed the ASRS report within ten days of the violation (AC 00–46D). An air carrier official described the importance of NASA's involvement in the development of ASRS:

> I think we all trusted NASA because our names were being removed [so] that no one else had access to the data. I know the FAA doesn't get it because it was in NASA's hands, not FAA's. So I know my certificate isn't at risk unless for some reason I get called in and I can pull my NASA receipt and be protected. (Air Carrier Interview D, 26/4/2010)

Aviation Safety Action Program

Created in 1997, the Aviation Safety Action Program (ASAP) is a voluntary disclosure program that allows employees of air carriers to report safety related events without the FAA or the carrier taking punitive action against the employee based on the information in the report. Unlike other voluntary programs, ASAP involves a partnership between three entities (FAA, air carrier, and the employee union) that is codified through a Memorandum of Understanding (MOU). A representative from the local FAA CMO, air carrier, and the employee union sit on an ERC to decide if an ASAP report should be accepted into the program and what corrective action, if any, is necessary to remedy the safety concern. ASAP provides the FAA and air carriers valuable safety information it would not otherwise have access to from those on the front lines of aviation. This information is used to pro-actively identify areas of risk and hazard in a carrier's operation and to develop corrective measures to address these potential safety concerns. One air carrier official noted that many employees were distrustful during the initial implementation of the pilot ASAP program at his air carrier:

> Pilots tend to be suspicious and conspiracy theorists. There is that kind of theme. When ASAP first came out in the mid-1990s, it was not immediately embraced because it was viewed as a snitch program and as another way for the FAA to find out what I did. It is just a camera in the cockpit. As time has gone on, there is more trust in the program and part of it is who has managed it and been on the ERC. (Air Carrier Interview D, 26/4/2010)

Today, there are over 200 active ASAPs spanning a variety of employee groups including pilots, mechanics, dispatchers, flight crew, and ramp operators. A recent account estimates that there are over 60,000 ASAP reports submitted annually with the number increasing by 20 per cent annually (Johnson, 2012). Analysing a survey of air carrier mechanics, Patankar and Driscoll (2004) found that maintenance personnel at air carriers with an ASAP program trusted their managers and FAA inspector more than at carriers without ASAP programs. This suggests that the existence of the program itself leads to improved relationships among regulators and firms, which can lead to increased trust over time.

ASAP, contrary to ASRS, is a national program that is implemented at the local CMO and air carrier level. The FAA does have a Voluntary Safety Programs Branch (AFS-230) at the national level responsible for issuing guidance and rules for voluntary programs including ASAP. However, most of the actual work is done at the local level. And there is often a great degree of variation in the implementation of ASAP across air carriers and even across employee groups (pilots vs. mechanics) in the same air carrier. One FAA HQ official noted:

> One reason ASAPs don't work well at some airlines is that they don't have a viable safety culture. The employees don't trust the carrier, the union doesn't trust the carrier or the FAA, the FAA doesn't trust the airline. You need that kind of nurturing environment for the voluntary programs to work.
>
> When I first got to the FAA, I'd been here six months and I went out to the west coast and I talked to an inspector of a major carrier and he referred to the carrier as 'my carrier'. I went to the east coast and I saw another inspector of another large carrier and he referred to the carrier as 'those bastards'. The relationship between the airline and the local FAA varies: some are professional and some are at each other's throats. (AFS-230 Interview B, 20/2/2010)

The differences in the level of trust in the ASAP process were very evident across different FAA CMOs in our interviews. For example, one air carrier official described a positive relationship with their FAA officials while describing his perception of other carriers' relationships:

> I can't complain about my group, but . . . FAA guys have a hard time coming into an ERC meeting and then going back to their CMO and not writing something up. There are inspectors in ERC meetings who forget to take off their inspector hat and be an ERC member. They go back to the CMO and they are writing enforcement actions based on all the information they got from the ERC meeting. Total contradiction to the entire program. I can't believe that the membership to the collective bargaining agreement or the company hasn't just pulled out.
>
> We don't have that issue here. [Inspector #1] and [Inspector #2] are my FAA guys. We talk about some sticky issues, I'm not going to lie. They are pretty good with keeping it discreet and confidential. We try to work it out in this room. (Air Carrier Interview A, 20/4/2010)

Another air carrier representative noted that while he had a good working relationship with his ERC representative, he had a less positive perception of other inspectors in the local FAA CMO:

> My relationship with [Inspector #1] is very open and very honest. If you're going to have a relationship with your FAA liaison you pretty much have to put everything on the table, you have to include them in everything you see. Without putting words in their mouth, I think they see me as the [air carrier] pilot, and a member of Air Lines Pilot Association (ALPA), but when I am on the ERC I am the management representative for this company. I would categorize our relationship as very good and very open. [Inspector #1] and I communicate quite a bit. Obviously we interact every week at the ERC meeting. We have a shared goal. He has a high-pressure position over there at the FAA and I'll be honest with you, there are a lot of Monday morning quarterbacks over there. He walks that fine line over there. (Air Carrier Interview E, 27/4/2010)

One of the central goals of the ASAP is to provide to both air carriers and the FAA valuable operational data from employees that can be used to proactively mitigate safety hazards. ASAP guidance requires that the air carrier maintain a database of de-identified ASAP reports that will be analysed annually to examine trends in reporting. Many carriers conduct a monthly analysis of their ASAP data and report the findings of that analysis to a variety of departments, including the quality assurance unit, which uses the data to change internal processes (Air Carrier Interview A, 20/4/2010). The local FAA CMO offices also use ASAP data trends within a single carrier to identify areas of risk and hazard within the operation. CMOs also are required to submit quarterly ASAP safety reports to the national FAA office that highlight the number of reports received and the types of corrective action taken.

In addition to using ASAP data at the local level, the FAA wanted to be able to mine this valuable source of data at the national level to look for systemic safety issues across air carriers. However, air carriers and employee unions were very concerned about turning identified ASAP reports over to the national FAA office to be shared among competitors. As one air carrier official noted, "The program lives and dies on confidentiality. As soon as that trust is violated, reports will dry up and no one will tell anything" (Air Carrier Interview D, 26/4/2010). In order to ensure the confidentiality of the air carrier and the employee in ASAP reports, the FAA decided to contract with the MITRE Corporation to provide computer servers at each participating air carrier to house their de-identified ASAP data. The FAA, in consultation with MITRE, developed Aviation Safety Information Analysis and Sharing (ASIAS), which is a collaborative government and industry initiative on data sharing and analysis to proactively discover safety hazards, leading to timely mitigation and prevention. ASIAS studies of ASAP data are approved by the ASIAS Executive Board, comprising industry and government members. Once approved, MITRE then conducts queries of ASAP reports on its servers so that the actual data does not leave the carrier's premises, and the compiled dataset is de-identified by carrier. The ASIAS program manager described why the FAA agreed to structure the program in this manner:

> The data collected in ASIAS is solely used for safety. We don't use the data for oversight. This is why we were able to have the operators voluntarily submit their de-identified data because of MITRE Corporation, who runs the external ASIAS for us. There are MOUs between each of the airlines and MITRE that describe how the data will be used, how it will be protected, how it is de-identified (we don't know pilots' names, plane number, etc.). We don't care about identifying information. We are looking for systemic issues. We have these organizations giving us proprietary data and one of the things that they wanted to be assured of was that you wouldn't have people, namely the FAA, in the data trolling around. (ASIAS Program Manager Interview, 24/2/2010)

The ASIAS program manager went on to note the importance of the voluntary nature of the data exchange process:

> Airlines always have the ability to walk over to their server and shut off the switch. Don't forget, their data resides at the airline, it never comes to MITRE. It comes to MITRE in a queried/aggregate format. Anytime one of those airlines wants to turn off that server, it is the end of our data coming from that airline. It says at the bottom of the MOU that the program can be terminated by either party, so all they have to do is pull the plug. (ASIAS Program Manager Interview, 24/2/2010)

Today, all major mainline and regional air carriers in the U.S. participate in ASIAS because they trust in the confidentiality of the data.

Voluntary Disclosure Reporting Program

The Voluntary Disclosure Reporting Program (VDRP) is a program that offers certificate holding air carriers reduced regulatory enforcement actions if they voluntarily report systemic problems within their operation and work collaboratively with their local FAA office on designing a comprehensive fix to the problem. For example, an air carrier could self-disclose to the FAA that they were out of compliance with an airworthiness directive (AD) that calls for monthly inspections of rudders on 757s. Additionally, an air carrier could self-disclose that its pilot training manuals were out of compliance with current FAA regulations. In order for the FAA to accept a self-disclosure, it must be reported within 24 hours of the air carrier learning of the violation and be the first time the FAA has learned of the violation. Once the violation is self-disclosed to the FAA, the agency and the air carrier work collaboratively to ensure that they have identified the root-cause of the violation and any systemic issues that led to the apparent violation. Once the air carrier and the local FAA agree on a corrective action, they work collaboratively on implementing the corrective action within the carrier. The local FAA office also uses the information contained in the self-disclosures to better target its inspections of the air carrier.

One of the major differences between other voluntary disclosure programs and VDRP is that the former are employee reporting programs while the latter is a company or air carrier disclosure program. This difference in the level of disclosure coupled with the need to collaboratively fix the problem identified in the self-disclosure introduces a different decision-making process from that found in employee-level programs:

> In the self-disclosure process, the company is strategic about what corrective actions it recommends. If we have a known issue with the computer system, we are not going to go out and buy a new computer system just because there is a quirk with it. Could it be fixed? Sure it could be fixed, anything could be fixed. Does it make sense to do it? Hell no. (Air Carrier Interview D, 20/5/2010)

As was the case with both ASRS and ASAP, there was a lack of trust in VDRP during the initial implementation of the program. As one air carrier official recollected:

> All the information in the SD (self-disclosure) then becomes ammunition against the airline in the LOI (letter of investigation). We have in the past acted strategically. When this first came out, yes we were sensitive to what the impact was because if it goes to a LOI, there could be a financial impact, civil penalty (FAA fine) to that LOI. When we first got into this program, there would be discussions as to what is the impact, how screwed up are we, what is the likelihood that the FAA will discover this on their own. (Air Carrier Interview D, 20/5/2010)

The same official went on to praise the carrier's relationship with their local FAA CMO and how that relationship has altered their behaviour: "If there is a screw up today we tell the FAA because we have trust in the CMO. I trust the program, with our CMO at least. There has never been a time when a SD was used as an enforcement action" (Air Carrier Interview D, 20/5/2010).

While VDRP is used by all major commercial air carriers, the number and amount of fines issued by the FAA to air carriers even with the opportunity to self-disclosure suggests that there are clearly air carriers that have a lack of trust in their local FAA CMO. According to our analysis of FAA enforcement actions, in 2012, the FAA fined air carriers a total of 233 times for over $14 million. If a violation qualifies for the program, the only plausible reason an airline would not disclose it – qualifying for immunity from regulatory action beyond a warning letter – is if it does not trust the FAA to hold to its side of the bargain: it cannot be sure the information submitted would not be used in an enforcement action (echoing Potoski and Prakash's insight that rigid enforcement undermines collaborative mechanisms by giving industry incentives not to comply). However, as we will illustrate, there are also cases where there is too much trust between air carriers and local FAA CMOs.

SOUTHWEST AIRLINES: WHEN REGULATORS TRUST TOO MUCH

As an inspector for the FAA at the Southwest Airlines (SWA) CMO, Charalambe Boutris was responsible for inspecting the airframe and systems of the airline's fleet of Boeing 737 jets. In the course of his inspections and as early as 2003, Boutris found that SWA records of ADs did not meet the requirements of the law. He informed the SWA maintenance officials and recommended on numerous occasions to his Supervisory Principal Maintenance Inspector (SPMI) Douglas Gawadzinski that they file a letter of investigation (LOI) against SWA. Gawadzinski refused the request by Boutris and instead told him that a safety attributes inspection (SAI) would be conducted to see if the airline was in compliance with federal regulations. SAIs are internal audits conducted by the air carrier and reviewed by the FAA on a routine basis. One year later, when Gawadzinski approved the SAI with Boutris in charge, SWA maintenance officials met with Gawadzinski to have Boutris replaced with a "more friendly supervisor" (U.S. House of Representatives, 2008). This once again delayed the SAI, which according to FAA records was three years overdue.

On 15 March 2007, SWA informed Gawadzinski that 47 of their aircraft had over-flown the required fuselage fatigue inspection. On 19 March 2007, SWA filed a VDRP claim with the FAA. However, after the VDRP claim was filed, Boutris learned that the affected aircraft continued flying in passenger operations until 23 March 2007 and that six of these aircraft had up to 4-inch cracks in the fuselage, which can lead to a larger breach of the aircraft frame and the rapid depressurization of the cabin (U.S. House of Representatives, 2008). On the VDRP application, Gawadzinski falsely confirmed that SWA had ceased operations of the planes after they discovered the crack in the fuselage. In reality, SWA allowed the 47 aircraft to continue in service for up to 30 months after they were due to be inspected.

On 3 April 2008, the House Committee on Transportation and Infrastructure, chaired by Representative James L. Oberstar D-MN, conducted a hearing into safety issues at SWA, and possible lapses in FAA oversight. In the testimony following the discovery of the violations, it became clear that Gawadzinski had fallen prey to the "relaxed culture" in the SWA CMO. Specifically, it was determined that Gawadzinski had allowed the non-compliant aircraft to continue to operate because of a close personal relationship with the Manager of Regulatory Affairs at SWA, who also happened to be a former subordinate of Gawadzinski's at the FAA. This relationship led Gawadzinski to trust the intention and general competence of the manager and SWA, even as evidence of lapses accumulated. An investigation of phone records also found that FAA inspectors were in some instances calling SWA maintenance staff to inform them ahead of time of what inspections were coming in order to file VDRP claims before the FAA inspectors discovered the same violations.

In response to the congressional and public concern arising from the SWA incident, the FAA ordered an immediate and nationwide audit of other airlines, to see if they too had any compliance problems with any ADs that affected their fleets. Each FAA office that oversees air carriers with aircraft seating ten or more passengers (so-called "Part 121" carriers, since the regulations governing them are found in Chapter 121 of the Code of Federal Regulations) was asked to audit 10 per cent of the ADs applicable to each aircraft type they operate. As a direct result of these "special emphasis" AD audits, problems quickly surfaced with American Airlines' fleet of MD-80s. On 25 and 26 March 2008 FAA inspectors found discrepancies with some of American Airlines' MD-80s, and American grounded part of its fleet, cancelling a few hundred flights. On 7 April 2008, just three days after the congressional hearings arising from the SWA events, FAA inspectors re-inspected 17 of AA's MD-80s and found 16 of them to be out of compliance with AD 2006–15–15. On April 8, faced with the prospect of imminent enforcement action by the FAA, American Airlines chose to ground its entire fleet of MD-80s (more than 350 planes), putting these planes back into service only when the AD requirements had been completely met, and were to the FAA's satisfaction. From 8 to 11 April, American Airlines cancelled 3,100 flights, stranding or inconveniencing more than 250,000 passengers (U.S. DOT 2008).

DISCUSSION

The case studies above demonstrate the positive and crucial rule trust played in developing the voluntary disclosure programs and using them to improve air safety. A few insights related to the role of trust and regulatory oversight can be drawn. First, it is clear from all three programs, that trust takes time to build and evolves over time (Black, 2008). An example of the evolution of trust was the FAA's decision to create institutional mechanisms to prevent the "betrayal" of trust. For ASRS, this meant allowing a third party (NASA) to control the voluntarily disclosed data. For ASAP, it meant that the national FAA could only receive de-identified information via a third party (the MITRE Corporation). In this way, the FAA made the programs work despite existing mistrust of the FAA willingness to forgo punitive action by airlines and their employees. Over time, each actor's needs and perception of the other changed, necessitating more institutionalization and delineation of roles and responsibilities (Fryxell et al., 2002). This suggests that the level of trust in regulatory environments is dynamic and each party must be flexible if voluntary arrangements are to succeed over time.

A second finding is that there is a significant difference in how trust is fostered and viewed at the organizational and individual levels. Trust is viewed through the RRT deterrent-based trust lens at the organizational level. Many inspectors and high-ranking officials frequently remind air carriers and their personnel that if they do not report violations (particularly large-scale systemic ones) to ASAP, ASRS, or VDRP, the FAA retains the right to take severe punitive action. At the local level, however, trust has been fostered through repeated interactions over time, which has allowed the regulated employees to internalize the values of the regulator (safety in our case). Consistent with SDT, trust between airline employees and inspectors grew as a result of the programmatic elements of ASAP and VDRP that allow regulated employees to develop autonomy, competence, and relatedness. Autonomy is evident through the collaborative fix processes in both ASAP and VDRP as employees are encouraged to participate and help attribute to identifying causality for violations (Ayers and Braithwaite, 1992; Gunningham and Sinclair, 2009). Competence is demonstrated through the feedback loops inherent in ASAP and VDRP that can lead to regulatory change (Six, 2013). Importantly, the ERCs that are a critical component of ASAP help to build trust between regulators and regulated employees through the specific procedural mechanisms enacted by all parties of the ERC (Murphy, 2004). Contrary to the work of Hedgecoe (2012), the building of trust in ASAP and VDRP does affect both regulators and air carriers and a violation of that trust would have consequences both financially and reputationally on all actors involved in the programs.

Third, the level of trust between airline employees and FAA inspectors varied quite drastically across locations. For example, of the ERCs we observed, some had very collegial and collaborative relationships between air carrier, union, and FAA officials while others had very adversarial relationships. This finding is consistent with the work of Heimer and Gazley (2012), who found similar differences across HIV clinics. There are several potential explanations for this finding. First, it is possible that employees of the regulated air carriers were not able to internalize the values of the regulators because of pressure from management not to do so. Second, it could be that the regulators in these instances were more focused on "sticking it to" the air carriers rather than ensuring safety. If the regulated employees were to internalize such a value, it could lead to the hiding of violations and a lack of disclosure.

Another key finding from our analysis is that there is also a dark side to excessive trust in regulatory environments. The SWA incident highlights Möllering's (2008) concept of the suspension of belief that a partner will engage in deception. Many in the FAA believed that the alternatives of submitting a self-disclosure to VDRP or facing the possibility of a fine would be a sufficient incentive to prevent deception. However, as Möllering notes, poor deception-detectors are often overconfident of their abilities to detect deception, which was evident in the SWA case. The SWA incident also illustrates how excessive or misplaced trust can catch regulators by surprise when they suspend belief of deception. Following the revelation that Southwest aircraft had been operating out of compliance for more than 30 months, the FAA did not look to revise its voluntary program guidance or restructure the Southwest CMO, but instead conducted a very command and control-oriented mandatory audit of all aircraft in the United States. Not only was the mandatory audit evidence of the FAA's belief of deception after the SWA incident, but also it eroded trust among other carriers participating in voluntary programs.

Finally, the SWA incident illustrates the danger of regulators who internalize the values of the regulated industry and then take action to further those values at the expense of public values and provides an excellent example of Kwak's conceptualization of cultural capital. Because the FAA's lead inspector for Southwest had a very close personal relationship with the director of regulatory affairs for the air carrier (himself a former FAA inspector for SWA), it was more likely that the agency would be culturally captured because many current employees were in the inspector's social network. Balancing the two sides – the need for trust in effective cooperative regulatory environments with the spectre of capture – is not easy. Importantly, an effective way to prevent capture is for both regulated firms and regulators to acknowledge the role that each has to play in ensuring both the safety of industry and the financial health of a firm. While the concern of capture is real, the substantial benefits of the collaborative programs suggest that doing away with them or undermining them comes at too high a cost.

CONCLUSION

The central theme of the role of trust in voluntary disclosure programs is one of balance and vigilance. While the level of trust between regulators and firms at all organizational levels is one of the most important indicators of success in process-oriented regulatory regimes such as voluntary disclosure programs, regulators and their political overseers must be vigilant in ensuring that a high degree of trust does not result in too cosy a relationship that turns a blind eye to incidents of non-compliance. The case of the FAA's voluntary programs illustrates that in order for process-oriented approaches to regulation to be effective, regulators must take great care in designing structural elements and policies that foster trust to encourage firms and their employees to provide the agency with valuable information on incidents of non-disclosure that can help the agency and firm implement corrective action to improve safety. However, as process-oriented tools such as voluntary reporting programs become trusted and routine over time, the agency runs the risk of becoming too trusting and abdicating their regulatory responsibility.

Our analysis indicates that structural elements such as visible data analysis and process improvements, the use of third parties to operate programs, and the building of relationships at the local level through repeated interactions and the development of autonomy, competence, and relatedness of the regulated firm can help foster trust and lead to successful voluntary disclosure programs. Future research in this area should focus on comparative case analysis, both nationally and cross-nationally, of voluntary programs to identify structural and potential cultural variables that influence the level of trust in voluntary disclosure programs.

REFERENCES

Alberini, A. and K. Segerson (2002), 'Assessing voluntary programs to improve environmental quality', *Environmental & Resource Economics*, **22**(1), 157–184.
Ansell, C. and A. Gash (2008), 'Collaborative governance in theory and practice', *Journal of Public Administration Research and Theory*, **18**(4), 543–571.

Ayers, I. and J. Braithwaite (1992), *Responsive regulation, transcending the deregulation debate*, New York: Oxford University Press.

Black, J. (2008), 'Constructing and contesting legitimacy and accountability in polycentric regulatory regimes', *Regulation & Governance*, **2**(2), 137–164.

Braithwaite, J. and T. Makkai (1994), 'Trust and compliance', *Policing and Society*, **4**, 1–12.

Carpenter D. and D.A. Moss (eds) (2014), *Preventing capture: special interest influence in regulation and how to limit it*, New York, NY: Cambridge University Press.

Costa, A.C., and K. Bijlsma-Frankema (2007), 'Trust and control interrelations: New perspectives on the trust–control nexus', *Group & Organization Management*, **32**, 392–406.

Dana, D. and S. Koniak (1999), 'Bargaining in the shadow of democracy', *University of Pennsylvania Law Review*, **148**(2), 473–559.

Deci, E.L. and R.M. Ryan (2000), 'The 'what' and 'why' of goal pursuits: Human needs and the self determination of behavior', *Psychological Inquiry*, **11**(4), 227–268.

Downer, J. (2010), 'Trust and technology: The social foundations of aviation regulation', *British Journal of Sociology*, **61**(1), 83–106.

Fryxell, G., R. Dooley and M. Vryza (2002), 'After the ink dries: The interaction of trust and control in U.S.-based international joint ventures', *Journal of Management Studies*, **39**(6), 865–886.

GAO (U.S. Government Accountability Office) (2006), *FAA safety efforts generally strong but face challenges*, GAO 06–1091T, Washington, DC: GAO.

Gilad, S. (2010), 'It runs in the family: Meta-regulation and its siblings', *Regulation & Governance*, **4**, 485–506.

Gore, A. (1997), White House Commission on Aviation Safety and Security Final Report. [Last accessed 12 February 2014.] Available from URL: http://www.fas.org/irp/threat/212fin%7E1.html

Gormley, W.T. (1986), 'Regulatory issue networks in a federal system', *Polity*, **18**, 595–620.

Gunningham, N. and D. Sinclair (2009), 'Organizational trust and the limits of management-based regulation', *Law & Society Review*, **43**(4), 865–900.

Gunningham, N. and D. Sinclair (2012), *Managing mining hazards: Regulation, safety and trust*, Sydney: Federation Press.

Hedgecoe, A. (2012), 'Trust and regulatory organisations: the role of local knowledge and facework in research ethics review', *Social Studies of Science*, **42**(5), 662–683.

Heimer, C.A. and J.L. Gazley (2012), 'Performing regulation: transcending regulatory ritualism in HIV clinics', *Law and Society Review*, **46**, 853.

Johnson, B. (2012), Looking for the big ASAP success story. Aviation Pros, July 13 [Last accessed 12 February 2014.] Available from URL: http://www.aviationpros.com/article/10726469/looking-for-thebig-asap-success-story

Kwak, J. (2014), 'Cultural capture and the financial crisis', in D.P. Carpenter and D. Moss (eds), *Preventing capture: special interest influence in regulation, and how to limit it*, Cambridge, MA: Cambridge University Press, pp. 71–98.

Leach, W.D. and P.A. Sabatier (2005), 'To trust an adversary: integrating rational and psychological models of collaborative policymaking', *American Political Science Review*, **99**(4), 491–503.

May, P.J. (2005), 'Regulation and compliance motivations: examining different approaches', *Public Administration Review*, **65**(1), 31–44.

Mills, R.W. (2010), 'The promise of collaborative voluntary partnerships: lessons from the Federal Aviation Administration', *IBM Center for the Business of Government*, Washington, DC.

Mills, R.W. and D. Reiss (2014), 'Secondary learning and the unintended benefits of collaborative mechanisms: the Federal Aviation Administration's voluntary disclosure programs', *Regulation and Governance*, **8**(4), 437–454.

Möllering, G. (2008), 'Inviting or avoiding deception through trust? Conceptual exploration of an ambivalent relationship', *MPIfG Working Paper 08/1*, Köln: Max-Planck-Institut für Gesellschaftsforschung.

Mouawad, J. and C. Drew (2013), 'Airline industry at its safest since the dawn of the jet age', *The New York Times*, 11 February, p. A1.

Murphy, K. (2004), 'The role of trust in nurturing compliance: a study of accused tax avoiders', *Law and Human Behavior*, **28**(2), 187–209.

Nielsen, V.L. and C. Parker (2009), 'Testing responsive regulation in regulatory enforcement', *Regulation & Governance*, **3**, 376–399.

Niles, M. (2002), 'On the hijacking of agencies (and airplanes): the Federal Aviation Administration, "agency capture" and "airline security"', *Journal of Gender, Social Policy & the Law*, **10**(2), 381–442.

Patankar, M.S. and D. Driscoll (2004), Published in the Proceedings of the First Safety Across High-Consequence Industries Conference March 9 and 10, St. Louis, Missouri pp. 97–102.

Perrow, C. (1984), *Normal accidents*, New York: Basic Books.

Potoski, M. and A. Prakash (2004), 'The regulatory dilemma: cooperation and conflict in environmental governance', *Public Administration Review*, **64**(2), 152–163.

Potoski, M. and A. Prakash (2009), *Voluntary programs: a club theory perspective*, Cambridge, MA: MIT Press.

Raymond, L. (2006), 'Cooperation without trust: overcoming collective action barriers to endangered species protection', *Policy Studies Journal*, **34**(1), 37–58.

Rousseau, D.M., S.B. Sitkin, R.S. Burt and C. Camerer (1998), 'Not so different after all: a crossdiscipline view of trust', *Academy of Management Review*, **23**(3), 393–404.

Short, J.L. and M.W. Toffel (2008), 'Coerced confessions: selfpolicing in the shadow of the regulator', *Journal of Law, Economics and Organizations*, **24**, 45–71.

Six, F.E. (2013), 'Trust in regulatory relations: how new insights from trust research improve regulation theory', *Public Management Review*, **15**(2), 163–85.

U.S. House of Representatives, Committee on Transportation and Infrastructure (2008), *Critical Lapses in FAA Safety Oversight Of Airlines: Abuses Of Regulatory Partnership Programs*, 110th Congress, April 3.

U.S. Department of Transportation, Independent Review Team (2008), *Managing risks in civil aviation: a review of the FAA's approach to safety*, Washington, DC: U.S. Government Printing Office.

Yin, R. (2003), *Case study research: design and methods*, London: Sage Publications.

APPENDIX A

Summary of Interviews Conducted

The researcher conducted a total of 13 interviews and attended a total of two ERC meetings to gather data on the FAA's voluntary safety programs.

FAA interviews

- AFS-230 Interview A, Program Manager. 6 November 2009.
- AFS-230 Interview B, Program Manager. February 22, 2010.
- ASIAS Interview. Official. February 24, 2010.
- FAA CMO Interview A, Inspector. February 18, 2010.
- FAA CMO Interview B, Principal inspector. February 18, 2010.
- FAA CMO Interview C, Inspector. April 7, 2010.
- FAA CMO Interview D, Inspector. April 20, 2010.

NASA interviews

- NASA Official Interview. 1/4/2010.

Air carrier interviews

- Air Carrier Interview A, ASAP Program Manager. 20 April 2010.
- Air Carrier Interview B, ASAP Program Manager. April 26, 2010.
- Air Carrier Interview C, Director of SMS. May 14, 2010.
- Air Carrier Interview D, Director of Regulatory Compliance. May 20, 2010.

Trade association interviews

- Aviation Trade Association Interview. General Council. 1 June 2010.

Event review committee meetings

- Event Review Committee Observation. 27/4/2010.
- Event Review Committee Observation. 13/5/2010.

APPENDIX B

List of Acronyms Used

AD	Airworthiness directive
AFS	FAA flight standards service
AFS-230	FAA Voluntary Safety Programs Branch
ALPA	Air Lines Pilot Association
ASAP	Aviation Safety Action Program
ASIAS	Aviation Safety Information Analysis and Sharing Program
ASRP	Aviation Safety Reporting Program
ASRS	Aviation Safety Reporting System
ATOS	Air Transportation Oversight System
CMO	Certificate Management Office
DOT	Department of Transportation
DOT-IG	Department of Transportation Inspector General
ERC	Event Review Committee (ASAP)
FAA	Federal Aviation Administration
FAR	Federal Aviation Regulation
GAO	Government Accountability Office
IJV	International joint venture
LOI	Letter of investigation
MOA	Memorandum of Agreement
MOU	Memorandum of Understanding
NASA	National Aeronautics and Space Administration
RRT	Responsive regulatory theory
SAI	Safety attributes inspection
SD	Self-disclosure
SDT	Self Determination Theory
SPMI	Supervisory Principal Maintenance Inspector
SWA	Southwest Airlines
VDRP	Voluntary Disclosure Reporting Program

3. When the going gets tough: exploring processes of trust building and repair in regulatory relations

Frédérique Six and Hans Van Ees

In their literature review Six and Verhoest (Chapter 1) conclude, among others, that the dynamics of processes of trust building and repair are under studied. In this chapter we begin to address this gap. Over the past decades several models taking different approaches have been proposed for processes of trust building. The first from Zand (1972) focuses on the interactive nature of interpersonal trust building and the role of intentions, expectations, behaviour and perceptions. A second, often cited, model focuses on three stages of trust development: calculus-based, knowledge-based and identification-based trust (Lewicki and Bunker, 1996). We question the usefulness of the distinction of these three stages in regulatory relations. First, calculus-based trust is an unhelpful concept as Janowicz-Panjaitan and Noorderhaven (2009) argued; it is more useful to see calculation and trust as two distinct drivers of cooperative behaviour. Second, identification-based trust, that is, trust "based on identification with the other's desires and intentions" (Lewicki and Bunker, 1996, p. 122), is undesirable in most regulatory relations. At best, empathy with the other's desires and intentions may be a good quality in regulatory relations, but not identification since that would lead to regulatory capture (Levine and Forrence, 1990). This only leaves knowledge-based trust as a relevant stage in trust development in regulatory relations, so there is not much development left to go through. We therefore start with Zand's model and tentatively extend it to interorganizational regulatory relations.

After a brief overview of trust, trust building processes and Zand's model, we introduce our case study design and the two cases. We performed a detailed reconstruction of the regulatory processes between a public regulator – Dutch water boards in charge of water management, licensing and enforcement – and a public regulatee – Dutch local authorities developing new housing districts; in other words, relationship 7 in Six and Verhoest's mapping of trust relationships in regulatory regimes

(Chapter 1). The empirical data were collected with the question what happens in the interaction processes between water boards and local authorities, why do these interactions sometimes get into trouble and what may explain the different outcomes? It turned out that processes of trust building and (attempts at) repair provide a fruitful conceptual lens through which we can understand and explain what happens. We construct an adaptation to Zand's model with tentative propositions, with new insights about organizational-level conditions for trust building and repair. We conclude with suggestions for further research and implications for practice.

CONCEPTUALIZATION OF TRUST

Trust is a complex concept that has many definitions. There is growing consensus that trust is best defined as the intention to accept vulnerability to the actions of the other party, based upon the positive expectation that the other will perform a particular action that is important to the trustor (Kramer and Lewicki, 2010; Nooteboom, 2002; Rousseau et al., 1998). Dietz (2011), however shows that this definition only covers one of three phases of trust within the trust process: (1) trustworthiness: the beliefs; (2) the trust decision; and (3) trust-informed actions. Trust is a judgement based on knowledge about another party's trustworthiness and in its turn provides the basis for "trust-in-action" (cf Dietz, 2011). Research into interpersonal trust building processes emphasizes the crucial role of expectations and perceptions (Nooteboom, 2002; Zand, 1972). Trust is ultimately based on the perceptions of the trustor and multiple interpretations of the trustee's actions and intentions are possible. In the first chapter of this book, a more elaborate review of the literature is provided.

Trust Building Processes

In general, trust is built between two interacting actors when over time positive expectations are met and they gradually get to know one another better. The interactive nature of the trust building process implies that the trustor's predisposing beliefs and expectations are crucial as they determine his or her initial attitude (Olson et al., 1996). These expectations are based on trustworthiness beliefs that the trustor has about the trustee (Dietz, 2011). The self-fulfilling prophecy of beliefs (Zand, 1972) implies that an actor's beliefs are most likely to be confirmed through the impact of the actor's actions – driven by these beliefs – on the other actor. The predisposing beliefs "guide" how information is interpreted, especially ambiguous information; and usually this information is interpreted in line with what

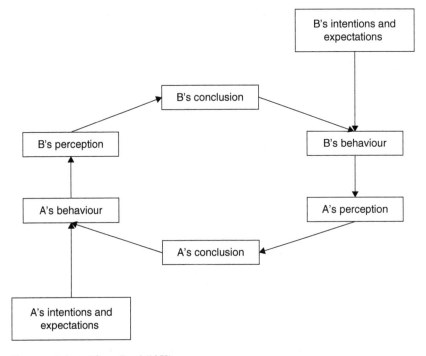

Source: Adapted from Zand (1972)

Figure 3.1   Trust building process

was expected (Olson et al., 1996, p. 217). In upward spiralling processes of positive trust experiences, A's trust in B is confirmed, that is, B acts according to A's pattern of expectations and trust is built. If A concludes that B is sufficiently trustworthy, A will act to make herself vulnerable to the actions of B; B in turn will perceive A's action as indications of A's trustworthiness and will likely act in line with A's expectations, which will be perceived as confirmation of A's initial trust (Figure 3.1).

If, on the other hand, A's initial expectation is that B may not be trusted, A's behaviour is likely to be suspicious and cautious, which is likely to be perceived by B as such. B is likely to conclude that he is uncertain about A's trustworthiness and will be cautious, on guard, maybe even suspicious in his actions. A, in turn, is likely to observe that and feel reinforced by her initial suspicion and caution.

Trustworthiness encapsulates a distinction between ability (or competence) and intention (Kramer and Lewicki, 2010; Nooteboom, 2002). Apart from being able to perform the future actions that the trustor expects, trustees also need to convince the trustor of their good intentions. That is, they also need to be willing to go beyond direct self-interest, taking the trustor's interest into account (Hardin, 2002), wanting to maintain a mutually rewarding relationship (Lindenberg, 2000). The underlying system dynamics of both trust and distrust are thus based on confirmatory feedback (Deutsch, 1973; Zand, 1972), but with an important asymmetry. Trust builds up gradually and incrementally, reinforced by previous trusting behaviour and previous positive experiences (Lewicki and Bunker, 1996; Zand, 1972), while distrust is more catastrophic (Lewicki and Bunker, 1996). Part of the explanation lies in the fact that it is easy to find evidence of untrustworthy behaviour while it is difficult to prove trustworthiness (Gambetta, 1988).

Trouble

It thus seems more likely that someone's good intentions are misperceived and reciprocated with suspicion than that trust can be built (Deutsch, 1958). And the chances of suspicion, and maybe even distrust, occurring are even greater when two parties trying to collaborate come from different fields, each with their own logic, implicit assumptions and sense making processes; as is the case in regulatory relations (Weick, 1995). When parties find it difficult to properly convey their intentions and competence, trouble often occurs. Trouble events disrupt the trustor's expectations of trustworthiness; such an event "produces a sense of disruption of trust, or profound confusion" (Zucker, 1986, p. 59). Trouble, if handled ineffectively, is likely to create or affirm distrust.

Unexpected events, which we call "trouble", are likely to trigger what psychologists call "attributional processes", where attribution is a form of explanation or interpretation (Pyszcsynski and Greenberg, 1981). People want to be able to explain what happens and make sense of events; as such an explanation is "a logical account of a particular event" (Anderson et al., 1996, p. 272). Unexpected events overthrow our existing explanations based on our existing beliefs and therefore require new explanations. The accuracy of this new explanation will depend on the degree to which the actor intends to form an accurate impression of the other actor, rather than just accomplish a specific task with the other party (Miller and Turnbull, 1986). The fundamental attribution error (Ross, 1977) states that we tend to over attribute behaviour to the properties of the actor (such as ability, intention and effort) and under attribute to situational factors (constraints). This is likely to impact trust building processes.

The trustor who experiences trouble, apparently caused by a trustee, needs to decide what this implies for the trust (s)he can place in the trustee in the future and how to respond to the trouble event. What happens in these critical moments is crucial in determining the nature of the collaborative relationship in the future. It may lead to distrust, a deepening of trust, or anything in between (Six and Skinner, 2010).

Interorganizational Trust

Research into organizational trust is not as well developed as individual trust (see overview provided by Six and Verhoest, Chapter 1). There is growing consensus that both organizational characteristics and interaction with people representing the organization (the boundary spanners, cf Williams, 2002) are relevant for trust in that organization (e.g., Kroeger, 2012; Kroeger and Bachmann, 2013; Möllering, 2005; Sydow, 1998, 2006). In line with Janowicz-Panjaitan and Krishnan (2009) we assume that only people can trust, but they can trust organizations or systems. The focus of this study is on individuals' perceptions of the other organization's actions and characteristics, and the conclusions they draw based on these perceptions and beliefs concerning the trust they have in the organization. Given the relational nature of trust, a party is both trustor and trustee, in other words, to properly understand how trust is built we must look at trust building and repair from both perspectives.

Trust in Regulatory Relations

The dynamic described above has been empirically tested in interpersonal work relations and inter-organizational business relations (e.g., Zaheer et al., 1998; Zand, 1972), but not yet in regulatory relations. John Braithwaite and colleagues have repeatedly stressed the importance of the actual interaction between the inspectors and the members of the regulated organization they are in contact with (e.g., Braithwaite et al., 2007). Mascini and Van Wijk's (2009, p. 40) research provides some examples of the psychological aspects of the trust process, "entrepreneurs react based on how they perceived an inspection rather than based on the inspector's intention [. . . and] entrepreneurs certainly do not always perceive the enforcement style in the same manner as was intended by the inspector". Braithwaite and Makkai's (1994) finding that regulatees' perception of regulator trust in them increased future compliance by regulatees illustrates the reinforcing dynamic of trust processes.

METHOD

Given our interest in the micro processes of trust building and repair within regulatory relations, the research design is qualitative and aimed at reconstructing the interactions, perceptions, intentions and expectations of the actors involved: the boundary spanners – participating officials – of the regulator who interact with the boundary spanners of the regulated organization. Within the setting of water governance regulation in the Netherlands, we tentatively build theory about trust building and repair processes in regulatory relations. This setting was selected because it focuses on regulating public organizations, which is an understudied regulatory relation (Six and Verhoest, Chapter 1).

Case Setting

Water boards in the Netherlands are the regulator in charge of licensing and enforcement for water management, in other words flood prevention and water quality control. Local authorities, when developing property and housing districts, need to obtain licences from water boards to ensure they comply with flood prevention and water quality regulation. In the Netherlands, both water boards and local authorities have a direct mandate from voters and hence democratic legitimization. In the past, when local authorities were developing large new districts with houses, public or commercial property and roads, water boards were usually only involved towards the end of the planning process when licences were needed to be obtained before the actual construction could commence. Often, requirements that water boards wanted to include in the licence were deemed disproportionately expensive, due to choices made earlier in the planning process. This often led to conflicts between parties. It was therefore decided at the national level that water boards should be included earlier on in the planning process, so that their requirements could be incorporated early on, when choices could still be made. Joined project teams were set up.

In this multiple case study, the case is a housing development project, as described above, within the context of the larger, long-term regulatory relationship between the two public organizations. In each relationship, the projects studied were the first of a new kind: more intensive, more informal and with higher ambitions. Before, the relationships were hierarchical, like traditional regulatory relations, rather than the more horizontal relationships envisaged now. Each party came to the project with new intentions and new, untested, expectations. We did not prompt respondents about their prior relationship with the other party and none referred to it. Most respondents (boundary spanners) had not actually interacted with their individual counterparts prior to this project.

Case Selection

We used theoretical sampling (cf Yin, 1994) to select two cases based on the criteria that (1) the regulatory process was complex, i.e. the water management task had to be technically and relationally complex, and (2) the regulatory process was interdependent, i.e. the water governance objective could not be realized by the water board alone; and (3) the projects had run into trouble. We varied the cases on their outcome: in one case the organizations managed to restore the relationship, in the other they did not. In the first case, Big Lake Development, there were serious disagreements along the way, but these were resolved eventually, resulting in an improved working relationship between both organizations and acceptance of the project outcome by all. In the second case, Low Polder Development, the serious problems persisted, even legal procedures were pursued, and the relationship between city and water board continued to be very strained. The actual housing development (task achievement), however, is progressing.

Big Lake Development is a new district with some 1,200 houses, which is being built just outside of C-City, a midsize town in the centre of the Netherlands. Water played a prominent role in the realization of the district, since the district is situated around a big lake created by the extraction of sand. C-City aspired for waterfront plots for houses and a water recreation area and thus strived for high water quality in the district. After the master plan phase of the development project, C-City involved the water board, C-Water, in their water plans and an interorganizational working group was established to facilitate the regulatory process. This project team consisted of functional experts from both organizations. We interviewed the two C-City members and the project leader of the overall development project, one of the C-Water members (the other one was unavailable), the new account manager for C-Water (appointed after the start of the project) and their manager (six interviews in total).

Low Polder Development concerns the construction of a new living district with 1,500 houses in SW-City, a major city in the southwest of the Netherlands. This project required collaboration between the water board SW-Water and SW-City as well as regulation by SW-Water of SW-City, since water played a central role in the spatial planning. Low Polder Development is situated in a low polder area (some six metres below sea level), which has serious consequences for the water management. SW-City involved SW-Water at a very early stage. SW-Water was asked to become part of a city project group on water, helping to draw up the master plan for the development. We interviewed two functional experts from SW-City, SW-City's project leader, the key member from SW-Water in this project and another SW-Water member who was also involved in the project (five interviews in total).

Data Collection

Data collection was performed using in-depth semi-structured interviews with the above-mentioned participants in the project teams and collection of all the relevant documents. We conducted 11 in-depth interviews lasting between one-and-a-half and two hours. The interviews were recorded and transcribed to facilitate fine-grained analysis. Each transcript was sent to the respondent for a factual check. In addition, minutes, policy notes, communication such as e-mails and official letters, spatial plans and newspaper articles were analysed and used to triangulate and support the interviews and reconstruct the regulatory process.

The interview questions aimed to elicit individual and organizational perceptions, expectations and attitudes regarding the process and cooperation in the project. We explicitly asked each respondent to give us their perception of the goals that each organization in the project was pursuing, their expectations, their view on the critical incidents that occurred when the going got tough in the regulatory process, and their view on the outcomes of the project. We did not prompt the respondents on trust, since we did not want to guide them in this respect. Our focus was on concepts that are important for understanding trust building and repair: actions, intentions, perceptions and expectations. We did not explicitly "measure" trust or distrust and did not prompt respondents for these concepts. Several respondents explicitly mentioned trust and/or distrust.

This allowed for a fine-grained analysis and rich understanding of the dynamics of the regulatory process. Subsequently, two verification meetings supported the process of data collection and analysis. Each of these verification meetings supported our findings and conclusions, providing grounds for generalizing beyond these two cases to the wider practice in water governance regulation. The verification focused on checking the facts and care was taken that no undue influence was exerted on our conclusions.

Data Analysis

The data analysis aimed to make explicit the often implicit causal assumptions that guide individuals' behaviour and decision-making, akin to cause map analysis. Although we did not draw individual cause maps (Eden et al., 1992; Laukkanen, 1994), also called mental maps, we were inspired by this analytical tool and its focus on highlighting implicit causal assumptions. This helped to make explicit how differently participants in the same process perceived and interpreted the events unfolding. Where perceptions and interpretations are different, we asked respondents why they perceived or interpreted events this way and explanations were given that revealed their assumptions. These assumptions were not made explicit during the actual interactions. This way we could analyse the impact of intentions and expectations on perceptions of the other organization's behaviour and the quality of the relationship; and infer conclusions about trust. It is important to point out that an unsuccessful interaction did not necessarily imply distrust occurred. Especially for those focused on the task, this was often not the case.

First, we conducted within-case analyses for the two cases. For each respondent we constructed the perceptions of the process more generally and of the critical incidents specifically. We then compared these analyses within each organization to create organization analyses and finally compared the two organizations' analyses. Second, we conducted a cross-case comparison of the two cases.

CASE FINDINGS

For the within-case analyses we present the findings on the perceptions of intentions, expectations, the other organization's behaviour and inferred conclusions about trust.

Big Lake Development

Both organizations started with good intentions and positive expectations. We asked each respondent about their perception of both their own organization's goals and the other organization's goals. All members of the working group only mentioned task-related goals. Only C-Water's manager explicitly mentioned 'a good relationship with C-City' as a goal, but he did not participate in the working group and joined C-Water towards the end of the project.

Initially the regulatory process progressed smoothly. There was agreement on all fronts. C-City's project manager had hopes that "[C-City] could rely on C-Water to have all the [technical] expertise", but that expectation was not met. This instance of disruption of the flow of positive expectations could have led to lower trust, but the project manager did not make any reference to this, instead he simply stated the fact "in the end we hired Grontmij [an engineering firm with the required expertise]".

All members of the working group were working towards achieving swimming water quality in the neighbourhood. In C-Water's perception "we told them early on, if you want [this], you must make sure there are no storm water overflow discharges [in the neighbourhood]". C-Water was under the impression that C-City had agreed to this condition. C-City, on · the other hand, was at this stage not aware that C-Water would not accept storm water overflow discharges with swimming water quality in the neighbourhood: "as far as I know, it had not been mentioned before". Their perception was as follows: "it had been decided in the master plan that we would have storm water overflow discharges [in the neighbourhood]". This plan was a core document for the group. C-City was under the impression that C-Water had accepted this fact. In the perception of each party all was well and they had positive perceptions about the other party and positive expectations about future interactions. This suggests that at this point in the regulatory process trust had been built.

Then, trouble occurred when C-City presented the plans for the sewerage system. C-Water noticed the overflow discharges. In their perception, C-City reneged on the earlier agreement. And in the eyes of C-City it only then became clear that C-Water was strongly opposed to the overflows. The working group met several times but was deadlocked. All members worked under the assumption that the canals in the neighbourhood needed to meet swimming water quality standards. No one saw a way out. Alternative solutions proposed by C-Water in an attempt to break the deadlock were not acceptable to C-City. During this process, C-City got the impression "that [meeting] swimming water quality becomes a demand from C-Water". The officials in the project team started blaming each other for blocking progress.

The Big Lake Development project leader needed to move on: "I decided to step in [. . .] and contacted my [counterpart at C-Water]". C-Water's manager was new to the job, and therefore looked at the process afresh. He wanted to build constructive relationships with the local authorities in C-Water's catchment area and was therefore interested in getting an accurate picture of C-City. In an attempt to resolve the issue, the two managers joined in a meeting with the working group, but that was no success. C-Water's manager reflected that the meeting went on and on and was very technically oriented. "They were not cooperating at all [. . .] one side was making his argument and the other rebutted with their argument. [. . .] In particular, the person from C-City drawing all the plans was not flexible at all. [. . .] In a way I could understand his position". After the meeting, he told his staff that if C-City is not prepared to change the overflows, then C-Water will formally inform C-City "that they will not agree with designating the canals in the neighbourhood as swimming water". Once they had decided that, things got moving again. Interestingly, C-Water felt as if "they had had to give in a lot", even though it was not their original goal to have swimming water quality standards in the canals. Also, in their perception C-City was hurting, since they could not use the image of jumping into the canal for a swim from your back garden as a sales pitch to prospective house buyers.

Big Lake Development's project leader also saw a disturbed relationship during the meeting. He commented that "C-Water was confusing what they could legally require from C-City with what their wishes were". He found C-Water's resolution of the stalemate very acceptable, because he did not have swimming water in those canals as his goal. He is very satisfied with the emerging new district. He reflected that "C-Water is quickly developing more feeling for the urban challenges that local authorities face".

The troubled event was resolved to everyone's satisfaction; both organizations have learned more about each other and comment that the relationship is now good, even better than before they started this collaborative process, despite the conflict. The reconstruction of the interaction process suggests that trust has been built, challenged and rebuilt.

Low Polder Development

Both organizations started with good intentions and positive to neutral expectations concerning the results of the project. However, the stated and perceived goals for each organization were only concerned with the task at hand. No one mentioned developing a good relationship as an objective. Furthermore, each organization ascribed to the other organization the goal of off-loading as much of the costs as possible to the other organization. "[U]ltimately it always comes down to money". Also, SW-Water stated as its goal "to get something out of it" (in terms of improved water system in the polder), which appeared to have been perceived by SW-City as "trying to get your way".

Right at the start of the overall project, SW-City's project leader organized a meeting between SW-City's executive and SW-Water's chairman. He was the only other person present and remembers SW-Water's chairman saying "if this project realizes high quality, then SW-Water is prepared to financially contribute more than the minimum". Unfortunately, no one else from SW-Water was present and the chairman left soon afterwards. Within SW-Water the normal attitude towards any initiatives from local authorities was that all the costs would be borne by the local authority, since it was that party that wanted changes to the water system.

All those involved in the regulatory process agreed that it started very well. SW-Water was asked to actively participate in the Master Plan phase, which was SW-City's responsibility, and the result was a pleasant cooperation. SW-Water sent a letter to SW-City complimenting them on their cooperation. This suggests that at this stage the positive expectations were met and that trust was built.

Based on the Master Plan, an Environmental Impact Assessment (EIA) was drawn up and formally accepted. Among others, it proposed to build an extra pumping station. Both organizations had agreed to the EIA. But they had not made explicit what each assumed as a consequence. As it turned out, SW-City assumed that SW-Water would pay for the pumping station since pumping is the responsibility of the water board. However, SW-Water followed another logic: SW-City wants to build a new district and to accomplish that the station needs to be build; and the party that causes the costs, i.e., SW-City, needs to pay. This was how SW-Water always operated with any new developments. And as to the status of the preferred alternative, "that was not automatically a definitive choice, it needed further discussion first".

Each organization had a clear logic for its position and therefore never thought of explicitly checking whether the other organization followed the same logic. So, soon after the EIA was formally accepted and they entered the next planning phase, a conflict erupted over who should pay for the pumping station. A compromise was reached: SW-Water concluded that the extra pumping station was not needed after all. SW-Water reflected on this incident with "we got off well there", while SW-City reflected "the relationship was disturbed", i.e., trust was under pressure. SW-City interpreted SW-Water's behaviour as lack of effort and not showing good intentions. Therefore they did not respond sympathetically, although also not angrily, since a good compromise was reached.

The next phase of the process was the formal zoning plan. Formally, this is a responsibility of the local authority, but there is a legal requirement that the local authority and water board collaborate to address the implications for the water system. These are addressed in a water section in the zoning plan and ideally the water board formally approves the water section. Many of the houses that were planned would have their gardens facing the water. The polder was some six metres below sea level and, consequently, there was a big challenge for SW-Water to manage the water levels in the district to avoid houses being flooded during heavy rainfall. Managing water levels to avoid flooding is the primary task of a water board; and in the Netherlands they may be held financially liable when houses are flooded. SW-Water wanted to make sure that the commercial property developers would build the floors of the houses high enough relative to the planned water level. In this way it hoped to be able to mitigate the huge financial risk of having to pay compensation for damages after flooding. Its position was therefore that in the formal zoning plan a minimum floor level should be prescribed. SW-City took the position that it is legally impossible to prescribe this as a requirement in this plan and therefore did not include such a requirement. SW-Water then asked for a formal guarantee from SW-City that the floors in the houses would have a minimum level relative to the planned water levels, but SW-City was not willing to give such a guarantee. SW-Water formally appealed to the province that had to accept the zoning plan. This did not go down well with SW-City. "We are supposedly in a [collaborative] process with SW-Water. [. . . But] at the end of the process SW-Water distances itself from the product that we have made collaboratively and where we have given in to them very often, just to get more gains for themselves". It further lowered their trust in SW-Water, which had already been strained by the first incident. The appeal was turned down. The problems escalated further when the water board cooperated with a local newspaper to publish an article about the problems the water board had with the new development. The title of the article was "fear for wet feet", citing the (new) chairman of the water board. SW-City's response was that this behaviour "was truly outrageous and unheard of" and that "the trust in SW-Water has been seriously damaged" [in the Dutch language this implies distrust]. They severed the relationship with SW-Water for a while in this project. They resumed the relationship, but it is still not good (information provided during the verification meeting).

Both organizations retrospectively realize that they had a different approach to the regulatory process. SW-Water saw it as "an open-plan process where everything remains fluid until right at the end". SW-City, however, saw it as a "project process where milestones are decided along the way with no backtracking on decisions made earlier". C-City also wanted transparency on the cost side, expecting "SW-Water to contribute as partners".

Both organizations blamed the other organization for trying to off-load costs, holding the other responsible for the trouble. These perceived bad intentions and lack of effort led to anger. The explanation of events was always that it was the other organization that was behaving badly, not that situational factors were at play (cf the fundamental attribution error; Ross, 1977). And given the expectations regarding the goals and experiences along the way, each organization started to doubt the other's intentions and trustworthiness. For example, the SW-City project leader said "SW-Water wants to get its way". Eventually, distrust erupted and the relationship was temporarily put on hold by SW-City.

While in the previous case the trouble was resolved by the superiors of the project team members, in this case it was more complex. SW-City's project leader tried "to speak to [SW-Water's project member's] boss, but I could not get a meeting". The probable explanation was that he himself was a project member and too involved in the trouble to be credible as mediator. The next level up was the executive board level.

BUILDING TRUST IN REGULATORY RELATIONS[1]

The key underlying concepts in the cases above reflect the dynamics of trust and distrust. At the start of both projects, all organizations entered the new, collaborative form for the regulatory process with good intentions and neutral to positive expectations. In the early stage of each project, trust appears to have been built, since the positive expectations were met.

Proposition 1: The more both parties have good intentions towards the other party and positive expectations about the actions of the other party, and these expectations are met, the more likely it is that trust will be built.

But in each case, expectations were not explicitly communicated, shared and tested, which contributed to the trouble later on. For successful trust building, explicit attention needs to be paid to how parties want to work together, i.e., the process itself. Crucial is that organizations have as one of their goals to better understand the other party, including their needs and interests. In each project, both organizations focused on task accomplishment, while neglecting relationship objectives. This contributed in each regulatory process to the conflict that erupted. Trust research shows that to build trust, attention must not only be paid to the task at hand, but also to the relationship itself. Giving positive feedback and praise is among the most important relational behaviours that help build trust (e.g., Six et al., 2010; Six and Sorge, 2008). A relationship-orientation requires parties to have the necessary interpersonal, communicative and reflexive competencies. In the cases studied, actions that help building trust by addressing relational aspects were scarce (Six et al., 2010). We found only one example, where SW-Water gives SW-City a compliment: SW-Water wrote SW-City a letter thanking them for their productive cooperation.

Proposition 2: The more parties have both a relationship-orientation and a task-orientation, the more likely it is that trust is built.

In both cases the critical incidents that occurred revolved around process factors such as unmet expectations and differences in perceptions of the other party's intentions. These process factors can be considered as the main contributors to the hampered trust building processes. In the Low Polder Development case, SW-City's unmet expectation that SW-Water would contribute financially, combined with SW-Water's unmet expectation that SW-City would cooperate actively in guaranteeing that minimum floor levels in the houses would be achieved, led to the breakdown of the trust built in the earlier phase and ultimately to distrust. In the Big Lake Development case, C-Water misperceives C-City's sewerage plan as the city intentionally reneging on the earlier agreement that there would be no storm water overflow discharges. Having investigated both sides of the event, we suggest that a better explanation is miscommunication, in other words an unfortunate mishap (cf Six and Skinner, 2010).

Both cases show the important role of information exchange. Not only is it important to be aware whether information is available to both parties, attention also needs to be paid to whether it is properly studied and attention needs to be paid to how information is interpreted.

Proposition 3: The more both parties are aware of the challenge of trust building, such as managing expectations, avoiding misperceptions, checking if interpretations and attributions are correct, the more likely it is that trust is built and trouble is avoided.

In interorganizational interactions, structural arrangements also matter, in particular the ability to 'escalate' to higher hierarchical levels when conflict cannot be resolved at the lower level. If done constructively, this is not a sign of weakness of the lower level or a sign of distrust of the other party, but a sign of strength and determination to make the process work. In the case of Big Lake Development escalation was successful, probably because both managers cared for a good relationship. In the Low Polder Development case effective escalation to the management level was hampered because SW-City's overall development project leader participated in the water subproject team. During the verification meeting C-Water described their new structurally embedded arrangement to facilitate escalation. A C-Water official is charged with arranging regular meetings between the C-Water chairman and water executives of all local authorities in their "catchment area". He prepares the meeting with his counterpart at the local authority and with C-Water officials collaborating with that authority. Thus all relevant topics are on the agenda. Both officials attend the meeting and report results to the operational-level officials. This facilitates communication within and across the organizations and "normalizes" escalation when needed. It strengthens trust building processes.

Proposition 4: The more parties create opportunities for constructive escalation and regular meetings aimed at improving relations, the more likely it is that trouble may be resolved and trust is repaired.

CONCLUSIONS

This study looked at actual micro-level processes of trust building and repair in order to contribute further insights to responsive regulatory processes. We used Zand's (1972) model to focus on the role of intentions, expectations and perceptions of actors in trust building (Figure 3.1). We used this model as a conceptual lens to understand the micro-level reconstruction of the interaction processes in two cases. The cases studied started with similar situational characteristics, but varied in the outcome of the regulatory process. We found similarities in the way the regulatory relation progressed, with similar causes for the conflict. The way the conflict was subsequently dealt with, however, was different in important ways, which helped identify the underlying mechanisms and conditions of trust building and dealing with trouble events effectively. If intentions and expectations are explicitly shared, then this will affect perceptions and intentions of the other party, and thus that other party's conclusions and subsequent behaviour, according to Figure 3.1. This will likely lead to a positive trust dynamic as shown in the figure.

Our study showed the importance of looking at the micro-level process so as to understand the mechanisms for successful trust building in regulatory relations and also how the dynamics of distrust work and can be remedied. Trust building processes are more successful if expectations are explicitly shared and needs and interests are exchanged and acknowledged. Interacting organizations need to have both a task- and a relationship-orientation. When only a task-orientation is present, self-fulfilling effects of beliefs and expectations are more likely and misattribution of causes for trouble are more prevalent, which hampers trust building. In one case, Big Lake Development, the trouble was resolved to everyone's satisfaction with positive outcomes on both the relationship- and the task-level, because managers on both sides wanted to preserve a good relationship. In the other case, important differences regarding perceptions and in the interpretation and valuation of behaviour and results led to mistaken inferences regarding intentions. Extending existing knowledge about processes of trust building and repair to interorganizational relations, we found that structural arrangements matter, particularly the opportunities for escalation when trouble erupts.

The particular relationship between the two organizations that we studied is that of a public regulator and a public regulatee. The overall relationship between water boards and local authorities in the Netherlands is more complex though. In some situations, like the one in this study, the water board is the regulator and the local authority is the regulatee; while in other situations they are co-regulator and in yet others co-producing partners. This may make this case study particular. The micro-level study of the interaction, we argue, is more generic for how regulators interact with regulated organizations; and for public organizations aiming to collaborate while having different, sometimes conflicting interests. The formulated propositions, we tentatively suggest, apply to relationships 5–9 in Figure 3.1 (this volume, Chapter 3).

Implications for Research

Research into regulatory relations, collaborative and more hierarchical, focusing on micro-level perceptions, expectations and interactions is scarce, but badly needed for a better understanding of how successful interactions work and how unsuccessful ones can be turned around. Studying in detail each party's perceptions of events gave valuable insights into how each party viewed the relationship. Subsequent research is needed using this approach in other types of regulatory relations than relation 7, the one that we studied. Do the findings from this study also hold in those relations? In other words, are differences in perceptions and unmet expectations also important explanatory factors for other troubled regulatory relations and is success more likely when attention is paid explicitly to the relationship, rather than a pure task-orientation (success is in the eye of the beholder and will likely include productive interaction and outcomes that are acceptable for both parties)?

The approach may also be applied real-time, rather than retrospectively as we did. This will be action-research-type of research since it will influence the actual process of interaction, hopefully aiding the process as participants are triggered to reflect on events. Future research into the dynamics of regulatory relations can test our findings on what it takes to build trust and overcome trouble.

Implications for Practice

We distinguish two clusters of recommendations when we consider what leaders in public organizations can do to improve interorganizational regulatory processes. The first cluster deals with the intentions and interpersonal competencies of the boundary spanners (Williams, 2002). First of all, it is important that operational-level boundary spanners have both a task-orientation and relationship-orientation to the relationship. Second, the more aware they are of the different logics, mental maps and perceptions of each party, the more likely trust can be built. Third, the next step is that they can and will act on that awareness and improve their understanding of the other organization's logic and mental map. This requires self-awareness and reflexivity. When trouble occurs, it is important that they have the interpersonal and communicative competencies to address the trouble in a nonthreatening inquisitive way, so that the trouble may more likely be resolved.

The second cluster of recommendations is at the organizational level. Because trouble events are (almost) inevitable in regulatory relations, it is important that relations between organizations are maintained at different levels and that within each organization there is good internal, vertical, communication about the developments in the relationship. When trouble occurs at the operational level and immediate resolution is not possible, then it may be resolved at a higher management level. When setting up joint teams, beware that this 'escalation' mechanism can work (avoid hierarchically lopsided project teams, like in the Low Polder Development case). Also, pay attention up-front to the mandate and role that is given to the operational-level boundary spanners and provide transparency to all partners in this respect. This will only work if the organizational strategy, policies and practices actually support interorganizational processes.

This study showed that regulatory researchers and practitioners, if they want to better understand the key success factors of regulatory processes, need to pay attention to the micro-level processes of trust building and repair.

NOTE

1. As we discuss our findings and relate them to Zand's model, we *tentatively* formulate propositions. We realize that our empirical analysis is not sufficient basis for solid theory building.

REFERENCES

Anderson, C.A., D.S. Krull and B. Weiner (1996), 'Explanation: processes and consequences', in E.T. Higgins and A.W. Kruglanski (eds), *Social psychology, handbook of basic principles*, New York: The Guilford Press, pp. 271–296.
Braithwaite, J. and T. Makkai (1994), 'Trust and compliance', *Policing and Society*, **4**, 1–12.
Braithwaite, J., T. Makkai and V. Braithwaite (2007), *Regulating aged care,*

ritualism and the new pyramid, Cheltenham, UK and Northampton, MA, USA: Edward Elgar Publishing.

Deutsch, M. (1958), 'Trust and suspicion', *Journal of Conflict Resolution*, **2**(4), 265–279.

Deutsch, M. (1973), *The resolution of conflict: constructive and destructive processes*, New Haven: Yale University Press.

Dietz, G. (2011), 'Going back to the source: why do people trust each other?', *Journal of Trust Research*, **1**(2), 215–222.

Eden, C., F. Ackermann and S. Cropper (1992), 'The analysis of cause maps', *Journal of Management Studies*, **29**, 309–324.

Gambetta, D. (1988), *Trust: making and breaking cooperative relations*, New York, NY: Basil Blackwell.

Hardin, R. (2002). *Trust and trustworthiness* (Vol. IV), New York: Russell Sage Foundation.

Janowicz-Panjaitan, M.K. and R. Krishnan (2009), 'Measures for dealing with competence and integrity violations of interorganizational trust at the corporate and operating levels of organizational hierarchy', *Journal of Management Studies*, **46**(2), 245–268.

Janowicz-Panjaitan, M.K. and N.G. Noorderhaven (2009), 'Trust, calculation and interorganizational learning of tacit knowledge: An organizational roles perspective', *Organization Studies*, **30**(10), 1021–1044.

Kramer, R.M. and R.J. Lewicki (2010), 'Repairing and enhancing trust: approaches to reducing organizational trust deficits', *Academy of Management Annals*, **4**, 245–277.

Kroeger, F. (2012), 'Trusting organizations: the institutionalization of trust in interorganizational relationships', *Organization*, **19**(6), 743–763.

Kroeger, F. and R. Bachmann (2013), 'Trusting across boundaries', in J. Langan-Fox and C.L. Cooper (eds), *The Routledge companion to boundary spanning in organizations*, London: Routledge, pp. 253–284.

Laukkanen, M. (1994), 'Comparative cause mapping of organizational cognitions', *Organization Science*, **5**(3), 322–343.

Levine, M.E. and J.L. Forrence (1990), 'Regulatory capture, public interest, and the public agenda. Toward a synthesis', *Journal of Law Economics & Organization* **6**, 167–198.

Lewicki, R.J. and B.B. Bunker (1996), 'Developing and maintaining trust in work relationships', in R.M. Kramer and T.R. Tyler (eds), *Trust in organizations, frontiers of theory and research*, Thousand Oaks: Sage Publications, pp. 114–139.

Lindenberg, S. (2000), 'It takes both trust and lack of mistrust: the workings of cooperation and relational signaling in contractual relationships', *Journal of Management and Governance*, **4**, 11–33.

Mascini, P. and E. Van Wijk (2009), 'Responsive regulation at the Dutch food and consumer product safety authority: an empirical assessment of assumptions underlying the theory', *Regulation & Governance*, **3**, 27–47.

Miller, D.T. and W. Turnbull (1986), 'Expectancies and interpersonal processes', *Annual Review of Psychology*, **37**, 233–256.

Möllering, G. (2005), 'The trust/control duality, an integrative perspective on positive expectations of others', *International Sociology*, **20**(3), 283–305.

Nooteboom, B. (2002), *Trust: forms, foundations, functions, failures and figures*, Cheltenham, UK and Northampton, MA, USA: Edward Elgar Publishing.

Olson, J.M., N.J. Roese and M.P. Zanna (1996), 'Expectancies', in E.T. Higgins and A.W. Kruglanski (eds), *Social psychology: handbook of basic principles*, New York: The Guilford Press, pp. 211–238.

Pyszcsynski, T.A. and J. Greenberg (1981), 'Role of disconfirmed expectancies in the instigation of attributional processing', *Journal of Personality and Social Psychology*, **40**, 31–38.

Ross, L. (1977), 'The intuitive psychologist and his shortcomings: distortions in the attribution process', in L. Berkowitz (ed.), *Advances in experimental social psychology*, New York: Academic Press, pp. 174–221.

Rousseau, D.M., S.B. Sitkin, R.S. Burt and C. Camerer (1998), 'Not so different after all: a cross-discipline view of trust', *Academy of Management Review*, **23**(3), 393–404.

Six, F.E., B. Nooteboom and A.W. Hoogendoorn (2010), 'Actions that help build trust: a relational signaling approach', *Review of Social Economy*, **68**(3), 285–315.

Six, F.E. and A. Sorge (2008), 'Creating a high-trust organization: an exploration into organizational policies that stimulate interpersonal trust building', *Journal of Management Studies*, **45**(5), 857–884.

Six F.E. and D. Skinner (2010), 'Managing trust and trouble in interpersonal work relationships: evidence from two Dutch organizations', *International Journal of Human Resource Management*, **21**(1), 109–124.

Sydow, J. (1998), 'Understanding the constitution of interorganizational trust', in C. Lane and R. Bachmann (eds), *Trust within and between organizations, conceptual issues and empirical applications*, Oxford: Oxford University Press, pp. 31–63.

Sydow, J. (2006), 'How can systems trust systems? A structuration perspective on trust-building in inter-organizational relations', in R. Bachmann and A. Zaheer (eds), *Handbook of trust research*, Cheltenham, UK and Northampton, MA, USA: Edward Elgar Publishing, pp. 377–392.

Weick, K.E. (1995), *Sensemaking in organizations*, Thousand Oaks: Sage Publications.

Williams, P. (2002), 'The competent boundary spanner', *Public Administration*, **80**(1), 103–124.

Yin, R.K. (1994), *Case study research, design and methods*, Thousand Oaks: Sage Publications.

Zaheer, A., B. McEvily and V. Perrone (1998), 'Does trust matter? Exploring the effects of interorganizational and interpersonal trust on performance', *Organization Science*, **9**(2), 141–159.

Zand, D.E. (1972), 'Trust and managerial problem solving', *Administrative Science Quarterly*, **17**(2), 229–239.

Zucker, L.G. (1986), 'Production of trust: institutional sources of economic structure, 1840 – 1920', *Research in Organizational Behavior*, **8**, 53–111.

4. Interorganizational trust in Flemish public administration: comparing trusted and distrusted interactions between public regulatees and public regulators

Peter Oomsels and Geert Bouckaert

Questions about interorganizational trust and distrust are a topic of scarce interest for public administration scholars (Choudhury, 2008). This is peculiar considering the reform discourse surrounding public management, in which interorganizational trust is increasingly considered as an important characteristic of well-functioning administrative organizations, in particular ever since ideas of 'governance' have emerged in response to the rising complexity which compels organizations in public administration to join forces and cooperate more intensively (Pierre and Ingraham, 2010; Pollitt and Bouckaert, 2011; Edelenbos and Klijn, 2007). Network theory scholars in particular have argued that interorganizational trust is essential for contemporary public administration, as it facilitates, solidifies and increases the performance of interorganizational cooperation in complex decision-making networks (Edelenbos and Klijn, 2007).

Unfortunately, few scholars have treated interorganizational trust within public administration as the topic of their main interest (Choudhury, 2008; Klijn et al., 2010), although there are some notable exceptions, for instance research by Carnevale and Wechsler (1992) and Nyhan (2000). Most advances in interorganizational trust research are found in organizational studies.

In this chapter we will develop an analytical framework for interorganizational trust on the basis of organizational studies literature. We will then apply this framework to interorganizational interactions between regulated and regulating organizations in the Flemish public administration. In particular, we will compare interactions in which Flemish government organizations trust Flemish 'horizontal departments' with interactions in which they distrust Flemish horizontal departments. The objective of this chapter is to better understand interorganizational trust and the (perceived) characteristics of interorganizational interactions that contribute to its development.

INTERORGANIZATIONAL TRUST

Although trust is now one of the most frequently used social science concepts (Das and Teng, 2004), the detached accumulation of literature has led to "a conceptual morass" (Carnevale and Wechsler, 1992, p. 473), which remains daunting after two decades of trust research (Nooteboom, 2006). A full discussion of this conceptual morass would go well beyond the scope of this chapter. We will refer the reader to our previous work (Oomsels and Bouckaert, 2014a), and simply present our definition of interorganizational trust as "a subjective evaluation made by boundary spanners, comprising the intentional and behavioural suspension of vulnerability on the basis of their expectations about a trustee organization".

In the following paragraphs, we explain the role of boundary spanners and the subjective evaluation process in this definition.

Interorganizational Boundary Spanners

Our definition places 'boundary spanners' (Aldrich and Herker, 1977) at the core of interorganizational trust. Interorganizational relationships are actively conducted and managed by individuals on managerial or operational levels of organizations. Interorganizational relations are thus never 'faceless' (Zaheer et al., 1998). As individual boundary spanners operate on behalf of their organization in specific interorganizational interactions, their personal expectations, intentions and actions toward the counterpart essentially constitute interorganizational trust (Beccerra and Gupta, 1999). Our inquiry is therefore focused on the subjective trust evaluation made by such interorganizational boundary spanners.

The Subjective Trust Evaluation: A Universal Trust Process

Our definition of interorganizational trust largely corresponds to the seminal definition of trust as a "psychological state comprising the intention to accept vulnerability based upon positive expectations of the intentions or behaviour of another" suggested by Rousseau et al. (1998, p. 395). However, it differs from the definition by Rousseau et al. (1998) in that it follows others who have argued that trust is not just a psychological state, but a process comprising three dimensions, which are causally related to each other (McEvily and Tortoriello, 2011; Lewis and Weigert, 1985; Mayer et al., 1995; Fulmer and Gelfand, 2012; Dietz, 2011). This trust process is argued to comprise an assessment of the other party's trustworthiness, which can be operationalized as perceived ability (expectation that the other party has competence to successfully complete its tasks), benevolence (expectation that the other party cares about the trustor's interests and needs) and integrity (expectation that the other party will act in a just and fair way) of the counterpart (Mayer et al., 1995). If this assessment of perceived trustworthiness is positive, trustors are more 'willing to suspend vulnerability', which means that they are willing to assume that irreducible social vulnerability and uncertainty will be favourably resolved (Möllering 2006) in the interorganizational interaction. This willingness to suspend vulnerability must then be followed by a behavioural manifestation of risk-taking in dealings with the other party in order for trust to become a 'social reality' in the relationship (Lewis and Weigert, 1985; Mayer et al., 1995; Schoorman et al., 2007). Finally, it is argued that the outcome from such risk-taking behaviour updates the trustors' perceptions of the counterpart's trustworthiness, rendering trust a cyclically dynamic process (Mayer et al., 1995). Dietz (2011) has argued that this causal process represents a 'universal sequence' that applies to all trust problems, and is now well accepted among many trust researchers. In that respect, our definition of interorganizational trust can be visualized as shown in Figure 4.1.

However, although the internal dynamic of this 'trust process' is argued to be universally valid for trust problems in (interorganizational) interactions, trust has also been argued to be affected by different characteristics of the particular (interorganizational) interaction in which it occurs.

INFLUENCE OF INTERORGANIZATIONAL INTERACTION CHARACTERISTICS ON THE TRUST PROCESS

Since boundary spanners operate in the context of the institutional, cultural, organizational, relational and personal characteristics of particular interorganizational interactions, their subjective trust evaluations can be expected to be affected by their perceptions of these characteristics. Different authors have argued that the institutional (macro), interactional (meso) and personal (micro) – level contexts of boundary spanners' interorganizational interactions affect (interorganizational) trust (Zucker, 1986; Rousseau et al., 1998; Kramer, 1999). It follows that an analysis of interorganizational trust in public administration should focus on how the perceived macro-, meso- and micro-level characteristics of

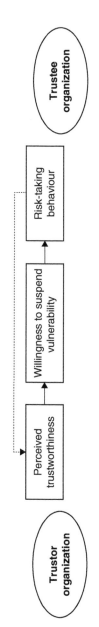

Figure 4.1   The universal trust process

interorganizational interactions affect boundary spanners' subjective trust evaluations. A framework for such an analysis is developed in the following paragraphs.

Macro-level Characteristics of Interorganizational Interactions and the Trust Process

Macro-level interaction characteristics refer to the institutions that encompass interorganizational interactions. Institutions can be defined as "systems of established and prevalent social rules that structure social interactions" (Hodgson, 2006, p. 2). Literature on 'institution-based trust' (Zucker, 1986; Bachmann and Zaheer, 2008; Bachmann and Inkpen, 2011; Rousseau et al., 1998) suggests that institutions enable trust on the basis of "internal organising principles and practices" (Perrone et al., 2003, p. 428) in the interaction, which can affect the trust process through the logics of consequences and appropriateness.

On the one hand, institutions are argued to affect the trust process through a logic of consequences, as they shape institutional templates (Bachmann and Inkpen, 2011), which may add to, or even substitute for direct knowledge or experience within a particular interorganizational interaction, thus providing a trustor with good reasons to consider a counterpart trustworthy, be willing to suspend vulnerability, and engage in risk-taking behaviour. This is why institution-based trust has been argued to play an important role in large and fragmented organizations, where formal and informal norms of behaviour are argued to form a bridge between unfamiliar actors (Sydow, 2006) by establishing a 'world in common' (Zucker, 1986). Sztompka (1998) proposes that, in order to support trust, institutions should be transparent, stable and morally jus-tifiable, provide normative certainty and accountability of power, allow enactment of rights and enforcement of duties, and safeguard autonomy. In addition to these 'substantive conditions', Sztompka (1998) argues that the consistent and sparing use of institutions are two essential 'operational conditions' to stimulate a culture of trust in the institutional environment.

On the other hand, institutions are argued to affect the trust process through a logic of appropriateness, by socializing boundary spanners through coercive, mimetic or normative isomorphism, a "constraining process that forces one unit in a population to resemble other units that face the same set of environmental conditions" (Dimaggio and Powell 1983, p. 149). Coercive isomorphism occurs when formal or informal pressure is exerted to adopt a certain mode of organization or behaviour (I trust them because I'm ordered to). Mimetic isomorphism occurs when high uncertainty and goal ambiguity drives individuals to adopt principles or behaviours that are already in general use in their institutional environ-ment (I trust them because we've always trusted them). Finally, normative isomorphism occurs when salient normative frameworks exert informal pressures on individuals to conform within their environments or networks (I trust them because my normative referents trust them) (Dimaggio and Powell, 1983).

Institutions are notoriously difficult to define and operationalize. In our empirical operationalization, we will distinguish between formal and informal institutions. With respect to formal institutions, we will consider formal rules and formal role attributions in interorganizational interac-tions, which are argued to allow shared understanding regarding appro-priate behaviour in interactions and establish institutional templates for mutual expectations (Kramer, 1999). With respect to informal institutions, we will consider informal routines and salient norms of boundary span-ners' political and administrative leaders in interorganizational interac-tions, as these characteristics are argued to establish interorganizational trust because they support internalized, taken-for-granted attitudes of mutual trust between organizations (Möllering, 2006) and exert normative pressure on boundary spanners' subjective evaluations in interorganiza-tional interactions by empowering a 'culture of trustfulness' (Sztompka, 1998).

Meso-level Characteristics of Interorganizational Interactions and the Trust Process

While macro-level interaction characteristics facilitate trust on the basis of 'institutional templates', meso-level interaction characteristics rely on direct experience with or evidence about a particular interaction or coun-terpart. On the meso-level of interorganizational interactions, 'calculative' and 'relational' characteristics have been argued to affect trust (Rousseau et al., 1998).

Calculative characteristics of interorganizational interactions
Calculus-based trust is presented as a utilitarian consideration of costs and benefits on the basis of available information about the counterpart and the extent of risk in the interaction, in which risk-taking occurs if doing so maximizes utility. The emphasis on such calculus-based trust is very much present in Rational Action Theory-based approaches to trust, such as transaction cost theory, resource dependence theory, and principal–agent theory (Zhong et al., 2014).

Some authors have argued that calculus-based trust is not trust, but mere rational action (Edelenbos and Klijn, 2007; Williamson, 1993). We disagree with this argument, because calculus-based trust goes beyond mere rationality. While a decision to engage in risk-taking behaviour can be calculated on the basis of information, the conditions of bounded rationality and radical uncertainty which are inherent to complex inter-organizational interactions, dictate that trustors must 'overdraw' on avail-able information (Luhmann, 1979) and make a 'leap of faith' (Möllering, 2006) in which they act *as if* they were completely sure of their decision, even though they are not. Since trust is a 'leap of faith' due to the willing-ness to suspend vulnerability, it goes beyond mere rational action, which makes calculus-based trust a relevant consideration in the subjective trust evaluation.

Calculus-based trust has been defined as "an on-going, market-oriented, economic calculation whose value is derived by determining the outcomes resulting from creating and sustaining the relationship relative to the costs of maintaining or severing it" (Lewicki and Bunker, 1996, p. 120). The cal-culation is particularly considered to depend on the availability of credible information about the risks, costs and benefits in the interaction (Lewicki and Bunker, 1996). In relations where resources are exchanged between actors, costs are often operationalized as the extent to which invested assets are difficult to gather and transfer (asset specificity) (Zhong et al., 2014; Katsikeas et al., 2009; Williamson, 1985; Zaheer et al., 1998). Such credible information about risks, costs and benefits may stem from direct relational knowledge about the trustee (for instance, through accumulated relational knowledge about the trustee), but may also result from other sources, such as formal institutional rules, third-party audit reports about the counter-part, or rumours about the trustee's reputation. Information about high risks, high costs and low benefits in an interaction is expected to negatively affect the trustors' willingness to suspend vulnerability (Schoorman et al., 2007).

Relational characteristics of interorganizational interactions

Some authors contend that trust cannot be explained on the basis of calcu-lative reasoning alone (Lyon et al., 2011). For instance, Bromily and Harris (2006) argue that calculative perspectives are very ineffective in explaining why trust emerges under circumstances where it is not rational to trust the counterpart. Therefore, relation-based trust (Rousseau et al., 1998) is also considered to reside at the meso-level of interorganizational interactions. The impact of relational characteristics on the trust process is emphasized in social exchange-based theories, such as social embeddedness theory (Zhong et al., 2014) or relational signalling theory (Six et al., 2010).

Relation-based trust rests upon reciprocated interpersonal care, concern and emotional attachment between boundary spanners, who establish a personal bond through interpersonal familiarity across their professional interaction experiences (Rousseau et al., 1998). Reciprocal behaviour (Blau, 1964) is argued to inspire boundary spanners to suspend more vulnerability in interactions. Furthermore, power equality is argued to affect (interorganizational) trust, as the amount of power that one actor has over another can affect the extent to which it is willing to make itself vulnerable to the other actor (Bachmann, 2001). Third, interpersonal familiarity, which grows from previous interaction experiences (Zand, 1972) and is associated with the age and the frequency of interactions, is linked to the emergence of shared values, mutual identity, interpersonal social norms, and a 'social memory' that helps partners understand and interpret each other's habits, customs and expectations (Zhong et al., 2014). Interpersonal familiarity thus acts as an 'incubator' for other relational characteristics which may affect the trust process.

It is important to note that relation-based trust does not exclude calculus-based trust. For example, we noted that interpersonal familiarity may be a source of credible information about costs, benefits and risks in an interaction, on the basis of which calculus-based trust is supported in interactions. However, while relation-based trust may thus build on or enter into rational calculations, it is argued to go beyond mere calculation, as it acquires value outside a strict self-interested discourse (Braithwaite and Levi, 1998).

Micro-level Characteristics of Interorganizational Interactions and the Trust Process

Finally, characteristics of the individual boundary spanners' personality, which are argued to stem from psychological (Sztompka, 1998), sociological (Glanville and Paxton, 2007) or even physiological (Zak, 2012) configurations, are argued to affect their subjective trust evaluations, and thus interorganizational trust. In particular, boundary spanners' generally stable 'willingness to trust others' (Frazier et al., 2013) or 'predisposition to trust' is often considered to be the most important micro-level characteristic (Mayer et al., 1995). While empirical research has found this to be an important determinant of trust (Grimmelikhuijsen, 2012), we will not consider these micro-level characteristics further and focus our own investigation on the macro- and meso-level characteristics of interorganizational interactions in the context of the Flemish public administration.

Integration of the Analytical Framework

Our theoretical framework can therefore be summarized as follows: in order to explain the interorganizational trust of organization A in organization B, we must investigate how the trust evaluation of organization A's boundary spanners is affected by perceptions about macro-, meso-, and micro-level characteristics of the interorganizational interaction with organization B. Figure 4.2 provides a graphic illustration of this theoretical framework.

METHODOLOGY: INTERORGANIZATIONAL TRUST IN HORIZONTAL DEPARTMENTS OF THE FLEMISH ADMINISTRATION

Nooteboom (2002) contends that the object, subject, context and situation of any trust study are of primordial importance and need to be defined clearly. Therefore, we will focus on specific 'trust problems' (Coleman, 1990) between regulated and regulating organizations in the Flemish administration, in which the regulated Flemish administration organizations are the 'trustor', and the regulating Flemish horizontal departments are the 'trustee'.

A 'trust problem' is a strategic interaction in which the trustor places some kind of resource at the disposal of the trustee, who has the possibility of either honouring or abusing trust (1), where the trustor prefers to grant trust if the trustee honours it, but regrets granting trust if the trustee abuses it (2), where there is no binding agreement that protects the trustor from the possibility that the trustee will abuse trust (3), and where there is a time lag between the behaviour of the trustor and the reaction of the trustee (4) (Barrera et al., 2011). In order to identify and study such trust problems in the Flemish administration, we have implemented a three-phase nested mixed-method research design (Lieberman, 2005). The research design consisted of a broad exploration of interorganizational interactions in the Flemish administration (phase 1), in which we nested a more targeted quantitative survey to compare 12 specific interactions with horizontal departments (phase 2), in which we nested qualitative interviews about the most frequently selected trusted interaction and the most frequently selected distrusted interaction with horizontal departments in the Flemish administration (phase 3). We discuss these methodological phases below.[1]

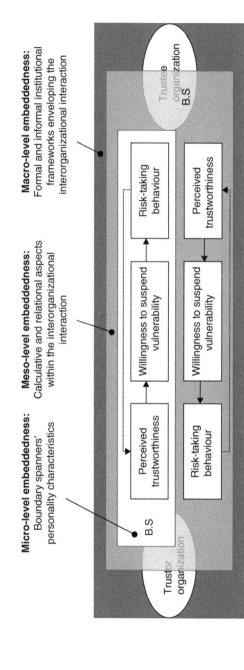

Figure 4.2   Interorganizational interaction aspects and the trust process

Phase 1: Exploration of the Flemish Administration

The Flemish administration governs the 6 million Dutch-speaking inhabitants of Flanders, the northern region of Belgium. At the time of our exploratory study, it employed almost 40,000 civil servants, and consisted of 13 'homogeneous policy areas'[2] (such as Agriculture and Fisheries, Environment and Energy, Public Works and Transport), each containing a department, internal and external agencies, and an advisory council. Policy preparation, monitoring and evaluation are the responsibility of the departments in each policy area, while policy implementation is the operational responsibility of the agencies, which operate at arms' length from the responsible member of the Flemish government with various degrees of autonomy. The three 'horizontal' policy areas DAR (Services for General Government Policy), BZ (Administrative Affairs) and FB (Finances and Budgeting) focus on regulating and coordinating the administrative entities in the entire Flemish administration for their respective tasks. As these departments occupy a central position in the network of interorganizational interactions within the Flemish administration due to the horizontal nature of their tasks, Flemish administrative entities engage regularly in interorganizational interactions with the three horizontal departments.

In prior exploratory research (Oomsels and Bouckaert, 2014b), we screened the occurrence of interorganizational trust problems in the Flemish administration in a variety of interorganizational interactions on the basis of an exploratory senior civil servant survey (n = 45) and exploratory senior civil servant interviews (n = 9). Our exploration indicated that trust problems primarily occurred in organizational interactions with the departments of the three 'horizontal policy areas' described above. In our subsequent research phases, we therefore focused on the subjective trust evaluations of boundary spanners (trustor) in interorganizational interactions with the horizontal departments (trustee) in the Flemish administration.

Phase 2: RI of Trust and Distrust in the Boundary Spanner Survey

The 'boundary spanner survey' was conducted between November 2013 and February 2014, and focused on boundary spanners in Flemish administrative entities who regularly interacted with the horizontal departments described above. The selection of respondents happened in two steps. In a first step, we screened all Flemish administrative entities for divisions in which employees would likely have regular interactions with horizontal departments (for instance, HR-divisions, financial divisions, strategy divisions, knowledge management divisions, communication divisions,

Senior Civil Servant support staff . . .). In a second step, 767 employees of selected divisions received an email with an introduction about the research, and an invitation to participate in a survey, if they considered that they had relevant interaction experience with horizontal departments (opt-in). In total, 145 respondents completed the full survey.

The survey requested boundary spanners to select a most trusted and a most distrusted Reference Interaction (RI) from amongst a list of 12 possible interactions with horizontal departments. The online survey software then automatically presented a list of Likert-scale items (see annex) measuring perceptions about macro- and meso-level interaction characteristics for the selected RI of trust. Then, the survey software automatically presented the same list of items for the selected RI of distrust. In other words, all respondents' most trusted and most distrusted RIs were automatically displayed as the referent interaction in a "three-part relation that restricts any claim of trust to particular parties and to particular matters" (Hardin, 2002, p. 7), allowing us to analyse and compare boundary spanners' perceptions about characteristics of interorganizational interactions for two quantitative samples: sample 1 (RI of trust) and sample 3 (RI of distrust).

Phase 3: Most Frequently Selected RI of Trust and Distrust in Qualitative Interviews

In phase 3, 20 respondents were invited for qualitative interviews based on the RI they had selected in the boundary spanner survey. Ten respondents were invited for interviews about the most frequently selected RI for interorganizational trust (the collection and use of horizontal information by B). The other ten interviews focused on interorganizational distrust, and were conducted with respondents who had chosen the most frequently selected RI for interorganizational distrust (the collection and use of horizontal information by A). For these interviews, the phase 2 survey items (see annex) were printed on plastic cards, which boundary spanners were asked to discuss in relation to the three dimensions of the trust process in their particular RI. This resulted in rich qualitative data which allowed us to analyse and compare how boundary spanners describe and relate perceived interaction characteristics with the trust process for two qualitative samples: sample 2 (the most frequently selected RI of trust) and sample 4 (the most frequently selected RI of distrust).

Samples and Sample Characteristics

Table 4.1 presents the four distinct samples on which our analysis is based. We note that we collected more completed answers for sample 1 (survey

Table 4.1   Number of respondents in quantitative and qualitative samples

	Reference interaction for trust		Reference interaction for distrust	
	Sample 1 (phase 2)	Sample 2: (phase 3)	Sample 3: (phase 2)	Sample 4: (phase 3)
Info collection/use by A	27	0	23	8
Info collection/use by B	30	8	10	0
Info collection/use by C	13	0	9	0
Policy evaluation by A	8	0	15	0
Policy evaluation by B	4	0	11	0
Policy evaluation by C	6	0	13	0
Policy monitoring by A	10	0	7	0
Policy monitoring by B	9	0	9	0
Policy monitoring by C	21	0	3	0
Policy preparation by A	18	0	20	0
Policy preparation by B	6	0	14	0
Policy preparation by C	6	0	11	0
Total	158	8	145	8

Note: Horizontal departments are anonymized.

module III) than for sample 3 (survey module IV), which is likely due to respondent fatigue and subsequent dropout. As shown in this table, information collection by horizontal department B was selected most frequently as referent of high interorganizational trust, whereas information collection by horizontal department A was selected most frequently as referent of high interorganizational distrust. It is interesting to note that in addition to being the most frequently selected referent for distrust in the survey, information collection by A was the second most frequently selected referent for trust in the survey, which indicates rather diverging subjective trust evaluations about department A.

The four samples are relatively comparable. All samples are characterized by 'rather high to high' micro-level predispositions to trust. The average respondent is about 50 years old, and average boundary spanning activity with horizontal departments is situated between 'at least every month' and 'multiple times a month' in all samples. Respondents come from various functional levels but mainly from the middle management level and level A (no managerial tasks), with a minority coming from the lower and top management levels. The large majority of respondents in all samples is male, has a master's degree, and has between ten and 30 years of experience in the Flemish administration, but we note that respondents with 20–30 years of experience are overrepresented in sample 2. Respondents come from a diverse set of organizational types in all four samples, but we note that boundary spanners from internal agencies with a limited degree of autonomy (IVAZRP) are overrepresented in sample 2 and external agencies with a large degree of autonomy (EVAPRP) are overrepresented in sample 4.

The findings of sample 1 and sample 2 (RI of trust) were combined and compared with the combined findings of sample 3 and sample 4 (RI of distrust). Although perfect equality between the four samples on all characteristics would have improved the comparability of the samples, we note that we have no reason to suspect that the diverging characteristics might distort our findings regarding the presence of interaction characteristics and their impact on the trust process.

FINDINGS

The comparison within and between quantitative (sample 1 and 3) and qualitative (sample 2 and 4) data provides a comprehensive understanding of how interaction characteristics are perceived by boundary spanners in trusted and distrusted interactions with horizontal departments in the Flemish administration, and how these perceptions affect interorganizational trust. Table 4.2 provides an overview of the findings regarding the perceived presence of interaction characteristics in interorganizational interactions with horizontal departments in the Flemish administration. The 'phase 2' column compares sample 1 and 3 on the basis of the confidence intervals around the mean values of the interaction characteristics we have measured in the boundary spanner survey. The 'phase 3' column compares qualitative information about these interaction characteristics in sample 2 and 4, and shows the extent of corroboration between the quantitative and the qualitative data.

In the following paragraphs, we will discuss these findings, and explain why perceptions of these interaction characteristics can be argued to affect interorganizational trust.

Macro-level Formal Characteristics in RI of Trust and Distrust

Phase 2 quantitative sample comparison: macro-level formal characteristics
No significant differences were found between the confidence intervals of the measured macro-level formal characteristics in sample 1 (RI of trust) and sample 3 (RI of distrust). This suggests that boundary spanners in RI of trust and distrust did not perceive a difference in the presence of

Table 4.2 *Perceived interaction characteristics in trusted and distrusted interactions*

	Interaction aspect	Phase 2 comparison (quantitative samples)	Phase 3 comparison (qualitative samples)
Macro formal	Formal rule framework	S1 = S3	Contradicts phase 2: Substantive/operational
	Formal role framework	S1 = S3	characteristics of institutional framework argued to differ between S2 and S4
Macro informal	Informal routine framework	S1 > S3***	Corroborates phase 2
	Confirmatory norms of administrative leadership	S1 > S3***	
	Confirmatory norms of political principals	S1 > S3***	
Meso-level calculative	Org. cost–benefit consideration	S1 = S3	Contradicts phase 2: org. cost–benefit considerations implicitly present in S2, but highly explicit in S3
	Asset specificity	S1 = S3	Contradicts phase 2: Asset specificity considered within acceptable limits in S2, but high in S4
	Pers. cost–benefit consideration	S1 = S3	Corroborates phase 2
	Dependency on rumour-based information	S1 = S3	Contradicts phase 2: irrelevant in S2, but source of suspicion in S4, specifically under institutional ambiguity
	No opp. motivations	S1 > S3***	Corroborates phase 2
	Perceived risk	S3 > S1***	Corroborates phase 2
Meso-level relational	Signalled trust	S1 > S3***	Corroborates phase 2
	Signalled distrust	S3 > S1***	Corroborates phase 2
	Value identification	S1 > S3**	Corroborates phase 2
	Power equality	S1 > S3***	Corroborates phase 2
	Quality pers. relationship	S1 = S3	Corroborates phase 2
	Heuristic formation	S1 > S3***	Corroborates phase 2
	Exp.-based expectations	S1 = S3	Corroborates phase 2: familiarity did not differ between S2 and S3, but appreciation of previous interactions was more positive in S2 than in S3
	Interaction age	S1 = S3	
	Interaction frequency	S1 > S3*	

Notes: S1: quantitative RI of trust sample; S2: qualitative RI of trust sample; S3: quantitative RI of distrust sample; S4 qualitative RI of distrust sample. Quantitative comparison of S1/S3 differences based on confidence intervals around mean values. $*$ = $p < 0.1$; $**$ = $p < 0.05$; $***$ = $p < 0.01$

clear formal rules or clear formal roles that clarify mutual tasks, rights and obligations in the interaction.

Phase 3 qualitative sample comparison: macro-level formal characteristics
Boundary spanners described the formal framework very differently in sample 2 (RI of trust) and sample 4 (RI of distrust), more specifically regarding substantive and operational characteristics. In sample 2, boundary spanners argued that stability, unambiguously defined rights and duties and a latent operational character of formal arrangements were characteristic of the institutional environment in the RI. In sample 4 however, boundary spanners argued that formal frameworks in information-exchange interactions were unclear or even (temporarily) absent, which led to formal opacity and ambiguity in the interorganizational interaction. Furthermore, the operational characteristics of the formal frameworks were argued to engender a culture of distrust, as formal rules and roles definitions were perceived to be used actively in order to coerce information exchange, which boundary spanners considered as a violation of organizational autonomy.

In the sample 2 and 4 interviews, these macro-level formal characteristics were argued to affect the three dimensions of the interorganizational trust process directly, through the institutional logics of consequences and appropriateness. First, macro-level formal frameworks with trust-supporting substantive and operational institutional characteristics were argued to positively affect perceived trustworthiness, because such formal norms acted as reference points for the horizontal departments' flexibility, compliance and ability, and to allow mutual benevolence in interorganizational interactions by establishing broad but clear boundaries to the horizontal departments' flexibility toward boundary spanners in information-collection processes. Second, such formal frameworks were also argued to affect the willingness to suspend vulnerability directly by creating a level playing field for all organizations that are required to share information with the horizontal department, thus reducing the vulnerability of the boundary spanners' organization to unfair behaviour by other organizations. Third, formal frameworks were argued to affect risk-taking behaviour directly through a logic of appropriateness. In sample 2, latent permissive and/or prohibitive formal frameworks were argued to clarify boundary spanners' mandate to engage in risk-taking behaviour on behalf of their organization. In sample 4 on the other hand, some boundary spanners argued that formal frameworks explicitly coerced them to exchange information with the horizontal department, thus breaking existing vicious cycles of interorganizational distrust (coercive isomorphism).

Macro-level Informal Characteristics in RI of Trust and Distrust

Phase 2 quantitative sample comparison: macro-level informal characteristics

All confidence intervals of measured macro-level informal characteristics were found to differ significantly between sample 1 (RI of trust) and sample 3 (RI of distrust). In sample 1 (RI of trust), respondents agree significantly more with the statement that unwritten routines offer a clear framework for mutual tasks, rights and obligations in their interaction with the horizontal department ($p < 0.01$). Furthermore, they also agree significantly more with the statement that their political ($p < 0.01$) and administrative ($p < 0.01$) leaders' normative preferences are in line with their own attitudes. These quantitative data thus suggest that clear informal institutional frameworks are considered to be present to a greater degree in trusted interorganizational interactions than in distrusted interorganizational interactions.

Phase 3 qualitative sample comparison: macro-level informal characteristics

Clear differences in the perceived presence of macro-level informal characteristics also appeared in our comparison of qualitative samples 2 (RI of trust) and 4 (RI of distrust). In sample 2, boundary spanners argued that stable routines were latently present in information-exchange interactions. Sample 4 respondents on the other hand argued that the interorganizational interaction was characterized by conflicting organizational routines, grounded in incompatible organizational cultures. Furthermore, sample 2 respondents argued that the salient norms expressed by their administrative leaders showed trust in the horizontal department. Sample 4 respondents emphasized salient norms of distrust expressed by their administrative leaders. In neither sample did boundary spanners argue to experience clear normative expressions of either trust or distrust by political principals. Finally, sample 2 respondents emphasized the presence of a macro-level informal characteristic we had not considered in our theoretical framework, which can be described as a 'culture of belonging to one single administrative community' with the horizontal counterpart, as they described the Flemish administration in terms of partnership, cultural unity and common challenges. Sample 4 respondents explicitly rejected this notion of 'belonging to one single administrative community', as they described the Flemish administration in terms of competition between entities and a patchwork of diverging organizational cultures.

In sample 2 and sample 4 interviews, macro-level informal characteristics were argued to affect all three dimensions of the interorganizational trust process directly, through logics of consequences and appropriateness. First, macro-level informal routines and salient norms of interorganizational trust expressed by administrative leaders were argued to positively affect perceived trustworthiness due to mimetic and normative isomorphism. Furthermore, the informal 'culture of administrative community' was argued to enable boundary spanners to make assumptions about the horizontal counterparts' trustworthiness on the basis of a 'cultural template'. In particular, sample 2 boundary spanners argued that the horizontal department was benevolent toward their own organization in order to maximize the common administrations' interest, and that the horizontal department faced similar standards of quality, performance and accountability and therefore had to be trustworthy in terms of its competence and integrity. Second, informal routines and the 'culture of administrative community' were argued to have a direct effect on the willingness to suspend vulnerability. Informal routines were argued to affect the willingness to suspend vulnerability due to mimetic isomorphism, and because they introduced predictability in the interaction, which was argued to extenuate vulnerability and thus render boundary spanners more willing to suspend vulnerability. The 'institutional culture of administrative community' was argued to affect the willingness to suspend vulnerability, as boundary spanners considered it their 'moral duty' to assume an attitude of openness and transparency toward the horizontal departments in the 'administrative community' (normative isomorphism). Third, informal routines and salient norms of administrative leaders were also argued to affect risk-taking behaviour. Informal routines were argued to support risk-taking behaviour, even though boundary spanners had little willingness to suspend vulnerability, because boundary spanners either did not question existing routines of information exchange (mimetic isomorphism) or if they did question the routines, breaking them was still considered an abnormal breach of professional norms in the Flemish administration (normative isomorphism). Finally, although respondents argued that it was theoretically possible for administrative leaders to coerce risk-taking behaviour against the will of boundary spanners, they argued that such did not occur, and that the influence of administrative leaders was normative rather than coercive.

Meso-level Calculative Characteristics in RI of Trust and Distrust

Phase 2 quantitative sample comparison: meso-level calculative characteristics

Two confidence intervals were found to differ significantly between sample 1 (RI of trust) and sample 3 (RI of distrust) for the measured meso-level calculative characteristics. First, boundary spanners reported significantly less knowledge about opportunistic interests of their horizontal counterpart in sample 1 than in sample 3 ($p < 0.01$). Second, boundary spanners perceived a lower degree of risk in sample 1 than in sample 3 ($p < 0.01$). The data did not show any difference between samples 1 and 3 regarding the asset specificity in the interorganizational relationship, or in the extent to which boundary spanners considered that their attitude towards the horizontal department depends on rumour-based information, personal or organizational cost–benefit considerations.

Phase 3 qualitative sample comparison: meso-level calculative characteristics

In our qualitative comparison of samples 2 (RI of trust) and 4 (RI of distrust), clear differences appeared regarding the presence of calculative interaction characteristics. In sample 2, boundary spanners downplayed the extent of personal and organizational cost–benefit considerations in information exchange with the horizontal department, arguing trust was maintained even though personal or organizational costs of information sharing with the horizontal department could outweigh benefits. Furthermore, sample 2 respondents argued that the asset specificity of information exchange with the horizontal department was within acceptable limits. In sample 4, boundary spanners explicitly and extensively emphasized the presence of costs and the absence of benefits of information exchange. Costs of information exchange were considered to be high due to asset specificity, as boundary spanners argued that resources were diverted away from core tasks in order to comply with the horizontal departments' frequent requests for information. Also, sample 4 boundary spanners strongly emphasized the risks of exchanging information with the horizontal department due to the possible (budgetary) consequences of undue, decontextualized or faulty interpretation and presentation of collected information. Sample 2 respondents argued that they suspected some opportunistic motivations in the horizontal department, but argued that these motivations were no larger than what was considered to be normal and healthy in any interorganizational interaction. In sample 4 on the other hand, boundary spanners argued that they suspected that the horizontal department had a 'hidden agenda', which ranged from 'bureau maximization' (Niskanen, 1971) to political-ideological motivations (i.e., cutting the cost and size of public administration rather than contribute to the quality of the Flemish public administration). In sample 2, rumour-based information about the horizontal department was not considered to be present. In sample 4 however, boundary spanners argued that their suspicions were partly based on information gathered from rumours, especially during temporary institutional ambiguity in the aftermath of the formation of a new Flemish government coalition.

Meso-level calculative characteristics were argued to have a particularly strong direct impact on the willingness to suspend vulnerability, a slightly weaker impact on perceived trustworthiness, and a mere indirect impact on risk-taking behaviour. First, meso-level calculative characteristics were argued to affect perceived trustworthiness. Suspicions about horizontal departments' opportunistic motivations were strongly suggested to negatively affect the perceived integrity and perceived benevolence of the horizontal department. Rumour-based reputational information was argued to inform such suspicions when other sources of credible information were absent. Second, several meso-level calculative interaction characteristics were argued to have a direct impact on boundary spanners' willingness to suspend vulnerability. The extent of perceived risk in an interaction was argued to affect the extent of vulnerability to be suspended in the interaction, and thus to affect the willingness of the boundary spanner to make a 'leap of faith'. Furthermore, as boundary spanners associated more benefits and fewer costs with the interorganizational interaction, they argued to have more 'good reasons' to be willing to suspend vulnerability, although they were more willing to suspend vulnerability when cost–benefit considerations are more implicit and internalized in the interaction. Third, the meso-level calculative characteristics were argued to only affect risk-taking behaviour indirectly, through their impact on the willingness to suspend vulnerability.

Meso-level Relational Characteristics in RI of Trust and Distrust

Phase 2 quantitative sample comparison: meso-level relational characteristics
Six out of nine confidence intervals for measured meso-level relational interaction characteristics were found to differ significantly between sample 1 (RI of trust) and sample 3 (RI of distrust). In sample 1, respondents reported that horizontal departments show significantly higher extents of trust ($p < 0.01$) and significantly lower extents of distrust ($p < 0.01$) in the respondents' organization. Furthermore, power distributions between the boundary spanners' organization and the horizontal department are considered to be more equal for sample 1 than in sample 3. Sample 1 is also characterized by a higher extent of value identification ($p < 0.05$) with the horizontal department than sample 3. However, samples 1 and 3 were not found to be significantly different regarding the quality of interpersonal relations. Some measures indicate a difference in familiarity between sample 1 and sample 3, while no difference is present in other indicators

for familiarity: there are significantly more 'interpersonal habits' between boundary spanners in sample 1 than in sample 3 ($p < 0.01$), and sample 1 is characterized by a higher interaction frequency than sample 3 ($p < 0.1$), but we do not find any difference for the interaction age and the extent to which expectations are based on previous interaction experiences.

Phase 3 qualitative sample comparison: meso-level relational characteristics
Our comparison of the qualitative interviews in samples 2 and 4 are in line with these quantitative differences and provide further clarification. In sample 2, respondents argued that the horizontal department expressed trust in their own organization, while sample 4 respondents argued that the horizontal department expressed a low extent of trust. While sample 2 respondents argued that the horizontal department did not express any distrust in their own organization, a minority of sample 4 respondents argued that the horizontal department expressed a high degree of distrust in their organization. Furthermore, sample 2 respondents emphasized that they could identify with the values of the horizontal department (in particular, neutrality and objectiveness). Sample 4 respondents argued that value identification was low, that their organizations were alienated from the horizontal objectives, and some even argued that the horizontal department had become so closely associated with the political ideology of its political principal, that it could no longer be considered neutral and objective in information-exchange interactions. Sample 2 respondents argued that power equality was empowered by the horizontal department's interactive approach to information collection, while sample 4 respondents emphasized the horizontal departments' top-down, one-directional approach. Furthermore, both sample 2 and sample 4 respondents argued that they had good professional interpersonal relations with counterparts in the horizontal department. Sample 4 boundary spanners in particular argued that their distrust was not directed at individual counterparts in the horizontal department, but at 'the horizontal department as such'. While one sample 2 respondent argued that mutual familiarity had fostered interpersonal habits in the interpersonal relationship with the counterpart boundary spanner, there was little further evidence that would support differences in interpersonal familiarity between samples 2 and 4. In both samples 2 and 4, respondents referred extensively to having previous interaction experiences. However, boundary spanners' appreciation of these previous experiences was very different between sample 2 and sample 4, as previous experiences were predominantly positive in sample 2, but ranged from mixed to extremely negative in sample 4.

Meso-level relational interaction characteristics were argued to have a strong impact on perceived trustworthiness in the trust process, little direct impact on the willingness to suspend vulnerability, and only indirect impact on risk-taking behaviour. First, meso-level interaction characteristics were argued to have a strong impact on perceived trustworthiness. Value identification in particular was argued to positively affect the perceived integrity of the horizontal department. Positive experiences (familiarity) were argued to be important determinants for all sub-dimensions of perceived trustworthiness, under the condition that formal rules and roles in the interaction would remain stable (macro). The expression of trust by the horizontal department was argued to affect the horizontal departments' perceived benevolence in information-exchange interactions. Furthermore, interactive feedback on information-exchange interactions was considered to enable more power equality, which was argued to positively affect the perceived benevolence of the horizontal department. The good quality of interpersonal relationships was argued to smoothen informal contacts and flexibility between boundary spanners, positively affecting the horizontal departments' perceived benevolence under the condition that the counterpart boundary spanner could make 'credible commitments' on behalf of their organization. Second, some relational interaction characteristics were argued to directly affect the willingness to suspend vulnerability. In particular, power equality was argued to decrease the extent of vulnerability toward the horizontal department in information-exchange interactions, which rendered boundary spanners more willing to suspend vulnerability. Furthermore, one respondent argued that signals of trust by the horizontal department directly affected their willingness to suspend vulnerability by inspiring 'mirroring' in the interorganizational interaction. Third, none of the relational interaction characteristics were argued to affect risk-taking behaviour directly. Instead, boundary spanners' arguments linking relational interaction characteristics with risk-taking behaviour all referred to their willingness to suspend vulnerability, suggesting that relational characteristics only affect risk-taking behaviour indirectly.

CONSOLIDATION AND DISCUSSION OF THE FINDINGS

The findings discussed in the previous paragraphs suggest that boundary spanners' perceptions of macro- and meso-level interaction characteristics explain why some interactions with horizontal departments are trusted while others are distrusted. Table 4.3 summarizes the relationship between perceived macro- and meso-level interaction characteristics and

Table 4.3 *Findings: impact of perceived interaction characteristics on the interorganizational trust process*

	Macro-level formal	Macro-level informal	Meso-level calculus	Meso-level relational
Perceived trustworthiness	**Direct:** logic of consequences – Formal frameworks act as reference point for expectations of integrity, compliance, and ability. – Formal frameworks also establish arena for cooperation with clear constraints, as such allowing flexibility within those constraints (benevolence).	**Direct:** logic of consequences/appropriateness – Informal routines and salient norms of administrative leaders socialize expectations due to mimetic and normative isomorphism. – Culture of administrative community fills 'gaps' in knowledge about the counterpart, on the basis of which assumptions about trustworthiness are made.	**Direct:** – Knowledge about opportunistic motivations affects perceived benevolence and integrity. – Dependency on rumour-based information is negatively related to perceived trustworthiness, especially when other sources of credible information are absent or boundary spanners are confronted with institutional ambiguity.	**Direct:** – Value identification affects perceived integrity. – Relational reciprocity affects perceived benevolence (particularly in RI of distrust). – Power equality affects perceived benevolence. – Quality of personal relationships affects perceived benevolence (if counterpart has ability to make credible commitments). – Familiarity: positive or negative previous experiences under counterpart control affect expectations of future trustworthiness (under condition of institutional stability).

Willingness to suspend vulnerability	**Indirect**: through perceived trustworthiness. **Direct:** logic of consequences – Latent presence of formal framework levels playing field, thus constraining vulnerability to third parties, providing good reason to suspend vulnerability.	**Indirect**: through perceived trustworthiness. **Direct:** logic of consequences/appropriateness – Informal routines introduce predictability and thus extenuate vulnerability. – Informal routines and culture of administrative community socialize willingness to suspend vulnerability due to mimetic and normative isomorphism.	**Indirect**: through perceived trustworthiness. **Direct:** – Perceived risks affect vulnerability, and thus willingness to suspend it. – More benefits and fewer costs positively affect willingness to suspend vulnerability, but more explicit cost–benefit consideration suggested to be negatively related to willingness to suspend vulnerability.	**Indirect**: through perceived trustworthiness. **Direct:** – Power equality reduces counterpart-dependent vulnerability, thus positively affects willingness. – Signals of trust affect willingness through 'mirroring'. – Familiarity: positive or negative previous experiences beyond counterpart control affect perceptions of vulnerability, and thus willingness to suspend vulnerability.

Table 4.3 (continued)

	Macro-level formal	Macro-level informal	Meso-level calculus	Meso-level relational
Risk-taking behaviour	**Indirect:** through willingness to suspend vulnerability. **Direct:** logic of appropriateness – Formal frameworks provide latent institutional permission or prohibition of risk-taking behaviour in trusted interaction. – Formal frameworks actively coerce risk-taking behaviour in distrusted interaction.	**Indirect:** through willingness to suspend vulnerability. **Direct:** logic of appropriateness – Informal routines create reluctance to challenge status quo and existing professional norms due to mimetic and normative isomorphism. – Administrative leaders' salient norms socialize behaviour due to normative isomorphism, coercion by administrative leaders argued hypothetically possible but empirically absent.	**Indirect:** through willingness to suspend vulnerability.	**Indirect:** through willingness to suspend vulnerability.

interorganizational trust, as discussed by boundary spanners in interorganizational interactions with horizontal departments.

Four core findings emerge from our analysis. Our first core finding is that there is no simple theory to explain and manage interorganizational trust of public regulatees in public regulators. Through our study of interorganizational trust as a process that is affected by macro-level and meso-level interaction characteristics, we found that different interaction characteristics directly affect different dimensions of the trust process through different mechanisms. In order to find solutions for the management of interorganizational trust in a particular interaction context, it is thus essential to understand the dimension-specific impact of the specific macro- and meso-level characteristics of that particular interaction. Our analysis indicated that perceived trustworthiness is strongly affected by macro-level institutional and meso-level relational interaction characteristics, while calculative characteristics are relatively less important for this dimension in the trust process. The willingness to suspend vulnerability is driven by 'good reasons' to take a 'leap of faith', and our findings indicate that macro-level institutional and meso-level calculative interaction characteristics were considered to be successful at providing such good reasons, while relational characteristics were found to have a more limited direct impact on this dimension. Finally, the risk-taking behaviour dimension of the trust process was found to be directly affected by macro-level institutional interaction characteristics, which constitute a framework of appropriateness for risk-taking behaviour through mechanisms of coercive, normative and mimetic isomorphism. The managerial implication of this finding is that management of interorganizational trust should start from an analysis of trust process dimensions in interorganizational interactions, followed by intervention aimed at shaping those interorganizational interaction characteristics with the strongest effect on any problematic trust process dimensions.

The second core finding is that macro- and meso-level interaction characteristics also have indirect impacts on trust dimensions, due to the trust process's internal causal logic. As perceived trustworthiness is argued to affect boundary spanners' willingness to suspend vulnerability, and the willingness to suspend vulnerability is argued to affect risk-taking behaviour, interaction characteristics that affect prior dimensions of the trust process will indirectly affect the process' subsequent dimensions. The managerial implication of this finding is that while relational and calculative interorganizational interaction characteristics may not affect risk-taking behaviour directly, they can have indirect effects on risk-taking behaviour under the condition that the internal causal dynamic of the trust process is safeguarded. An important area for further inquiry is therefore whether and how macro- and meso-level interaction characteristics affect the internal causal logic of the trust process. For instance, managerial interventions that strengthen the behavioural decision mandate of boundary spanners may be hypothesized to strengthen the causal link between willingness to suspend vulnerability and risk-taking behaviour in interorganizational interactions. Likewise, managerial interventions that increase the interdependency between trustee and trustor may be hypothesized to strengthen the causal relation between perceived trustworthiness and the willingness to suspend vulnerability. Further empirical research is required to test these hypotheses.

As a third core finding, we found that both the presence and the form of macro- and meso-level characteristics of interorganizational interactions are important to understand their impact on the interorganizational trust process. On the one hand, the extent to which certain characteristics are present in interorganizational interactions was argued to affect the trust process. Boundary spanners argued that the presence of clear informal routines, salient trusting normative frameworks of administrative leaders, an informal institutional sense of belonging to one single 'administrative community', value identification, expressed trust by the horizontal department, familiarity, power equality, knowledge about horizontal departments' opportunistic motivations, dependency on rumour-based information, perceived risk and expressed distrust by the horizontal department affected the trust process due to their mere presence. On the other hand, the form of some interaction characteristics, rather than their presence in interorganizational interactions, was considered to affect the trust process. The substantive and operational characteristics of macro-level formal frameworks were argued to affect interorganizational trust, rather than the mere presence of clear macro-level formal frameworks. Cost–benefit considerations were equally present in trusted and distrusted interactions, but they were argued to be implicit and 'automatic' in the former, and explicit and interaction-specific in the latter. Expectations based on previous interaction experiences were equally present in trusted and distrusted interactions, but their effect on the trust process was argued to be determined by the positive or negative nature of those experiences. The implication of this finding is that management of interorganizational trust should not only focus on introducing more institutional, calculative and relational 'reasons for trust' in the characteristics of interorganizational interactions, but also consider how the boundary spanners perceive and experience those characteristics in their interorganizational interactions.

Our fourth core finding is that macro- and meso-level interaction characteristics may be analytically separated, but are empirically interrelated.

Macro-level interaction characteristics shape meso-level interaction characteristics. Formal macro-level frameworks were argued to affect calculative characteristics of interorganizational interactions by levelling and delineating the playing field of interorganizational interactions, and by providing reliable information about possible costs, risks and benefits of interorganizational trust. The informal macro-level characteristic of an institutional culture of 'belonging to an administrative community' was argued to emphasize possible government-wide costs and benefits of trust over individual or organizational cost and benefits, thus affecting meso-level calculative considerations. In addition, such a culture was also argued to empower value identification in interorganizational interactions, thus supporting the meso-level relational characteristics on which interorganizational trust is built. As Giddens (1990) argues, macro- and meso-level interaction characteristics produce and reproduce each other through the perceptions, attitudes and behaviours of the individual boundary spanners in a continuous process of structuration. The implication of this finding is that understanding and managing interorganizational trust necessitates studying and managing both social structures (macro-level formal and informal institutions) and the interaction between trustor and trustee within such structures (meso-level calculative and relational considerations) in a theoretical framework which allows for long-term interaction between these characteristics.

However, these findings should be interpreted with due regard for two limitations of our research. A first limitation is that we investigated boundary spanners' *perceptions* of macro- and meso-level characteristics in interorganizational interactions with horizontal departments. We did not study objective differences between trusted and distrusted interactions, but differences as perceived and reported by boundary spanners in such interactions. Since interorganizational trust was argued to be a subjective evaluation of boundary spanners in interorganizational interactions, this approach can be justified. However, the question whether boundary spanners' perceptions are actual representations of objective differences between trusted and distrusted interactions remains unanswered in this research. A second limitation regards the external validity of this research. Are the results obtained here also applicable to other (public) regulatee–regulator interactions? Are they applicable to interorganizational interactions in a more general sense? Calder et al. (1982) argue that research into the application of general scientific theory does not necessarily require statistical generalization, since the theory is applied beyond the research setting, not the sample. In this respect, we argue that the theoretical model for this research can apply to interorganizational trust problems beyond the samples investigated here. However, the specific empirical results of this inquiry only apply to interorganizational interactions with horizontal departments in the Flemish administration. Generalization of empirical findings beyond this context requires replication of this research in other interorganizational interactions, within and beyond public administration and within and beyond public regulatee–regulator interactions.

CONCLUSION

In this chapter, we have shown how boundary spanners' perceptions of macro- and meso-level interaction characteristics affect interorganizational trust in trusted and distrusted interorganizational interactions with horizontal departments in the Flemish public administration. Our inquiry was based on a nested mixed-method analysis, in which a comparison of quantitative samples was integrated with a comparison of qualitative samples. Our core findings are first, that macro- and meso-level interaction characteristics affect the trust process through various direct impacts on perceived trustworthiness, the willingness to suspend vulnerability, and risk-taking behaviour. Second, interaction characteristics are also argued to affect the dimensions of the trust process indirectly, due to the internal causality of the 'universal trust process'. Third, both extent and form of macro- and meso-level characteristics in interorganizational interactions are important to understand how they affect the trust process. Fourth, macro- and meso-level interaction characteristics are interdependent, as they affect and shape each other in structuration processes.

Based on these observations, we suggest that any due understanding of interorganizational trust evaluations in public administration must acknowledge the multi-level embeddedness of the interorganizational trust process, and must therefore acknowledge that any single group of institutional, rational, or social exchange theories can only provide an incomplete perspective on interorganizational trust. Rather, a model is required that allows interdependent macro- and meso-level interaction characteristics to affect the trust process, in order to further a more comprehensive understanding of interorganizational trust.

NOTES

1. At the time of our study, the Flemish administration comprised 13 policy areas, 13 departments and 67 agencies, and employed nearly 39,401 people (departement Bestuurszaken, www.bestuurszaken.be/personeel, consulted on 12.11.2014). However, in

the 2014 coalition agreement, a number of reforms were announced to reduce the number of policy areas to 11, reduce the number of departments and agencies, and reduce the total number of people employed by the Flemish administration (Vlaamse Regering, 2014).
2. A more detailed discussion of the concepts, theories, methods, findings and conclusions presented in this chapter may be found in the first author's Ph.D. dissertation (Oomsels, 2016).

REFERENCES

Aldrich, H. and D. Herker (1977), 'Boundary spanning roles and organization structure', *Academy of Management Review*, **2**(2), 217–230.

Bachmann, R. (2001). 'Trust, power and control in trans-organizational relations', *Organization Studies*, **22**(2), 337–364.

Bachmann, R. and A.C. Inkpen (2011), 'Understanding institutional-based trust building processes in inter-organizational relationships', *Organization Studies*, **32**(2), 281–300.

Bachmann, R. and A. Zaheer (2008), 'Trust in interorganizational relations', in S. Cropper, M. Ebers, C. Huxman and P. Smith Ring (eds), *Oxford handbook of inter-organizational relations*, Oxford: Oxford University Press, pp. 533–554.

Barrera, D., V. Buskens and W. Raub (2011), 'Embedded trust; the analytical approach in vignettes, laboratory experiments and surveys', in F. Lyon, G. Möllering and M.N.K. Saunders (eds), *Handbook of research methods on trust*, Cheltenham, UK and Northampton, MA, USA: Edward Elgar Publishing, pp. 199–211.

Beccerra, M. and A.K. Gupta (1999), 'Trust within the organization: integrating the trust literature with agency theory and transaction cost economics', *Public Administration Quarterly*, **23**(2), 177–203.

Blau, P.M. (1964), *Exchange and power in social life*, New York: Wiley.

Braithwaite, V. and M. Levi (1998), *Trust and governance*. New York: Russell Sage Foundations.

Bromily, P. and J. Harris (2006), 'Trust, transaction cost economics and mechanisms', in R. Bachmann and A. Zaheer (eds), *Handbook of trust research*, Cheltenham, UK and Northampton, MA, USA: Edward Elgar Publishing, pp. 124–143.

Calder, B.J., L.W. Phillips and A.M. Tybout (1982), 'The concept of external validity', *Journal of Consumer Research*, **9**(3): 240–244.

Carnevale, D.G. and B. Wechsler (1992), 'Trust in the public sector: individual and organizational determinants', *Administration and Society*, **23**, 471–494.

Choudhury, E. (2008), 'Trust in administration: an integrative approach to optimal trust', *Administration and Society*, **40**, 586–620.

Coleman, J. (1990), *Foundations of social theory*, Cambridge: Harvard University Press.

Das, T.K. and B.S. Teng, (2004), 'The risk-based view on trust: a conceptual framework', *Journal of Business and Psychology*, **19**(1), 85–116.

Dietz, G. (2011), 'Going back to the source: why do people trust each other?', *Journal of Trust Research*, **1**(2), 215–222.

Dimaggio, P. J. and W.W. Powell (1983), 'The iron cage revisited: institutional isomorphism and collective rationality in organizational fields', *American Sociological Review*, **48**(2), 147–160.

Edelenbos, J. and E.H. Klijn (2007), 'Trust in complex decision-making networks: a theoretical and empirical exploration', *Administration and Society*, **39**, 25–50.

Frazier, M.L, P.D. Johnson and S. Fainshmidt (2013), 'Development and validation of a propensity to trust scale', *Journal of Trust Research*, **3**(2), 76–97.

Fulmer, C.A. and M.J. Gelfand (2012), 'At what level (and in whom) we trust: trust across multiple organizational levels', *Journal of Management*, **38**(4), 1167–1230.

Giddens, A. (1990), *Consequences of modernity*, Cambridge: Polity.

Glanville, J. and P. Paxton (2007), 'How do we learn to trust? A confirmatory tetrad analysis of the sources of generalised trust', *Social Psychology Quarterly*, **70**(3), 230–242.

Grimmelikhuijsen, S. (2012), 'Linking transparency, knowledge and citizen trust in government: an experiment', *International Review of Administrative Sciences*, **78**(1), 50–73.

Hardin, R. (2002), *Trust and trustworthiness*. New York: Russell Sage Foundation.

Hodgson, G. (2006), 'What are institutions?', *Journal of Economic Issues*, **XL**(1), 1–25.

Katsikeas, C.S., D. Skarmeas and D.C. Bello (2009), 'Developing successful trust-based international exchange relationships', *Journal of International Business Studies*, **40**, 132–155.

Klijn, E.-H, J. Edelenbos and B. Steijn (2010), 'Trust in governance networks: its impacts on outcomes', *Administration and Society*, **42**(2), 193–221.

Kramer, R. (1999), 'Trust and distrust in organizations: emerging perspectives, enduring questions', *Annual Review of Psychology*, **50**, 569–598.

Lewicki, R. and B.B. Bunker (1996), 'Developing and maintaining trust in work relationships', in R. Kramer and T.R. Tyler (eds), *Trust in organizations: frontiers of theory and research*, Thousand Oaks: Sage, pp. 114–139.

Lewis, J. and A. Weigert (1985), 'Trust as a social reality', *Social Forces*, **63**, 967–985.

Lieberman, E.S. (2005), 'Nested analysis as a mixed-method strategy for comparative research', *American Political Science Review*, **99**(3), 435–451.

Luhmann, N. (1979), *Trust and power*, Chichester: John Wiley.

Lyon, F., G. Möllering and M.N.K. Saunders (2011), 'Introduction: the variety of methods for the multi-faceted phenomenon of trust', in F. Lyon, G. Möllering and M.N.K. Saunders (eds), *Handbook of research methods on trust*, Northampton, UK and Northampton, MA, USA: Edward Elgar Publishing, pp. 1–18.

Mayer, R.C., J.H. Davis and F.D. Schoorman (1995), 'An integrative view of organizational trust', *Academy of Management Review*, **20**(3), 709–734.

McEvily, B. and M. Tortoriello (2011), 'Measuring trust in organizational research: review and recommendations', *Journal of Trust Research*, **1**(1), 23–63.

Möllering, G. (2006). *Trust: reason, routine, reflexivity*, Amsterdam: Elsevier.

Niskanen, W.A., Jr. (1971), *Bureaucracy and representative government*, New Brunswick, NJ: Aldine Transaction.

Nooteboom, B. (2002), *Trust: forms, foundations, functions, failures and figures*, Cheltenham, UK and Northampton, MA, USA: Edward Elgar Publishing.

Nooteboom, B. (2006), 'Forms, sources and processes of trust', in R. Bachmann and A. Zaheer (eds), *Handbook of trust research*, Cheltenham, UK and Northampton, MA, USA: Edward Elgar Publishing, pp. 247–263.

Nyhan, R.C. (2000), 'Changing the paradigm: Trust and its role in public sector organizations', *American Review of Public Administration*, **30**, 87–109.

Oomsels, P. and G. Bouckaert (2014a), 'Studying interorganizational trust in public administration: a conceptual and analytical framework for "administrational trust"', *Public Performance & Management Review*, **37**(4), 577–604.

Oomsels, P. and G. Bouckaert (2014b), *Working paper III: studying administrational trust in Flanders: prevalence of administrational 'trust problems' in the Flemish administration*. Leuven: SBOV.

Oomsels, P. (2016), *Administrational trust: an empirical examination of interorganizational trust and distrust in the Flemish administration* [diss.doc]. Leuven: KU Leuven.

Perrone, V., A. Zaheer and B. McEvily (2003), 'Free to be trusted? Organizational constraints on trust in boundary spanners', *Organization Studies*, **14**(4), 422–439.

Pierre, J. and P. Ingraham (2010), *Comparative administrative change and reform*, Montreal: McGill-Queens University Press.

Pollitt, C. and G. Bouckaert (2011), *Public Management Reform: A Comparative Analysis* (Third Edition). Oxford: Oxford University Press.

Rousseau, D., S.B. Sitkin, R.S. Burt and C. Camerer (1998), 'Not so different after all: A cross-discipline view of trust', *Academy of Management Review*, **23**(3), 393–404.

Schoorman, F., R.C. Mayer and J.H. Davis (2007), 'An integrative model of organizational trust: past, present, and future', *Academy of Management Review*, **32**(2), 344–354.

Six, F.E., B. Nooteboom and A. Hoogendoorn (2010), 'Actions that build interpersonal trust: a relational signalling perspective', *Review of Social Economy*, **68**(3), 285–315.

Sydow, J. (2006), 'How can systems trust systems? A structuration perspective on trust-building in inter-organizational relations', in R. Bachmann and A. Zaheer (eds), *Handbook of trust research*, Cheltenham, UK and Northampton, MA, USA: Edward Elgar Publishing, pp. 377–392.

Sztompka, P. (1998), 'Trust, distrust and two paradoxes of democracy', *European Journal of Social Theory*, **1**(1), 19–32.

Vlaamse Regering (2014), *Vertrouwen, verbinden, vooruitgaan*, Regeerakkoord Vlaamse Regering 2014–2019. Brussel: Vlaamse Regering.

Williamson, O.E. (1985), *The economic institutions of capitalism*, New York: The Free Press.

Williamson, O.E. (1993), 'Calculativeness, trust, and economic organization', *Journal of Law and Economics*, **36**(1), 453–486.

Zaheer, A., B. McEvily and V. Perrone (1998), 'Does trust matter? Exploring the effects of interorganizational and interpersonal trust on performance', *Organization Science*, **9**, 141–159.

Zak, P.J. (2012), *The moral molecule: how trust works*, New York: Dutton.

Zand, D. (1972), 'Trust and managerial problem solving', *Administrative Science Quarterly*, **17**(2), 229–239.

Zhong, W., C. Su, J. Peng and Z. Yang (2014), 'Trust in interorganizational relationships: a meta-analytic integration', *Journal of Management*, Online first.

[Last accessed 12 February 2014.] Available from URL: http://jom.sagepub.com/content/early/2014/08/07/0149206314546373.abstract

Zucker, L.G. (1986), 'Production of trust: Institutional sources of economic structure, 1840–1920', *Research in Organizational Behavior*, **8**, 53–111.

ANNEX

Boundary Spanner Survey Items

Interaction age	How long are you already involved in your interaction with *(REFERENCE INTERACTION)*
Interaction frequency	How often are you generally in contact with this organization?

Please indicate the extent to which you agree with the following statements about *(REFERENCE INTERACTION)*

Power equality	We are equal partners in most interactions with each other
Asset specificity	The content we share in this interaction (information resources, knowledge) is very specific and difficult to establish
Risk nature	This interaction with this organization implies certain risks to our organization

Please indicate the extent to which you agree with the following statements about *(REFERENCE INTERACTION)*

Signalled trust	This organization shows trust in us in this relationship
Org. costs and benefits	My trust in this relationship is determined by the balance between the advantages and disadvantages for our own organization
Value identification	I can identify well with the values of this organization in this relationship
No opp. motivations	As far as I know this organization has no interest to behave themselves opportunistically in this relationship
Exp.-based expectations	Based on previous experiences, I know exactly what I can expect of this organization in this relationship
Formal rule framework	Formal rules provide a clear framework for mutual tasks, rights and duties in this relationship
Heuristic formation	My attitude to this organization in this relationship has become a 'natural habit' over time
Quality pers. relation	I have a good personal relationship with my contact person(s) in this organization
Dependency on rumour-based information	Certain information about this organization could bring me here to reconsider my trust
Signalled distrust	This organization shows distrust in us in this relationship

Pers. costs and benefits	A trade-off between my personal advantages and disadvantages in this relationship determines my trust in this organization
Formal roles	My formal task or role description offers a clear framework for mutual functions, rights and obligations in this relationship
Informal routines	Unwritten routines in this relationship offer a clear framework for mutual functions, rights and obligations
Confirmatory norms of admin. leadership	My supervisor clearly has *(TRUST/DISTRUST)* in this organization with regard to this relationship
Confirmatory norms of political principles	My politically responsible Minister (s) clearly has (have) *(TRUST/DISTRUST)* in this organization with regard to this relationship

Notes: These phase 2 online survey items were also used during phase 3 interviews in the form of plastic cards, which boundary spanners were requested to discuss in relation the three trust process dimensions.

5. In vino veritas? The development of producer trust and its market effects in regulated French and Italian quality wine markets

Betsy Carter

Most economists contend that comparative production advantages arise by enabling producers to meet changes in demand and to lower costs of production. The cases of quality French and Italian wine producers present them with a dilemma: Quality French AOC wines are produced in a more rigid regulatory context than any other quality wines. Yet these quality French producers consistently earn higher prices for their wines than similar competitors, such as regulated Italian DOC producers. How can one explain the fact that producers who face higher production costs and who refuse to respond to changes in consumer preferences earn significantly higher market prices? What advantages are provided as a consequence of the French wine regulatory context? How is the Italian context different?

This article postulates French producers outperform their competitors due to the strength and legitimacy of producer organizations. These organizations fortify non-personal, institutional trust and weaken individual (personal) power discrepancies. Strong institutions lessen the risk of individual failure, and lead to greater market stability and predictability—at the cost of production flexibility. This article aims to both investigate the origins of divergent trust patterns as well as the relationship between trust and production strategies. I argue higher institutionalized trust—or 'trust in the rules of the game'—is associated with higher quality production, higher prices, less price-based competition, and less market concentration. And in the case of wine, market rigidities—and a producer refusal to follow the market—becomes a source of producer strength rather than weakness.

France and Italy have nearly identical private wine regulatory regimes—the Italian DOC system (*denominazione di origine controllata* 1963) was directly modeled on the successful French AOC (*appellation d'origine contrôlée* 1935) classification system. Both systems claim to protect *terroir*, a delimited area with a distinct cultural heritage and geographic characteristics. The regulations link geographic areas with specific rules of production, including allowable grape varieties, maximum yields, and grape growing methods. The producers themselves determine these production standards, and they theoretically act as a *de facto* quality indicator, where the protected location names serve as a shared brand. A quasi-governmental organization of wine professionals and experts determines which new groups receive the quality mark, and the Ministry of Agriculture ultimately issues this mark. These regulatory regimes are best classified as private as opposed to public, and the formal role of the Ministry of Agriculture is both indirect (appointing some members of the quasi-governmental body) and secondary (approving the recommendations posed to them by the quasi-governmental body). Despite the parallel regulatory apparatus, the two wine markets function differently. The majority of French consumers make wine purchases based primarily on regulated place names (appellation). Grape type, producer brand, and other considerations are secondary (d'Hauteville and Sirieix, 2007). Conversely, the best-selling wine in each Italian wine region is a local wine (ISMEA, 2008a), consistent with locally taught definitions of Italian quality. When Italian consumers venture beyond familiar local wines, wine guide scores play a significant role in comparison to the DOC regulation (Corrado and Odorici, 2004). So, despite the parallel regulatory structure, consumers rely on different quality guarantees in the two countries.

In the pages that follow, I investigate how the problem of trust is solved in the quality wine market. In both France and Italy, regulation developed as a means to create a protected market by guaranteeing a traditional, limited-quantity quality product. But consumer trust in the regulated mark varies significantly in France and Italy, and France manages to obtain higher prices for the regulated AOC wine than their Italian counterparts (Table 5.1).[1] I investigate whether the ways in which the regulatory regimes are structured and operate provide explanations for these observed differences. My findings indicate that differences in price premium obtained and consumer trust may be explained by three factors:

1. administrative historical legacy and government trust
2. trust among supply chain actors
3. market structure.

Variance among these three interrelated variables leads to differences in both business and citizen trust in the regulatory quality mark, resulting in different price premiums.

Table 5.1   French and Italian quality wine markets, compared

	French quality market (AOC)	Italian quality market (DOC/DOCG)
Average price for AOC/DOC(G)	€ 6.72	€ 3.14
Consumer behavior	Appellation	Local
Regulatory strength	High	Low
Production style	Traditional	Innovative

THEORY

According to George Akerlof, quality markets will cease to exist without a viable way to solve informational asymmetries (1970). *Informational asymmetries* exist when one party (typically the seller) has greater access to information on the product's quality than another party (typically the buyer). In his "The Market for Lemons" (1970), Akerlof argues that in the used car market, buyers and sellers have asymmetric information. If sellers are unable to convey qualitative variance to consumers, there is no economic incentive to sell higher quality goods. Akerlof proposes that quality uncertainty can be resolved through private certification—such as product guarantees or brands—or through public certification, such as professional licenses.

This point is reiterated in Lucien Karpik's analysis of luxury markets (2010):

> The only way to prevent the collapse of the quality market is to rely on the action of 'counter-institutions': guarantees, brands, certificates, diplomas, professional licensing, intervention of the state and private institutions, and of course, trust. In the absence of such mediations, the market collapses. Thus, under certain conditions, free competition leads to market self-destruction, while market continuity requires the regulation of competition. (p. 27)

Institutions, such as certification schemes, regulatory mechanisms, or private brands and guarantees are posited to solve the issue of asymmetric information. Karpik emphasizes the inherent connection between judgment devices and trust: "Judgment devices are also trust devices [. . .] To be effective, a judgment device must be credible; for it to be credible, it must be trusted by those who use it" (p. 55). He argues that judgment devices are a form of delegation, and this delegation is "a social relation [. . .] intimately bound up with trust" (p. 47). While Karpik links the notion of trust to judgment devices and luxury markets, he does not explain why certain devices are employed, nor does he explain consequences of different devices. This article intends to shed light on this dynamic.

In his book *Trust*, Francis Fukuyama explicitly develops this link between trust, institutional environment, and firm structure (1996). According to Fukuyama, both France and Italy are low-trust countries characterized by three factors: strong families, extensive government market intervention, and small firms. He argues these factors are inter-related: in low-trust environments, the state and the family step in to coordinate market transactions because actors do not trust the broader institutional context; smaller firms are a negative consequence of contracted trust networks. However, Fukuyama's analysis suffers from two critical flaws. First, his description of France as strong family and Italy as strong state overlooks decades of political economy research into the French and Italian cases (Ginsborg, 2003; Hall, 1986; Levy, 1999; Putnam, 1994). Aside from this gross error, he assumes vertical integration reflects high levels of institutional trust. In reality, vertical integration is one of many possible responses to *low* levels of institutional trust.

Klein et al. (1978) provide a more nuanced perspective on the problem of asymmetric information in the supply chain, adding here the problem of resource dependence, and how firms organize to resolve these two asymmetries simultaneously. They note three possible solutions to solve asymmetric information and resource dependence in the supply chain: vertical integration, state regulation, and interpersonal relations. The first two are formal and the third is informal, relying on implicit contracts within, what they call, "the market for reputation". According to this analysis, small firms could be evidence of strong, institutionalized relationships between firms.

Wei Zhao compares the classification regimes and institutional logics in the French and Californian wine industries and investigates their subsequent effect on prices (2005, 2008). He argues divergent classification schemes are an outcome of politics and institutions, without describing the mechanics of either. He emphasizes the role of *formal* regulation and classification categories on market construction and describes the French wine market as a vertically structured regulatory regime, classified primarily on appellation of origin, with an emphasis on tradition. By contrast, the Californian wine market is described as horizontally structured, brand dominant, classified primarily by grape variety, and reliant on scientific methods. Zhao assumes that regulations lead to predictable market behavior, but there is clearly a mechanism shaping wine market structure beyond formal rules, regulations, and classifications. These could include informal norms, formal organizations and associations, and personal relations—

each of which would be expected to shape producer risk and patterns of trust. Comparing the French and Italian wine markets enables one to explore the limits of Zhao's argument, as the Italian DOC system (*denominazione di origine controllata*, 1963) was directly modeled on the successful French AOC (*appellation d'origine contrôlée*, 1935) classification system, yet the Italian wine market *functions* in a manner similar to the California wine market—with fragmented producer cooperation and an emphasis on brands, scientific know-how, horizontal market structure and grape variety. Thus something links classification regimes and market structures beyond formal regulation.

Lane and Bachmann's research on trust in German and British industry (1996) is distinct from Fukuyama and Zhao because the authors consider the role of intermediary institutions in the construction of institutional trust. Luhmann (1979), like Zhao, emphasizes the importance of legal regulation in mitigating the risks of trust. Lane and Bachmann challenge this claim, arguing "law might not be the only environmental structure promoting the constitution of trust," and demonstrating instead how intermediary institutions such as trade associations can substitute for law, especially in cultivating trust in inter-firm relationships (p. 371). Business transactions rely either on systems trust or on personal trust based on a "taken-for granted" character constructed by expectations of the institutional environment. Systems trust, or institutional trust, is a type of generalized trust produced by reference to an institutional framework. Personal trust, conversely, is constituted on the basis of individual experience. Through the study of mining machinery and kitchen furniture, Lane and Bachmann find high institutional trust, strong intermediary (producer) institutions, and high institutional power are correlated with higher prices and the perception of higher quality in the German case. Conversely, a context of personal trust and a lack of cooperative governance mechanisms leads to greater flexibility but lower price points in the British case. The French and Italian wine markets offer the opportunity to test Lane and Bachmann's findings in a starkly different sector (agriculture versus industry), using different national cases.

In Bachmann (2001), the author shifts his focus to trust and power in the supply chain. He posits trust and personal power as inversely related, noting power is more often employed in social systems with low levels of institutional regulation. Networks of trust become more personal-based and more contracted in weak institutional systems, whereas in strong institutional environments, actors rely less on personal power and more on systems power, such as the power of the state to regulate. Is the link between supply chain trust in highly regulated institutional systems and the use of power to contract across the supply chain in weakly regulated institutional systems generalizable? My research tests his findings by applying these ideas in the French and Italian wine markets.

Finally, Giddens (1991) and Luhmann (1979) argue systems of regulations and control have greater density in a modern and complex society, and as a result impersonal system trust (rather than interpersonal trust) is more common as a solution to uncertainty (Hedgecoe, 2012). Walgenbach (2001) challenges this perspective, arguing certification schemes do not in themselves reduce the level of information asymmetry. He studies trust and legitimacy in the ISO 9000 certification in Germany, where he finds that close contacts and direct experiences of independent control systems weaken the trust regarding their impartiality and thereby their capacity to effectively regulate behavior. Walgenbach thus concludes legitimacy is a prerequisite for institutional-based trust. In the pages that follow, we will study impersonal regulatory systems to reveal the extent to which they rely on interpersonal trust.

Finally, one is left with the task of understanding the relationship between patterns of producer organization and consumer behavior. In other words, if producers recognize a regulatory regime as legitimate, does this influence consumer behavior in quality markets? Economic sociology provides us with a few tools to help us find the answer. According to both convention theorists and Pierre Bourdieu (1984), producers define quality for consumers. Convention theory emphasizes the role of producer behavior in constructing frameworks for consumer behavior (Diaz-Bone, 2009; Eymard-Duvernay, 2007; Boltanski and Thévenot, 2006; Becker, 1982). Conventions are collective schemata for the perception of quality, reflecting the culture and values embedded in networked relationships, such as in supply chains. According to sociologist Howard Becker, quality conventions are cultural logics that enable producers to coordinate to produce market goods collectively (Becker, 1982). Consumers do not create these frames: they are production regimes constructed by *producers* through repeated behavior over time. These conventions are routinized principles for the organization of production, which serve as a response to uncertainty.

Rainer Diaz-Bone applies the convention theory framework to the wine world. Specifically, Diaz-Bone analyzes the different wine supply chain conventions that link producers under shared understandings of quality, such as environmental conventions (green conventions), traditional and handicraft conventions (domestic conventions), or efficiency and price-based conventions (industrial and market conventions, respectively) (Diaz-Bone, 2013). Thus Diaz-Bone's framework allows for a conceptual linking between supply chain governance to shared cultural quality templates across the wine market.

Pierre Bourdieu's notion of homology provides a parallel explanation of how producer-driven quality conventions create consumer demand. According to Bourdieu, producers of cultural products meet demand without expressly having to seek it. Instead, consumers identify goods that "go together" because they are homologous, or situated in roughly the same social spaces. In the field of cultural production, "the supply always exerts an effect of symbolic imposition" (Bourdieu, 1984, p. 227).[2] Patrick Aspers describes the producer—consumer dynamic in status markets as more of a dynamic creation between buyers and sellers, where the two groups together co-create shared understandings of a status market (Aspers, 2009). In sum, the dominant thread of economic sociology literature of differentiated quality markets indicates that producer networks principally shape consumer behavior. Based on these significant findings, this article aims to shed light on consumer behavior through analyzing how producers organize production.

METHODS AND DATA SOURCES

The quality wine market relies upon an array of signals in order to convey the qualitative differences that price differentiation relies upon. The difference in wine quality may be perceptible, or it may not be; and qualitative differences may or may not be correlated with price. The question of a producer's success may depend less upon the product's observable characteristics and more on the perception of product differentiation. Producers in the French and Italian quality wine markets vary in how they solve the issue of market trust. Market trust here consists of two related dimensions: how producers guarantee quality within their supply chain, and how consumers guarantee quality at the point of sale. In both France and in Italy, regulation developed as a means to signal product quality and to construct market differentiation. But consumer trust in this quality mark varies greatly in France and Italy; and wine prices also differ significantly.

I focus primarily on how the issue of trust is solved within the supply chain, building upon the economic sociology literature indicating that producer networks principally shape consumer behavior. Thus how producers solve trust among themselves would be expected to influence how consumers solve the issue of trust at the point of sale. I further focus on the issue of trust between producers—specifically between those that grow grapes and those that buy the grapes and convert them into wine—due to the important reason that those who command high prices in the wine market distinguish themselves by their *terroir*. I will argue this strategy dominates only in situations where grape quality is perceived as reliably guaranteed within the supply chain, and where this distinction can be reliably conveyed to consumers.

I collected qualitative data for this project through 114 semi-structured interviews, which generally lasted for slightly over one hour in duration. The core of my questionnaire investigated the role of regulation in shaping producer strategy, how producers conveyed quality to consumers, and the patterns of trust and cooperation among producer groups. I selected my interview subjects in order to represent a range of regions, production volume, price points, and branding strategies to better understand variances between regions and between market segments. I conducted these interviews with an array of experts, producers, and policy makers, across the high and low end of the French and Italian wine sector, in a total of ten wine producing regions.

The specific breakdown of my interviews are as follows: producers (28 French, 17 Italian; including growers, winemakers, cooperative operators and directors, branded houses, retailers and distributors), government officials (11 French and 11 Italian; at the national, regional, and local level, including the officials of quasi-governmental producer organizations), professionals (12 French and 13 Italian; including lawyers, economists, and historians); actors from private associations (six in France, four in Italy; principal agents involved in luxury organizations), and 12 interviews with wine sector experts beyond the immediate French and Italian context. In France my interviews were conducted in Champagne, Burgundy, Bordeaux, Languedoc, and Paris over three visits totaling 15 months. I conducted my Italian interviews in three visits totaling six months in Sicily, Tuscany, Piedmont, Puglia, Lazio, the Veneto, and Emilia-Romagna. I triangularized my research with interviews with producers, political organizers, and wine lobbyists in both the U.S. (California and Oregon) and Germany (Rhineland-Pfalz); as well as with actors from luxury manufacturing in France and in Italy (producers, professors, and instructors at French and Italian fashion and technical schools, lobbying firms, producer organizations, and lawyers at top luxury houses).[3]

In the following pages I investigate relationships between various supply chain actors. I specifically focus on grape growers and the wine merchants who convert the grapes of wine into finished, bottled and labeled wine. To be clear, there can be some variance about how winemaking tasks are divided between these two groups, with some growers making their own wines, for example. But one thing remains the same: growers are numerous, often interchangeable, and they may struggle to guarantee quality and earn fair prices when they sell their product to relatively scarce wine merchants. The actual tasks performed in different contexts do not change the trust and power dynamic between these two actors. "Producers" refers to any actor who grows grapes, makes wine and/or bottles it. It does not refer to actors who distribute wine or sell it in retail outlets.

RESEARCH FINDINGS: FRENCH AND ITALIAN QUALITY WINE MARKETS IN COMPARATIVE PERSPECTIVE

Since the 1970s, the global wine market has undergone dramatic transformations. This was the first time that it appeared probable that international competitors might threaten the singular French dominance of the quality wine market. Californian wines beat top French Bordeaux in blind tastings in the 1976 Judgment of Paris (Taber, 2006), and Italian wines began to receive global recognition for their high-quality "Super Tuscan" table wines. These turning points were accompanied by three other important trends: the decline of wine consumption in traditional wine-consuming countries (most pronounced in France and Italy), the European Union's attempt to actively decrease the number of vineyards in order to stabilize table wine prices via the Common Agricultural Policy (CAP), and improvements in the quality and volume of wine produced in the "New World," as well as in the volume of wine consumed. Indeed, a recurring story in today's wine world is the diminished significance of French wine, specifically, and of "Old World" wine—such as Italian wine—more broadly.

Despite these dramatic changes in the international wine market, French and Italian producers continue to dominate wine production in terms of both price and volume. In 2014, France led global production with 47 million hectoliters and Italy came in second with 45 million (OIV, 2015). In 2014, French wine exports totaled €7.7 billion and Italian wine exports totaled €5 billion (OIV, 2015), making these countries the global leaders in wine export value. However, there is an important distinction between these dominant producers: Italian and French wine have similar per unit prices for both table wines and for their lightly regulated "protected geographic indicator" (PGI)[4] wines (Chever et al., 2012). However, the difference in the value conferred by regulated quality wine is significant. France's *appellation d'origine contrôlée* (AOC) wines average €5.20 per liter (€6.72 if one includes Champagne), whereas Italian *denominazione di origine controllata* (DOC) and *denominazione di origine controllata e garantita* (DOCG) price averages €3.14 per liter (*ibid.*) (Table 5.2).

Thus the difference between French and Italian wine value is found almost completely in their different appellation of origin (PDO[5]) wine values. The rules governing these regulated appellation wines require that a minimum of 85 percent of the grapes come from a given geographic area,

Table 5.2   Comparative PDO (AOC, DOC/DOCG) wine prices per liter,
2010

Protected designation of origin wines	
France (including Champagne)	€ 6.72
France (without Champagne)	€ 5.20
Italy	€ 3.14

impose yield restrictions, and guarantee producer-determined production rules (including allowable grape varieties). Regulation of these wines theoretically represents legal recognition of traditional local winemaking practices. But while regulated AOC wine producers capture 82 percent of French wine value, Italy's regulated DOC and DOCG wines capture only 47 percent of Italy's wine market value (ISMEA 2008b, p. 219, data excludes sparkling wines). While there are over 360 DOCs in Italy, many have annual production volumes of zero, as the value gained by the DOC mark is less than the per-bottle fee incurred to apply the DOC sticker (personal interview, Corrado and Odorici, 2010). And DOC production is concentrated: fewer than 100 DOCs account for over 80 percent of DOC output (Corrado and Odorici, 2009). To put this another way, France accounts for 35 percent of European PDO (AOC) wine production and 54 percent of European sales value, whereas Italy, its closest competitor, produces 20 percent of PGO (DOC/DOCG) sales volume and only 4 percent of its value. Thus the appellation sticker dominates quality wine production in the French context, while in the Italian context, the majority of appellation stickers confer limited value on protected producers.

Indeed for French consumers, wine origin is the primary determinant of their wine purchases (d'Hauteville and Sirieix, 2007). For Italian consumers, the drivers of consumption are harder to discern. According to the research arm of the Italian Ministry of Agriculture, ISMEA, the best selling wine in each Italian wine region is a local wine both for table wine and for DOC/DOCG markets (ISMEA, 2008b), reflecting a long-standing tradition of local wine consumption. This parallels studies on Italian wine consumption that emphasize that the principal driver of consumer behavior is "tasted the wine previously" (Casini et al., 2009, p. 69). Overall, "wine origin," or appellation, exerts more than double the effect on consumer purchasing choices in France in comparison with Italy (*ibid.*). Expert opinion ("I read about it") exerts a strong influence on Italian consumer behavior but no measurable impact on consumer decision-making in the French market context (*ibid.*).[6] French and Italian consumers and businesses, then, trust different judgment devices. I investigate whether the way in which the regulatory regimes are structured and operate provides explanations for these observed differences. My findings indicate that variance among three factors accounts for differences in trust in the regulation, leading to different ways of competing and to different price premiums:

1.   administrative historical legacy and trust in government
2.   trust among supply chain actors
3.   market structure.

I now investigate each of these three interrelated variables in turn.

Administrative Historical Legacy and Trust in Government

France
The impact of administrative heritage on wine regulation can be observed in both how producers organize for and how consumers respond to state-backed regulation. These two factors are closely related: producers are more likely to organize for state protection when they believe state protection has the ability to influence consumer preferences. In the French case, producers organized for state protection (1935) in part due to the historical role played by the state in regulating and defining quality. In the Italian case, producers sought regulatory protection (1963) due to the observed market successes in the French case. However, the Italian market lacked the administrative heritage, which I argue was critical for the construction of state-defined quality in the French case. Here I apply institutionalist logic from political science and argue that this organization arises based on past experiences and subsequent expectations with state quality regulation.

The French state has played a significant role in regulating quality production dating from the seventeenth century (Shonfield, 1965, p. 79), constructing centralized, hierarchical definitions of quality (such as the AOC). During this time, the Sun King (Louis XIV) determined quality, regulated by his finance minister Colbert, and the King's taste would be replicated by his court and through the social hierarchy. Consumers demonstrated their sophistication by converging on the King's definition of quality (Elias, 1978). In the French case, the perceived legitimacy of the state—especially given their history of centralized quality regulation—helped the regulation gain legitimacy. Indeed, the perceived power and legitimacy of the state influenced the decision of the producers to organize themselves, as they feared if they did not push their own regulation upon the state, the state would push their own regulation on producers, as they did in the bulk wine market segment (Loubère, 1978) and in a number of industrial sectors during the Interwar period.

Both the French model of AOC production and consumption are oriented towards and reward deep principles of class and exclusion that characterized the *ancien régime*. The French AOC mark is not the sign of quality, but rather it is a mark of tradition. Implicit here is the idea that producers who have been making wine through history have superior methods (and thus a superior product) than market newcomers. The French AOC is a unique type of structure. Created by producers in 1935, it enables producers to determine quality, then to use state regulation as a means to legitimate their definition. The quasi-governmental organization charged with regulating the AOC, the *institute national des appellations d'origine* (INAO), does not have the direct power to create quality production guidelines, they only have the power to accept or reject the quality proposals presented by organized producer groups. The principle underlying the AOC is the notion that producers and the state know quality, and consumers should align themselves with producer's tastes (Geneviève Teil, INRA, personal interview, 2007).

French producers repeatedly expressed this idea that producers, rather than consumers, know quality. Thus they reject the idea of quality consumption as something evolving, "meritocratic", and earned. Quality, rather, is demonstrated by the lack of market evolution:

> Definitely I think the whole idea of terroir is fascinating because in the US people say that terroir was a marketing invention of the French to kill the competition, which is absolutely untrue. The whole idea of terroir is the fact that you *don't stick to the market*. People are still making the same wine on this terroir for generations but obviously the market has changed a lot. . . This is absolute proof that they don't want to stick to the market. (Eric Texier, Burgundian Wine Merchant, personal interview, 2011)

Texier's logic, and the reasoning of other quality French producers, reflects the notion that quality is given by birth, heritage, and tradition (*noblesse du robe*) rather than something that can be acquired (*noblesse d'epée*). In other words, title and distinction are inherent and "God-given" rather than something attained through effort and merit (Fourcade, 2012). For wine categorizations *other* than the AOC—for example, the less-regulated French IGT or even the Italian DOC or DOCG—any group of producers can theoretically obtain the know-how to produce quality wine (provided that soil and climate are conducive to quality wine production). The elite structure of the AOC resonated with a certain sense of identity on the part of consumers who want to differentiate themselves. By attributing value to a feature that is impossible for most to perceive—the process of production—the French created both a restricted market supply (providing them with greater control over both price and distribution) and—among consumers—a clear group of "insiders," differentiated by their defined and refined taste. This is because taste and knowledge must be slowly acquired and built up; it cannot be bought, and cannot be faked by the "nouveau bourgeois." In other words, the AOC was homologous to the French system of class, differentiation, and distinction. Politics and history, then, influence which structures resonate with consumers as legitimate.

Producers repeatedly expressed the notion that they create demand for consumers, rather than respond to it. When asked how he markets his wine to consumers, a Bordeaux producer explained to me "we don't 'sell' our wine, our wine sells itself" (December 2007). This perspective, too, reinforces the notion that quality is not defined by success in responding to the market, but rather in its resistance to follow the market. Quality producers in Champagne and Bordeaux also indicated in interviews their dominance over other supply chain actors—notably retailers and distributors: "We know who sells our wine, where they sell it, and what they charge. If we are not satisfied (with this), we do not (give) them wine the next year". This supports the notion of hierarchical (producer-defined), limited access distribution structures, further reinforcing the idea of elite, inaccessible, producer-dominant quality markets in the French case.

It is important to note, however, that the French case is not monolithic. In general, there is an inverse relation between success of the AOC and perception of the AOC as political. Champagne, the region with the highest average AOC wine prices in France, is also the region where interview subjects reported the highest levels of trust and satisfaction with both institutions (local and national) and with other supply chain actors. In the Languedoc, the former table wine producing region that now has the lowest average AOC wine prices in France, producers were much more likely to perceive the AOC institutions as political.[7] One local interprofessional leader noted that AOC approval for the Languedoc was helped when you have a personal contact: "things move faster when you know someone in Paris" (personal interview, Languedoc, 2009). This perceived foot-dragging may not be coincidental; a member of the main AOC governing body in Paris, the INAO, explained to me: "we are trying to move away from the association of the AOC from quality to traditional production. So new quality producers, like Cité de Carcasonne (in the Languedoc), will produce a great wine, but not an AOC wine." This approach defends the rents of those who have already secured an AOC while more broadly protecting an elite-defined notion of quality, reinforcing the notion that quality is born, not made.

Thus the French AOC reflects and maintains a top-down, producer-defined notion of quality, legitimized by the centralized state. This elite structure creates clear insiders and outsiders, and the idea that quality, like taste, is born and not created, excludes market newcomers. This hierarchical quality definition resonates with consumers looking to distinguish themselves by the deep principles of class and exclusion, which has characterized the French market since the *ancien régime*.

Italy

Italian administrative heritage stands in sharp contrast to the French example. The Italian state is perceived to rely on clientelistic ties to create political linkages and to consolidate power. Unlike its French counterpart, the young Italian state (Italy united only in 1861) had no history of regulating quality. Quality was hierarchical and defined by the local courts; a centralized, national quality hierarchy never emerged. Quality knowledge is deep in Italy, but it is not centralized. It is taught at the local level.

Undeniably, in any sociopolitical hierarchy, some actors have access to opportunities that other producers do not. In the Italian wine sector, these advantages are sometimes economic: some producers can afford to hire enologists, winemakers, and build cellars, and other producers cannot. But my interview subjects indicated a perception that economically powerful wine producers operate under a different set of rules than the rules that inhibit other producers, thereby weakening trust in "neutral" political institutions. The local division comes not from an inequity in opportunities—though this exists—but from a perception of differential political access.

The perception of the state as a weak guarantor of quality effects how producers organize, the type and depth of protection they pursue, and the extent to which consumers rely on state-backed regulation to guide their purchases. In the Italian context, producers and consumers perceive quality wine regulation as an outcome of clientelistic ties. In each of my interviews, except for one, producers and consumers indicated they believed DOCs were primarily the result of political connections. DOCs are granted by an expert para-public committee, the *comitato nationale della vita del vino*, which parallels the French national *Institute national d'origine et de la qualité* (INAO) committee. However, the only person I encountered who attempted to argue that the *comitato* was fair and apolitical was himself a member of the *comitato*. No other actors I spoke to in the Italian wine industry shared this opinion. Instead, producers and wine writers perceive the *comitato* as a means for local leaders to deliver economic protection to their local constituencies. "In Italy we have a political committee who decides, instead of technicians" (Ziliani, personal interview, July 2009). Even the assistant to the *comitato* member who defended the organization said (after his boss left the room) "yes, giving the DOC is a bit political." The assistant also said that *comitato* members were primarily beholden to regional interests over national interests (interview, July 2010).

Vincenzo Zampi, an economist at the University of Florence, echoed this view: "Agriculture and politics are intertwined. Favors. You want to protect your constituents" (July 19, 2010). Wine Journalist Franco Ziliani provided a handful of concrete examples of powerful producers receiving appointments to the *comitato* and then granting themselves DOCGs. A top winemaker in Emilia-Romagna told me about the political nature of the DOC in a more oblique manner: "Soon the EU will grant DOC status [. . .] this reduces the ability of political actors to improve their local standing by securing DOCs for their constituents [. . .] it is perceived it will be more difficult to secure DOC protection at the European level." According to economists Corrado and Odorici, "Instead of [distinctions like DOC and DOCG] being a selection of 'the best among the good wines,' based on actual quality, fame and diffusion, denominations became a tool of local institutions for promotion of their territories and productions" (Corrado and Odorici, 2008, p. 8).

Not only does the perception of patronage undermine trust in the regulation directly, but if indeed it is accurate that the regulation is given as a favor, then this regulation can undermine the evolution of Italian wine quality, as the political nature of the DOC can inhibit the regulation from delivering effective results. "When you want to create a new area, you need to allow people to experiment, learn, and find the best quality. Instead, politicians are in a rush to give a value-added to their constituents" (Zampi, personal interview, 2010). Instead, the DOC provided a quality guarantee to many wines that had not yet found their highest quality production practices as a means to secure political patronage (personal interviews: Franco Ziliani, 2009; wine industry expert, 2009; Italian enologist, 2010; Vincenzo Zampi, 2010). Political patronage harms the wine sector in three ways. First, it slows down the process of innovation (at least among some producers). Second, it stigmatizes the shared local geographic brand, if the region is associated with a low-quality wine. Third, the protection of lower-quality wines weakens the value of other DOCs, as the mark no longer signifies an effective quality guarantee. Italian producers sought to emulate successful French AOC wine regulation in the hopes that it would add value to Italian wine producers, as it had for French wine producers (Zampi, personal interview, 2010). However, given the different administrative and institutional contexts, the regulation had different market consequences in our two cases.

Fukuyama claims generalizable trust is low in both France and Italy due to a strong familial legacy and a strong reliance on the state to coordinate market transaction. In reality, the French and Italian relationships to both the state and to the family follow two very different trajectories: France has traditionally been categorized as *étatist*, whereas the role of the family and of local networks occupies a more central role within Italian political economy literature (Berger and Locke, 2001). One sees this pattern in the wine sector, where French producers capitalize on the administrative and regulatory heritage of the state. Italian producers, on the other hand, capitalize on personal networks.

These divergent heritage patterns laid the foundation for divergent levels of institutionalized trust in our two cases. The next section considers how producers organized themselves to address trust and risk within the supply chain.

Trust among Supply Chain Actors

The wine sector provides insight into the mechanisms of both informational asymmetries and power asymmetries. Information asymmetries exist not only at the final point of sale, but in any transaction throughout the supply chain. In the case of the wine supply chain, growers have knowledge of their grape quality, but the ability of a wine merchant[8] to reliably verify the quality of large grape quantities is constrained. While there is an information asymmetry that benefits growers (in that growers know the quality of their product better than merchants), merchants possess a *power asymmetry* in the absence of institutionalized cooperation. In other words, there are many growers who sell to a limited number of wine merchants. The merchant sets the price, and the grower has little choice but to accept the price, even if the price is below production costs. This puts downward price pressure on growers, who may skimp on quality by increasing yields, or attempt to increase their revenues by illegally adding sugar to increase alcohol levels.[9] In order to ensure quality production, these two market asymmetries—information and power—must be solved.

Our two cases sharply diverge in how producers organize to solve these market asymmetries. In the French context, producers rely on institutional power and generalizable trust, organizing themselves into "corporatist" cooperative producer structures that typically characterize quality German industrial organization. These structures are intended simultaneously to balance power and informational asymmetries by institutionalizing decision-making bodies which split power evenly between growers and merchants. Italian production initially followed the French model, but producer institutions were later reformed to equate voting power with production volumes in the hope that this shift would encourage small Italian producers to be more responsive to market signals. As a result, the French model attempts to equate power between different groups, and the Italian model institutionalizes and formalizes existing power asymmetries.

France

Trust among supply chain actors varies greatly between our two cases. In the French quality wine market, producers solve informational and power asymmetries primarily through producer organizations. The producer associations facilitated the establishment of trust in "the rules of the game," and producers generally believed other supply chain actors followed agreed upon rules of production. While the AOC is under the quasi-governmental INAO, the AOC rules are made and enforced by the producers themselves, through local interprofessional councils. In the French case, the interprofessional council (the local regulatory body) has a corporatist structure, and power is divided evenly between growers and merchants, with each producer given one vote, regardless of output. Growers and merchants have the same number of elected union representatives in the producer organization (interprofessional council), and the presidency alternates between the two groups. The bargain reached between the two groups is essentially the following: growers agree to produce wine according to codified production standards, and merchants agree to limit their grape inputs to growers within the interprofessional council. The local growers' union is charged with auditing the local growers, to ensure they meet the agreed-upon production standards. In order to use the geographic place names—such as Champagne, *Côtes du Rhône*—merchants need to purchase grapes from growers in the interprofessional council. If a merchant were to use grapes from outside the region, they could forfeit the right to use a shared geographic label.

Producer organizations were established upon a history of national quality regulation, as previously mentioned, and also upon some history of producer cooperation (Loubère, 1978), notably in the late nineteenth century. After the AOC was established in 1935, the specificity of the regulation increased over the first two decades of the AOC (Loubère, 1990), as confidence in their regulatory model increased alongside its market success. The dense regulation in the French case helped solve the problem of asymmetric information, and buyers and sellers within the supply chain were willing to pay more for products perceived to be of a higher quality.

As growers began cooperating with wine merchants (*négociants*) and developing trust-based, institutionalized relationships, they ensured that high grape quality and adherence to traditional production became

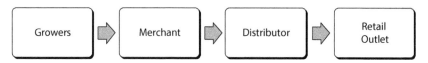

Figure 5.1   Simplified wine supply chain

profitable for actors throughout the production chain. For example, Champagne grape growers have a monopoly over grape production, enabling them to earn as much as €5.50 per kilo. Champagne *négociants* pay more for their wine grapes than any other *négociant*. But instead of making Champagne uncompetitive, the quantity of Champagne is severely constricted, leading buyers to bid up prices in the luxury market: Champagne sells for an average of €21.34 per liter, four times the average price of regulated French wines (Chever et al., 2012). This protects farmers, but wine merchants are better off as well, as both parties benefit from the restricted supply, the perceived qualitative difference, and the notion of Champagne as a status product.

Success in the French case is dependent upon strong grower groups, legitimate grower-merchant institutions, and legitimate state recognition. Corporatism has the potential to change the balance of political power in favor of the weaker groups in a capitalist market society (Grant, 1985, p. 25). The French institutional structure tends to equalize power between two previously unequal players: traditionally weak, numerous and interchangeable grape growers and the larger, more powerful wine merchants.[10] As suggested by Bachmann, there is an inverse relationship between personal power and institutionalized trust. The French model capitalizes on a strong institutional context and the trust it engenders, decreasing transaction costs, enabling growers with higher costs to find buyers (the merchants in their interprofessional council) and enabling wine merchants to have reliable quality guarantees regarding the grapes they purchase.

Producer groups, and the national regulation AOC that protects them, are perceived to be central to the continued French dominance of the quality wine market. Efforts at the EU level to weaken and refine the AOC and other protected geographic regions were met with a fierce resistance from the Ministry of Agriculture and the producer-dominated INAO. Eventually, French producers secured the ability to maintain their strict production rules, despite the fact that the same regulation (the aforementioned PDO) offers greater producer flexibility in other European markets (Smith et al., 2007). According to a producer and interprofessional representative from the Languedoc region: "We cannot lose the AOC [. . .] it is fundamental to protect our wine tradition and our market share." This point was reiterated in my interviews at the Ministry of Agriculture (2007, 2008, 2009) and at the INAO (2008, 2011).

Thus the French solved the issue of supply chain trust by strong intermediary associations in a strong institutional context. This limited their ability to compete at lower prices and to respond quickly to market signals, but it enhanced their perception as a distinct product and strengthened the legitimacy of the wine regulation from the perspective of both producers and of consumers. The issue of supply chain trust is particularly important in supply chain relationship between growers and merchants, because the ability to guarantee quality of the grape enables producers to create a production strategy that emphasizes the unique characteristics of the grape specifically and the *terroir* (the land, climate, and production know-how) more broadly. This differentiated strategy can only be pursued when merchants can reliably solve the information asymmetry. I explore this argument explicitly in the section on market structure.

Italy

Weaker levels of trust among producers characterize the Italian wine market. Actors did not trust other actors in their appellation, and neither they nor consumers trust the DOC mark. These producers tend to either suffer in asymmetrical relationships, or construct small, vertically integrated firms. Italian growers have historically remained more fragmented than their French counterparts (Loubère, 1978), weakening their ability to tightly link wine quality to a geographically-based (and limited quantity) grape. Instead, wine quality is defined principally by individual brands. This is true both of large quality producers, who dominate their suppliers and tend to blend both mass market and quality-value production, and of small quality producers. The tendency toward individualist market orientation—as opposed to associative political logic—harms the shared geographic brand and fails to correct asymmetries of power and of information.

Whereas French wine regulation emerged as a political response to perceptions of unequal economic power and class divides between growers and merchants (Loubère, 1978), Italian producers had similar political divisions but effective political structures were not created to remedy this imbalance. Today, the Italian wine market continues to be characterized by a demarcation between wine's "market insiders" and "market outsiders," even in quality regions. Specifically, several Italian interview subjects repeated the idea that some grape growers suffered from a "farmer mentality" (or a "peasant mentality"), were free riders with no sense of how markets work, and had only a limited interest in making quality wines (personal interview, quality winemaker in Emilia-Romagna, July 2010; wine promoter, Sicily, July 2010; economist, Florence, July 2010; wine merchant, Emilia-Romagna, July 2010).[11] Other experts (including growers, writers, academics, market leaders, and agro-tourism promoters) cited the previously mentioned endemic system of corruption and patronage in national and local wine politics as the principal problem in Italian wine regulation. Several interviewees expressed both perspectives at the same time: that the powerful were corrupt and the less powerful lacked marketing savvy. On both sides, the effect of these divides is to perpetuate weak local institutions: less successful farmers distrust successful farmers, and successful farmers have little interest in cooperating with less market-oriented "backwards producers".

This insider/outsider divide in the Italian wine industry has become institutionalized into local Italian *consorzii*. In the French interprofessional council, decision-making authority is divided evenly between grape growers and wine merchants. In the Italian case, since 1992 the voting structure in the *consorzio* is determined by production volume, regardless of position in the supply chain. These voting procedures shift local decision-making power toward large, export-oriented producers in regions where ownership is concentrated.[12] For example, large export-oriented producers may prefer to adapt their local wine variety to the currently popular "New World" wine style. In practice, this means favoring international grape varieties over local varieties, enhancing wine colors, increasing the taste of oak, etc. Even when powerful producers are unable to formally change the *disciplinario* production rules, they have been able to push the taste and color of Italian wines toward a more international style. In one major Italian wine-exporting region, large producers used their power to put themselves on a DOC's "blind" wine tasting panel, where select *consorzio* members taste a wine sample for "typicalness" before the wine receives the DOC stamp. A key player in breaking the Brunello fraud scandal,[13] Franco Ziliani, described how these large producers used their voting influence to "stack the deck" on the tasting panel. Once they dominated the panel, they used their voice to push the taste of Brunello in a particular direction:

> The *consorzio* is very political—[the people] who judge the wine in the "blind tasting" are the same people who make the wine. They like their style of wine. In Montalcino, it happened more than once; the best producers were 100 percent sangiovese from Montalcino. They played by the book. And the wine was boycotted from the test panel because there was too much sangiovese. This was not the official reason. They find other reasons. But fake Brunellos passed without any problems.

The concentration of political power in the Italian wine sector both changes the taste of wine and inhibits the voice of small producers. According to my interviews, local power asymmetries weaken local cooperation because vulnerable actors fear retribution (personal interview, Agro-Tourism Operator in Emilia-Romagna, July 2010; personal interview, France Ziliani, 2010).[14] When asked why so many producers kept quiet though they knew about the wine fraud, Franco Ziliani explained:

In Montalcino, the majority of producers respect the rules. At the same time, they justify what the big producers are doing. Everyone is a little bit guilty. With so many rules, everyone is guilty of having broken a few rules. Small producers don't feel that they are powerful enough to stand up to the large producers. The most important producers know the secrets of the small producers. So their hands are dirty, and this is known.[15]

These findings parallel the findings of Bachmann (2001): In a weak institutional context, actors within the supply chain will rely on power as opposed to trust to coordinate transactions and to control social relationships when the risk of trust betrayal by someone is perceived to be relatively high. In a strong institutional context, actors rely on the institutional environment to guarantee transactions and personal trust is replaced by a broader systems trust. Our next section considers the impact of these two institutional contexts on production strategy and market structure.

Trust and Market Structure

France
French interprofessional councils function as an intermediary institution that help address the problems of information and power asymmetries. Unable to distinguish themselves by low prices or by market responsiveness—the institutional structure prevents this type of market adaptation—French producers instead distinguish themselves by emphasizing the quality of one of their production inputs—the grape. Grapes are perceived to be unique expressions of terroir. French wine merchants have some degree of confidence that the grapes they purchase from growers meet certain specifications that may be correlated with higher prices and higher quality. As a result, wine merchants will employ winemaking techniques that emphasize grape uniqueness rather than standardizing or correcting a grape by technology. Wine maker Eric Texier expressed this commitment to making a unique wine, which emphasizes grape distinction: "We make the wines that the *terroir* makes, not the wines the market wants." He continued to describe how he creates the best wines he could make with his *terroir*, and he trusted that, despite fluctuations in consumer trends, his wines would continue to find quality-conscious consumers without needing him to adapt to consumer demand (July 2011). Given that producers in any national context can access technology (including oak barrels and oak chips, made-to-order yeast strains, micro-oxidation, reverse osmosis), wines that rely less on a standardizing technology can distinguish themselves in a different—albeit pricier—production style. Thus the commitment to making a unique terroir-driven

wine has the potential to launch quality producers into a particular, and rare, market segment.

However, this type of production only exists when trust is established in the supply chain: specifically, when merchants are certain of grape quality. The strong institutionalized French context guarantees grape quality for merchants, guarantees agreed-upon prices for growers, and, importantly, indicated to consumers that any wine with the shared AOC geographic brand will have a certain taste palate and quality standard. This allows small firms to survive, despite the fact that they do not have individual brand recognition. These findings challenge Fukuyama's assertion that French firms are small because they have weak levels of trust. In reality, small French firms have the possibility to survive due to producer networks that move power from the individual to the institution. These institutions explicitly restrict larger actors (such as wine merchants) from squeezing smaller actors (such as small growers), ensure product quality within the organization, and enable consumers to reliably purchase an AOC wine without direct knowledge of the specific wine merchant. In cases where the AOC is especially effective in creating value-added (such as in Champagne), wine distributors and retailers are limited in their ability to squeeze wine merchants. While some might see this limit on competition as a market hindrance, this limit allows growers and wine merchants to maintain their methods of production and, as a result, their perception of luxury and their high prices.

Italy
Whereas French producers describe the importance of resisting market trends, Italian wine producers equate quality success with market success. The reliance on market signals rather than political signals is related to low levels of institutionalized trust in the Italian context. This is true from the point of view of consumers, as observed by reluctance to buy based on government-backed regulation. But it is also true of producers, who equate quality production with economic success and high prices. One Italian interview subject described the market as an accessible path for a producer hoping to build a better life in a manner that did not rely on political dealings (personal interview agro-tourism firm owner, Emilia-Romagna, July 2010). Other Italian producers turn a blind eye toward political "problems" so long as they perceive they have a chance to achieve a level of market success: "There was a magical moment when everything was selling and everybody was making money. Any bottle which said Brunello would sell for $50. People say 'America has to have wines like this, America buys wines like this, so what's the problem?' Everyone was ignoring or playing blind. The press, the importers, the *consorzio*" (Ziliani, July 2010).

Unable to reliably trust the government-backed mark, Italian producers and consumers rely on personal networks of trust. As a result, many power asymmetries remain in market organization, and small growers in known wine regions increasingly vertically integrate, as they are unable to receive fair prices for their grapes (personal interview, Piedmont producer, July 2010; Sicilian wine promoter, 2011; ISMEA interview, 2010). As most of the value in the Italian wine market is with wine merchants instead of grape growers (ISMEA, 2008a), vertical integration can theoretically enable growers to capture more value-added from their wine. Vertical integration, however, leads to a proliferation of individual brands, which is difficult for the consumer to navigate, especially given the absence of shared geographic brands. Thus these firms solve the supply chain problem between growers and merchants, but they ultimately face problems when they sell their wines to distributors and retailers. Firms who have successfully circumvented this dilemma tend to do so by relying on personal distribution networks, notably by contracting with family members in the Italian diaspora who work in or have contacts in foreign Italian restaurants (personal interview, Italian wine producer in Lazio, 2007).

For the majority of Italian producers, the Italian structure frequently divides small producers—who try to compete on a differentiated product—from large producers, who produce on economies of scale. This may provide a short-run market advantage to some large firms, but overall it inhibits quality producers from attaining product attributes associated with singularity, uniqueness, and higher prices. Specifically, the differences in the location of supply-chain power shape French and Italian wine styles. As noted above, technology masks grape flaws. As a result, standardizing technology becomes important when winemakers have grapes of variable or of unknown quality. This may be a more common problem in markets with fragmented cooperation among supply chain actors. The wine blog *The Zinquisition* summarized these differences between French (*terroir*-driven) wines and Italian (style-driven) wines:

> *Terroir*-driven wines are often associated with wines of a 'natural' style [. . .] with limited human intervention. Style-driven wines are wines where a winemaker strives to create a wine of a certain style [. . .] These wines are also thought by critics to reveal less of their *terroir* as those subtleties are masked by the (human) intervention. (cited in Corrado and Odorici, 2009, p. 115)

Robert Parker makes a similar point: technology (the domain of the winemaker) brings "standardization to such a point that it becomes difficult to distinguish between an Italian, a French, a Californian or an Australian Chardonnay" (Parker's *2002 Wine Guide*, cited in Karpik, 2010).

Table 5.3   Implications for power and informational asymmetries

	Patterns of trust	Producer cooperation	Institutional environment	Patterns of power
France	High systems trust	High levels of vertical supply chain cooperation	Strong national regulatory legitimacy	High systems power
Italy	Low systems trust	Power asymmetries within the supply chain	Weak national legitimacy	High personal power

Finally, technology also becomes important when brand "consistency" drives product strategy.

The difference in market structure and definitions of quality, then, affects the extent to which a product distinguishes itself from similar competitors. French quality is perceived to be above concerns of market demand, as the *terroir* principle protects "tradition" and explicitly inhibits market adaptation. The Italian wine strategy on the other hand, orients production to the changing consumer tastes, in part by anticipating market demand (personal interview, Ziliani, 2010).

In summary, intermediary producers' organizations and a strong institutionalized trust contest play a central role in cultivating trust in supply chain relations in the French quality wine market (Table 5.3). Conversely, Italian producers operate in a system with lower levels of institutional regulation, causing them to rely more heavily on personal trust both within the supply chain at the final point of sale. The effects of these different trust patterns are two-fold. First, producers who operate in a strong systems trust environment secure greater quality guarantees in the supply chain, leading to a manner of production securing both higher prices for all supply chain actors, but also a higher final price in the market and a higher perception of quality. Conversely, markets with lower levels of systems trust and higher levels of personal trust exhibit market flexibility, though the producers are found at a lower price point. Secondly, patterns of institutional/systems trust shape how consumers consume, and if they buy products they are already familiar with, or if they will try a new product based on a government-backed guarantee (Table 5.4).

Table 5.4   Summary comparison of French and Italian wine markets

	France	Italy
Name of state quality regulatory regime	*appellation d'origine contrôlée*	*denominazione di origine controllata*
Average price per liter, 2012 (euros)	6.72	3.14
Administrative heritage	Quality historically state defined and state regulated, perception of state bureaucracy as legitimate guarantor of quality Strong centralized government with history of quality regulation	Quality historically locally defined, perception of state bureaucracy as overly bureaucratic and captured by elite interests
Business/citizen trust in government regulation	Low in industry, high in agriculture. Consumers learn quality nationally	Low in industry, low in agriculture. Consumers learn quality locally
Market structure	Quality-based Perception of quality as traditional and resistant to mass markets demand, calls for slow moving market structures/regulation	Price-quality intersection Perception of quality and innovation and tradition together, calls for similarly dynamic market structures/regulation
Trust among supply chain actors	High levels of system trust	Low levels of system trust, reliant on personal trust

CONCLUSIONS

Different systems of trust lead to distinct systems of production and subsequent quality definitions in our two cases. Ultimately my conclusions support the main findings of Lane and Bachmann: French quality wine makers operate in a context of high system trust, strong intermediary organization, and, as in their example of German industry, these producers dominate at the high end of the market. Italian quality wine producers, however, operate in a context reliant on personal trust, voluntaristic intermediary organization, and, as in the case of British industry, a more flexible but lower price point than the "high system trust" counterpoint. But again, these divergent outcomes emerge in a formally identical regulatory environment, which puts my findings at odds with the wine research of Zhao.

French producers opted for a political solution of government-backed private quality guarantees and strong local organizations; Italian producers formally had the same structure but informally relied on personal knowledge and networks to distinguish their individual brands. This possibly reflects different views on the market and on politics in our two cases: historically, an array of quality French producers have relied on political protection from market fluctuations, whereas quality Italian producers have seen the market as meritocratic in comparison to the Italian political system (personal interview, Agro-Tourismo Director in Emilia-Romana, 2011).

Consumer trust is not an independent, stand alone concept, but rather consumers find themselves in a market context in which producers first need to solve how they will guarantee product quality within the supply chain. Consumers respond to and generally reflect differentiated supply chain producer networks (Bourdieu, 1984; Diaz-Bone, 2013). In instances where producers exhibit high levels of "taken for granted" institutionalized trust, consumers respond to institutionalized quality signals. In systems where producers rely on personal trust networks to signify quality within the supply chain, consumers rely on personal knowledge and wine reviews. Thus there is a symmetry between the patterns of trust within the supply chain and consumers' behavior.

Despite the same formal rules, French producers faced a higher likelihood of success with their regulatory protection for two reasons: First, producers and consumers had a long history of relying on government-backed quality guarantees in the market. Conversely, a historical trust of government-backed regulation never emerged in the Italian case. Secondly, the French were advantaged being the "first movers" in the market, and they had the possibility to convince consumers that their product was worthy of market protection. For the Italian producers, introducing this legislation before quality production emerged only served to further undermine trust in the DOC guarantee. Thus French producers had an advantage in informal norms, and producer organizations were able to profitably build upon these.

The two systems analyzed here posit different views on the benefits of collective action versus individualism, and these perspectives are reflected in how producers organize, how they define quality, and how consumers consume. The social and political context—or how wine regulations are embedded in relationships—are not a linear outcome of their regulatory context. This raises important questions on the limits of regulation and formal classification to reshape markets and to construct networks of trust and cooperation. Importantly, the insights gleaned here point to the idea that strong producer organizations are not equally likely to arise in any given institutional context. Yet when they do arise, they can solve critical production problems and can support the establishment of high quality and high value production.

NOTES

1. Note that less regulated wine categories are nearly the same for both French and Italian wines, indicating that the French "brand" does not explain the difference in wine prices.
2. Bottero and Crossley explicitly compare Bourdieu's concepts of homology and cultural fields to Becker's concepts of conventions and art worlds in their 2011 article "Worlds, fields and networks: Becker, Bourdieu and the Structures of Social Relations." In brief, the authors argue that the concept of networks and social connection is underdeveloped with regard to cultural production.
3. My secondary data included price data, production data and data on consumer behavior. In addition to these data sources, I relied heavily on export data collected through the Wine Economics Research Centre at the University of Adelaide.
4. 2010 PGI prices averaged €1.85 per liter for French producers and €1.66 per liter for Italian producers (Chever et al., 2012: 47). PGI wines specify a relatively large geographic area but they allow producers to choose which grape varieties they plant. Producers face stricter yield limits than table wine producers but more generous limits than the PGO ("protected geographic origin," for example AOC or DOC) producers.
5. PDO, or Protected Designation of Origin, is the European Union's term for the most regulated geographic production methods, including the AOC, DOC, and DOCG.
6. In the Italian context, "I read about it" exerts a stronger effect on consumer behavior than "wine origin" for well informed consumers at all points of sale, as well as for all consumers making on-premises wine purchases. "Read about it" is important for Italian wine consumers in all measured purchasing contexts except for less involved consumers purchasing in the retail segment (Casini et al., 2009: 69, 71, 73).
7. In the Languedoc, producers often expressed mistrust of both AOC institutions and of other producers. For example, one producer described how she witnessed fraud on a blind tasting panel, which was charged to make sure all AOC wine samples have abided by the producer-defined rules: "at a recent AOC tasting, one taster recognized cabernet in a wine and rejected it from the appellation. But two other tasters said yes it wasn't legal but it was good so keep it in the appellation anyway" (grower-merchant personal interview, Languedoc, 2011). An employee at the local interprofessional described seeing empty bags of sugar left on the roads next to vineyards, implying local producers "didn't follow their agreed-upon rules" of production (interprofessional council interview, Languedoc, 2009). Producers in other French regions would describe instances of individual producer fraud, and note that these deviations were not the norm and did not pose a challenge to the quality or reputation of the region.
8. The wine merchant purchases grapes, wine must, or wine from grape growers, and s/he blends, bottles and labels the wine.
9. Adding sugar to wine, or chapitalization, is legal in some contexts, and illegal in others. Adding sugar can increase the alcohol context; higher alcohol levels historically earn producers a higher price.
10. The actual tasks performed along the supply chain vary greatly by sector and in the case of wine, by region. In many contexts (especially in Italy and in the Languedoc in Southern France), one sees the proliferation of the grower-merchant, or someone who grows grapes, makes wine, bottles it and labels it. Additionally, there can be a blending of tasks across the supply chain, i.e., some growers may sell must of wine to merchants, as opposed to grapes.

11. One example of this "farmer mentality" included Southern farmers' resistance to wage-based economic arrangements. "Wine producers have beautiful cellars that are not used. Producers were given capital (from the EU), but still have an aversion to a wage-based economy" (personal interview, wine promoter, Palermo Sicily, July 2010). A local agricultural leader in Puglia told me a similar story. This *consorzio* president organized producers of an array of village products—olive oil, wine, cheese, pasta—with one producer of each product represented in this particular *consorzio*. Yet despite the fact that EU funding made this promotion nearly free for participating producers, there was a pervasive sense of competition, despite the fact that producers in the organization made complementary products (personal interview, Lazio, March 2008).

12. As a result, when I describe the French case I discuss the two groups that share power equally: growers and merchants. As the Italian *consorzio* distribute votes based not on supply chain position but on production volume, I describe Italian producer politics along this distinction.

13. In the Brunello fraud scandal, more than 20 producers were accused of adding grapes other than sangiovese to Brunello wine in order to increase production volumes and to keep down costs. According the Brunello regulation, only sangiovese can be used in Brunello wine.

14. Leo Loubère also put forward this idea in his historical account of Italian wine politics in *The Red and the White*. He described the particularly apolitical nature of southern Italian grape growers, where asymmetries of power and fear of political retribution are most acute (1978).

15. Retribution affected Ziliani himself after he broke the Brunello scandal: he was kicked off the board of a major Italian wine journal after he broke the story in 2008. Another interview subject described the retribution that befell a local distributor when he stood up to the powerful players in the wine market in the Emilia-Romana regions.

REFERENCES

Akerlof, G. (1970), 'The market for "lemons": Quality uncertainty and the market mechanism', *Quarterly Journal of Economics*, **84** (3), 488–500.

Aspers, P. (2009), 'Knowledge and valuation in markets', *Theory and Society*, **38**(2), 111–131.

Bachmann, R. (2001), 'Trust, power and control in trans-organizational relations', *Organization Studies*, **22**(2), 337–365.

Becker, H.S. (1982), *Art worlds*, Berkeley, CA: University of California Press.

Berger, S. and R.M. Locke (2001), 'Il caso italiano and globalization', *Daedalus*, 85–104.

Boltanski, L. and L. Thévenot (2006), *On justification: Economies of worth*, Princeton, NJ: Princeton University Press.

Bourdieu, P. (1984), *Distinction*, London: Routledge.

Bottero, W. and N. Crossley (2011), 'Worlds, fields and networks: Becker, Bourdieu and the structures of social relations', *Cultural Sociology*, **5**(1), 99–119.

Casini, L., A.M. Corsi and S. Goodman (2009), 'Consumer preferences of wine in Italy applying best–worst scaling', *International Journal of Wine Business Research*, **21**(1), 64–78.

Chever, T., C. Renault, S. Renault and V. Romieu (2012), *Value of production of agricultural products and foodstuffs, wines, aromatised wines and spirits protected by a geographical indication (GI)*, Final Report, Brussels: European

Commission. [Last accessed 12 February 2014.] Available from URL: http://ec.europa.eu/agriculture/external-studies/2012/value-gi/final-report_en.pdf

Corrado, R. and V. Odorici (2004), 'Between supply and demand: Intermediaries, social networks and the construction of quality in the Italian wine industry', *Journal of Management and Governance*, **8** (2), 149–171.

Corrado, R. and V. Odorici (2008), Tradition or Control? Change of Product Categories in the Italian Wine Industry, SSRN Working Paper. [Last accessed 12 February 2014.] Available from URL: http://papers.ssrn.com/sol3/papers.cfm?abstract_id=1145309

Corrado, R. and V. Odorici (2009), 'Winemakers and wineries in the evolution of the Italian wine industry: 1997–2006', *Journal of Wine Research*, **20**, 111–124.

d'Hauteville, F. and L. Sirieix (2007), 'Comprendre le consommateur de vin en 2005' in J.-P. Couderc, H. Hannin, F. d'Hauteville and E. Montaigne (eds), *Bacchus 2008: Enjeux, stratégies et pratiques dans la filière viti-vinicole*, Paris: Dunod, pp. 105–135.

Diaz-Bone, R. (2009), 'Qualitätskonvention als Diskursordnungen in Märkten' in R. Diaz-Bone and G. Krell (eds), *Diskurs und Ökonomie: Diskursanalytische Perspektiven auf Märkte und Organisationen*, Wiesbaden: Springer VS, pp. 309–337.

Diaz-Bone, R. (2013), 'Discourse conventions in the construction of wine qualities in the wine market', *Economic Sociology*, **14**(2), 46–53.

Elias, N. (1978), *The civilizing process*, New York: Urizen.

Eymard-Duvernay, F. (ed.) (2007), *L'économie des conventions: méthodes et résultats*, Paris: La Découverte.

Fourcade, M. (2012), 'The vile and the noble: Between natural and social classifications in the French Wine World', *Sociological Quarterly*, **53**(4), 524–545.

Fukuyama, F. (1996), *Trust*, New York: Free Press.

Giddens, A. (1991), *Modernity and self-identity: Self and society in the late modern age*, Redwood City, CA: Stanford University Press.

Ginsborg, P. (2003), *A history of contemporary Italy*, London: Palgrave Macmillan.

Grant, W. (1985), *The political economy of corporatism*, London: Macmillan.

Hall, P. (1986), *Governing the economy*, Ithaca: Cornell University Press.

Hedgecoe, A. (2012), 'Trust and regulatory organizations: The role of local knowledge and facework in research ethics review', *Social Studies of Science*, **42**(5), 662–683.

Istituto di Servizi per il Mercato Agricolo Alimentare (ISMEA) (2008a), *Filiera vino, Volume II* [Wine Industry, Volume II], Rome: ISMEA.

Istituto di Servizi per il Mercato Agricolo Alimentare (ISMEA) (2008b), *Vino da tavola: Report economico finanziario* [Table Wine: Economic and Financial Report], Rome: ISMEA.

Karpik, L. (2010), *Valuing the unique: The economics of singularities*, Princeton: Princeton University Press.

Klein, B., R.G. Crawford, and A.A. Alchian (1978), 'Vertical integration, appropriable rents, and the competitive contracting process', *Journal of Law and Economics*, **21**(2), 297–326.

Lane, C. and R. Bachmann (1996), 'The social constitution of trust: Supplier relations in Britain and Germany', *Organization Studies*, **17**(3), 365–395.

Levy, J. (1999), *Tocqueville's revenge*, Cambridge: Harvard University Press.

Loubère, L. (1978), *The red and the white: A history of wine in France and Italy in the nineteenth century*, Albany: SUNY Press.

Loubère, L. (1990), *The wine revolution in France: The twentieth century*, Princeton: Princeton University Press.

Luhmann, N. (1979), *Trust and power*, Chichester: Wiley.

OIV (International Organization of Vine and Wine) (2015), *OIV report on the world vitivinicultural situation,* Paris: OIV. [Last accessed 12 February 2014.] Available from URL: www.oiv.int/oiv/info/en-Bilan_OIV_Mainz_2015

Putnam, R. (1994), *Making democracy work*, Princeton: Princeton University Press.

Shonfield, A. (1965), *Modern capitalism*, New York: Oxford University Press.

Smith, A., J. De Maillard, and O. Costa (2007), *Vin et politique: Bordeaux, la France, la mondialisation*, Cambridge: Cambridge University Press.

Taber, G.M. (2006), *Judgment of Paris*, New York: Simon and Schuster.

Walgenbach, P. (2001), 'The production of distrust by means of producing trust', *Organization Studies*, **22**(4), 693–714.

Zhao, W. (2005), 'Understanding classifications: Empirical evidence from the American and French wine industries', *Poetics*, **33**(3), 179–200.

Zhao, W. (2008), 'Social categories, classification systems, and determinants of wine price in the California and French wine industries', *Sociological Perspectives*, **51**(1), 163–199.

6. Being everybody's accomplice: trust and control in eco-labelling

Lovisa Näslund and Kristina Tamm Hallström

In the modern world, as a consequence of globalization, it has been argued that trust based on personal relations will increasingly become replaced by trust in abstract, faceless systems, in other words, by trust in organizations (Giddens, 1990). Such organizational trust in essence is trust in the norms and rules that guide or even determine the behaviour of the members of that organization (Kroeger, 2011). Organizational trust may therefore also be described in terms of trust in systems of regulation and control (Hedgecoe, 2012). Regulatory actors, one might argue, could therefore be seen as examples of organizations borne out of this consequence of modernity, designed to and dependent on their ability to elicit trust. Through the introduction of a network of intermediaries, certification and accreditation bodies, market interaction shifts from interpersonal trust to impersonal system trust, with actors being able to put their faith in the controlling ability of intermediaries and allowing for collective control to supplement interpersonal trust in networks (Sydow and Windeler, 2003). This ability to instil trust furthermore depends not only on the trustworthiness of the norms and rules of the organization, but also in their ability to engage in and influence the sense-making process of the actors it interacts with (Fuglsang and Jagd, 2015; Weber and Glynn, 2006). In order to be able to function as an intermediary between citizen and organization, and play their part in the regulatory trust triangle described by Six and Verhoest earlier in this volume, regulatory regimes thus need to be skilful in trust creation. The legitimacy of regulatory regimes depends on this ability, which enables them to play the role of trust intermediaries, and legitimately and with credibility play the role of accomplice to both citizens and organization (regulatee) at the same time. For private regulators, whose clients have the options of whether they want to become regulatees or not, choose this certifying body or that, or even no certification at all, the ability to create trust becomes even more critical. A voluntary regulatory regime, which furthermore is financially dependent on its regulatees, runs an obvious risk of regulatory capture. Therefore, a voluntary private regulatory regime needs to balance the need for an appearance of low trust or even distrust towards regulatees (in order to attain legitimacy as independent regulators) with the ability to create a trusting relationship with them (Power, 2003, 2011; Shapiro, 1987). Such a mutually trusting relationship with the regulatees is necessary for two reasons: firstly, in order to maintain a business relationship, and be chosen by the client organizations, and secondly, in order to ensure their compliance (Murphy, 2004; Hedgecoe, 2012).

However, displaying such distrust or lack of trust openly in the interaction with the regulatees, as this volume as well as earlier research shows, may prove detrimental to the ability to create regulatee compliance with regulations (Costa and Bijlsma-Frankema, 2005; Six, 2013; Smets et al., 2013; Weibel, 2007). Nevertheless, from the citizen's perspective, the legitimacy and authority of voluntary private regulators stems from the perception that they are independent from the organizations they regulate, and thereby able to be objective and untarnished by the interest of these organizations in their quality assessment (Hatanaka et al., 2005; Tanner, 2000). Regulators can thereby make plausible that they have the benevolence and integrity, as well as the value affinity, necessary to appear trustworthy in the eyes of citizens (Lang, 2013). In a further development of the model of the role of trust in different relationships within regulatory regimes described in the introduction of this volume, the specific context of voluntary private regulation of private organizations can thus be summarized as seen in Figure 6.1 below.

How the regulators solve the paradox of at once trusting (in order to build a client relationship and ensure compliance), and appearing not to trust (in order to appear trustworthy and valuable to the citizens) the regulator has rarely been studied (for one recent example, see Hatanaka and Busch, 2008), and we seek in this chapter to address this gap. The question

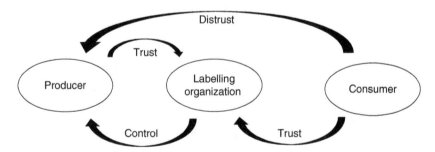

Figure 6.1   *Overview of trust relationships in the context of voluntary private regulation of private organizations*

discussed in this chapter, put simply, is how they do it, and how the conflicting demands put on the regulator in terms of combining trust and distrust, monitoring and compliance are solved in practice by these labelling organizations. How do they manage to become everybody's accomplice in this system of relations? The purpose is to thereby contribute to the ongoing discussion in research on how trust relates to control (cf Bijlsma-Frankema and Costa, 2005; Costa and Bijlsma-Frankema, 2005; Das and Teng, 1998; Inkpen and Currall, 2004; Six, 2013; Skinner and Spira, 2003; Weibel, 2007), and furthermore how regulatory regimes incorporate both trust and distrust in the regulatee relationship, in that they entice the trust that enables compliance, while signalling distrust by way of monitoring (Braithwaite and Makkai, 1994; Murphy, 2004; Walgenbach, 2001).

This form of voluntary regulatory regime, moreover, has become increasingly common on many global markets, as private regulators are able to act as *guardians of trust* that help bridge the social and spatial distance between actors who as a result of the increasing complexity of the economic system have no direct relationship, and thus little opportunity to build trust (Eden et al., 2008; Shapiro, 1987). The result is a market for trust production, where guardians of trust enable impersonal trust, by offering assurance of control that will ensure that the producers' behaviour will be trustworthy in the eyes of the consumers. This organizational solution can be described in terms of a chain of trust that enables citizens or consumers to trust the products, even if they do not know enough about the producers to trust them, as seen in Figure 6.1 above. This is the case not least in the agrifood sector, the empirical focus of this study (Almeida et al., 2010; Hatanaka et al., 2005). It should be noted that the role of guardian of trust, as seen in the agrifood sector, is not based on the logic of third-party trust, in that it is built on links of interpersonal trust. Rather, it is based on a chain of strangers, as described by Luhmann (1979), and thus the knowledgeable and skilful assessment of the producer. In order for this assessment to seem legitimate and authoritative, it has to have the appearance of independence and integrity. The underlying logic is thus fundamentally different: third-party trust may well be stronger the closer the intermediary seems to the trustor, but for a guardian of trust, such closeness would be detrimental for the trustworthiness of the assessor, because this trustworthiness is based on the notion of a chain of strangers, and impersonal, system trust (Shapiro, 1987). Therefore, a guardian of trust cannot appear too close and trusting with a regulatee, while interpersonal third-party trust, on the other hand, depends precisely on such closeness and trust.

In recent years, consumer interest for organic and environmentally friendly goods has grown in the European market, and the prognosis is that it will continue to do so. However, since the organic and sustain-ability quality of household goods is to a large degree a credence quality, one that cannot be ascertained before or even after consumption by the consumers, the purchase of these goods typically presents a trust problem for the consumers (Perrini et al., 2010). The problem, however, is that the consumer herself lacks the means of verification, and the globalization of the agrifood system and consolidation of the retail industry has largely moved these questions away from local public governance (Gundlach and Cannon, 2010; Hatanaka et al., 2005). The globalization and growing com-plexity of the food industry means that consumers are rarely able to have direct contact or interaction with producers of retail goods, and thus lack the means to gain direct information or control the goods they are buying. Since consumers are increasingly displaced from the food production system, and the food is increasingly processed before it reaches the con-sumers, consumers have increasingly voiced concerns about the safety and nutritional value of the foods they buy (Sapp et al., 2009). In the wake of highly publicized food scandals, recent instances being for example when horsemeat was found in frozen beef lasagne across Europe (Neville, 2013) or Italian virgin olive oil was found to be counterfeit, manufactured out of soybean oil coloured with chlorophyll (Hooper, 2008), perceptions of food risk and uncertainty has likely amplified (Sapp et al., 2009).

In other words, while trust is demanded, and producers thus need to find some means of creating consumer trust in their products, this has to be achieved in a context where consumers have been given ample reason to view producers with wary indifference at best, and distrust at worst (Almeida et al., 2010). This demand for quality assurance systems has created an opening for institutional entrepreneurs, in the form of voluntary private regulators that act as third-party certification bodies, emerging as the organizational innovation that has been able to address this problem, providing consumers with the cues necessary to distinguish qualities which are not apparent from the product itself (Almeida et al., 2010; Eden et al., 2008).

In the case of organic and environmentally friendly consumer goods, this third-party certification is provided by eco-labels. Consequently, these labels have become more prominent and gained importance in retailing in recent years, as the need for producers and retailers to entice the trust of consum-ers has increased, while scandals and other sources of distrust have made it difficult for retailers or producers to gain the direct trust of consumers (Elder et al., 2014). In addition, third-party certification bodies in the food industry are often encapsulated by oligopolist retailers, who, through the introduction of certification, are able to shift costs of marketing and quality control to the producers. While certification is ostensibly voluntary, in practice it might not be, as retailers demand of producers that they should have certain certifications in order for their goods to be sold, and retailers thus not only have a heavy hand in what labels are used, but moreover are also often engaged in the certification bodies themselves, in order to legitimize the standards that would be most profitable for the retailer (Almeida et al., 2010; Elder et al., 2014; Hatanaka et al., 2005). Therefore, although ostensibly voluntary, in practice producers of organic foods not unlikely perceive some pressure to adhere to the regulatory regimes of eco-labelling.

The effectiveness of the eco-label thus hinges on their ability to gain the trust of both consumers (citizens) and producers (regulatees), so that consumers trust them to control the producers, and producers trust them to deliver the trust of the consumers. The legitimacy and trustworthiness of these regulatory regimes hinges on their intermediary, and thereby presumably independent, position. However, this independence might well be questioned. Since the producers double as regulatees and clients for the labelling organizations, this poses a potential problem for the latter, as they have to balance the trust necessary for a successful client relationship with the control necessary to be able to act as a convincing guardian of trust in the eyes of the consumer. The intermediary position, which on the one hand enables the existence of these regulatory regimes, at the same time poses a problem, as its puts contradictory demands on the organization. In this chapter, we will investigate how such private regulators organize to solve this dilemma. While the empirical focus of this study is organic labels in the food industry, this problem is not unique to them, but rather a problem common for many audit and certification systems, that depend on their ability to independently and objectively monitor and control their clients (Bartley, 2011). The construction of independence, as a crucial legitimizing value necessary for authority, private voluntary regulations, or indeed auditing in general, given the possible conflict of interests that comes from financial dependence on the auditee, is a well-known problem that has recently attracted new scholarly interest (Dogui et al., 2014; Goldman and Barlev, 1974; Jamal and Sunder, 2011; Power, 2011; Kouakou et al., 2013).

CONSTRUCTING AUTHORITY AND LEGITIMACY AS AN INTERMEDIARY

As argued, the intermediary position is problematic. Firstly, because neither legitimacy nor authority of a voluntary regulatory regime is given, but has to be constructed, and secondly, because the position of middleman in itself puts contradictory demands on the regulator in their relations to citizens and the organizations they regulate. In order to understand the middle-man dilemma, we will therefore take a closer look at these two areas.

As we have seen, the regulator, in this case the labelling organization, has the task of providing the consumer with relevant social cues to assist decision making under uncertainty, and enable them to make a judgment on the unobservable qualities of the goods in stores (Eden et al., 2008; Polidoro, 2013). In this role, their authority, that is, their legitimate power (Boström and Tamm Hallström, 2010; Cutler et al., 1999; Weber, 1948) largely depends on the perception that they are independent of the producers, and thus can be trusted to scrutinize them with integrity (Tanner, 2000). What complicates their role as a regulator however, as becomes evident when analysing them not only as regulators but also as intermediaries, is that third-party certification regimes as well as other voluntary standard frameworks are not provided with a given mandate, or authority to develop and enforce rules. Instead, they compete in a market for standards (Brunsson and Jacobsson, 2000) where they have to contend for authority.

As stated earlier, the trustworthiness of these third-party certification agents is seen as based to a large degree on their independence from producers whose goods they evaluate (Power, 2011). However, it should be noted that this independence is not unproblematic, as eco-labels are often financed by licence fees, and their regulatees therefore double as clients. Being financially dependent is not necessarily a convincing recipe for independence from those that fund you. Furthermore, as most contemporary international standards and certification systems, eco-labels as examples of voluntary regulatory regimes lack legal enforcement mechanisms, and have to depend on some other means of authority to enforce compliance to their regulations (Bartley, 2011; Boli, 1999; Brunsson and Jacobsson, 2000; Tamm Hallström, 2004).

The literature engaged in explaining the construction of authority within transnational governance, many of which draw on studies of transnational standard setters (Boli, 1999; Boström and Tamm Hallström, 2010; Cutler et al., 1999; Djelic and Sahlin-Andersson, 2006; Tamm Hallström, 2004) and recently also on the few studies of certification and accreditation bodies (Bartley, 2011; Gustafsson and Tamm Hallström, 2013; Tamm Hallström and Gustafsson, 2014), show that the authority of voluntary, non-state regulatory regimes is fragile and evidently something these organizations continuously struggle for. They obviously need to attract standard users that in the world of standards often are manufacturing companies and other organizations that must find the requirement of the standards acceptable, and be willing to pay for the standards and certifications (Tamm Hallström, 2004). However, there are also a number of other stakeholders that standard setters depend on for their legitimacy and specifically need to convince about their suitability as relevant, competent and independent regulators (*Ibid.*). Here we find consumers buying the labelled products and services as well as a range of other organizations acting as guardians of trust, such as governmental organizations, consumer organizations, environmental organizations and ranking institutes (*Ibid.*; Tamm Hallström and Boström, 2010). In sum, third-party certification regimes are situated in a delicate intermediary position in between regulatees on the one hand, and consumers, citizens and various guardians of trust, on the other, and for organizations in this position the issue of authority is constantly present.

The above-referred literature also reveals that these types of intermediary organizations engage in considerable organized efforts to construct authority: by way of organizing the internal regulatory activities in a rational, legitimate way (Meyer and Rowan, 1977; Weber, 1948) that in this context typically mirrors ideals of neutrality and independence (Boli, 1999; Tamm Hallström, 2004), by communicating an image of virtuosity and rationalization of society (Boli, 2006; Drori and Meyer, 2006), and by seeking recognition from other more authoritative organizations (Jacobsson and Sahlin-Andersson, 2006; Tamm Hallström, 2004). In recent studies of the emergence and organization of third-party certification regimes a separation between the standard-setting and certification functions is also observed, as a way to emphasize the perceived independence of the regime (Loconto and Busch, 2010; Tamm Hallström and Gustafsson, 2014). Another organizational effort identified is that external organizational structures in terms of a certification of the certifier (often labelled accreditation) tend to develop over time as a consequence of legitimacy problems about insufficient independence (Bartley, 2011; Bernstein and Cashore, 2007; Loconto and Fouilleux, 2014; Reinecke et al., 2012), but also as a preventive action against anticipated legitimacy problems (Gustafsson and Tamm Hallström, 2013; Loconto and Busch, 2010; Tamm Hallström and Gustafsson, 2014). What the latter group of studies that use a constructionist approach also show is that decisions about various organizational efforts often involve negotiations between stakeholders with diverse ideologies and interests, meaning that to some extent such decisions are vulnerable and open to criticism.

Finally, yet another organizational dimension discussed in this literature regards the ownership of regulatory activities. As pointed out, the problem at the transnational level is the lack of a world state with authority to set and enforce rules across national borders (Brunsson and Jacobsson, 2000; Drori and Meyer, 2006; Tamm Hallström and Boström, 2010), in turn opening up for a multiplicity of non-state actors to engage in various voluntary governance activities. At a closer look at contemporary standard setters and labelling organizations, some are initiated and run by environmental organizations alone, independently from both producers and consumers, while others are multi-stakeholder organizations with (preferably limited) involvement of business interests and sometimes also governmental organizations (Tamm Hallström and Boström, 2010). However, studies that go beyond the standard-setting body and include the set of organizations often involved and interrelated in third-party certification regimes are still rare. Moreover, knowledge is lacking about the way various organizational efforts aiming at constructing authority interrelate with the ownership of organizations that are part of the third-party certification regime, including the specific role of the state in these contexts (Gustafsson and Tamm Hallström, 2013).

When it comes to the trust of the consumers in the case of third-party certification it will likely not be based on any interpersonal relationship, but rather on trust in the quality assurance system of the labelling organization (Carriquiry and Babcock, 2007). Such system trust is based on a belief in the validity and correctness of the abstract principles and procedures in and of social and technical systems – a regulatory system, as described above in terms of elements such as certification and accreditation, which thus are expected to be impersonal and thereby also impartial, a bureaucratic machinery that will pass judgment based solely on incoming data, not on considerations of loyalty or willingness to please (Sydow and Windeler, 2003). Arguably, the complex and globalized nature of modern life makes it rational for consumers, for example, to invest trust in well-designed institutions, rather than individuals (Skinner and Spira, 2003). In order for such systems to elicit trust, it would seem that personal interaction and experience from the auditing process is counter-productive, as closer knowledge of this process reveals that this independence is not unproblematic or self-evident. Indeed, audit systems are likely to be less trusted the more one becomes acquainted with them, simply because it is not possible to keep complete control over those subjected to the audit, especially as it in many cases consists of scrutinizing documentation rather than actions, which a closer encounter will make clear (Walgenbach, 2001).

In the next section we now focus on the middle-man position, and the implications this will have for the regulator.

THE MIDDLE-MAN DILEMMA: TRUST, CONTROL AND COMPLIANCE

As was described in the introduction, the function of third-party certifica-tion as an example of voluntary private regulators might be described in terms of a guardian of trust (Shapiro, 1987). As such, the regulator col-lects information on and evaluates agents, or producers in this case, that consumers lack the means and/or knowledge to evaluate themselves, thus bridging the physical and social distance between actors that emerges as a result of globalization. On an organizational level, a middle-man such as a labelling organization thereby provides a convenient solution to the conundrum of distrust faced by consumers and producers alike: consum-ers want to buy ecological goods, but cannot trust the producers to be as eco-friendly as they proclaim themselves to be, and producers want to sell their ecological goods, but are unable to convince the consumers that they really are ecologically sound, not just engaged in greenwashing. By acting as guardians of trust, the labelling organizations can vouch for the trust-worthiness of certified producers, as they make it believable that they have the means to evaluate the qualities of the producers' goods, while being distanced enough from them to remain objective and independent in their judgment (Shapiro, 1987). Fulfilling this role of trust builder, however, puts certain demands on the intermediary, who cannot appear biased or interested solely in attaining cooperation between the two parties, but rather should appear to care mainly about the issue at stake, daring a conflict with either side if necessary, and be concerned about preserving honesty – in other words, have some integrity (Kydd, 2006).

One complication that arises due to the use of independence as a legiti-mizing value for the authority of third-party certification regimes concerns the relationship with the regulatees, the producers of labelled products in this particular case. As labelling organizations are financially dependent on the regulatees, this relationship usually doubles as a customer relationship. The relationship between labelling organizations and producers thus has to be able to harbour contradictory notions of trust and distrust, of control and customer relations and of independence and dependence. Therefore, the legitimacy based on independence and integrity is at least to some extent challenged by the need to also make the client happy, and estab-lish a good working relationship. Therefore, if the perception of auditor independence is achieved, it is the result of careful construction from the auditor, a result of sense-making strategies such as storytelling and proce-dural mechanisms that allow auditors to latch on to prevalent concepts of professional and independent auditing (Dogui et al., 2013).

Arguably, in order to gain their trust and thereby their voluntary collaboration, the labelling organizations need to be able to show the producers that they have their good interest at heart, and have no wish to frame them or make unreasonable demands, but the best of intentions in helping them ensure the trust of the consumers. A label awarded by a third-party certification body potentially provides a competitive advantage, setting the producer's goods apart from those of other producers, less worthy of the consumers' trust. The signalling value of the certification does not depend primarily on a tight coupling between the certification standards and the underlying capabilities of the organization, but moreover in how it sets the product apart from others in the market, and possibly deters competitors from entering it (Polidoro, 2013). However, for the relationship between the regulator and the regulatee to work the labelling organization must trust the regulatee to adhere to the rules and standards, but the regulatee must also trust the regulator, and have faith in its regulatory authority, since otherwise it could be highly unlikely that they would want to collaborate, much less comply (Hedgecoe, 2012).

In the food system, citizens' trust in institutional actors depends on their perception of the actor's competence and fiduciary responsibility. The latter especially, that citizens believe that the actors feel an obligation to act on behalf of the citizens, rather than on behalf of producers or out of self-interest (Kydd, 2006; Sapp et al., 2009). In the empirical context of the studies reported in this chapter, the main goal is helping the cause of sustainability, and making sure that products that bear an organic label therefore are trustworthier than those that do not. By trusting the labelling organization to verify that organic goods are bona fide, and that they would not trust the producers so much that they would take their word for it, but suspending trust until verification can be ensured, the consumers thus trust that labelling organizations distrust the producers enough to disable deceit (Gundlach and Cannon, 2010). Audit systems, such as third-party certification, may therefore be seen as embodiments of distrust – in this context, of consumer distrust (Skinner and Spira, 2003). Since producers, due to the social and spatial displacement of the consumers from the food system, will find it difficult to make a control system depending on disinterested self-regulation seem trustworthy in the eyes of consumers, this surveillance will be contracted out to independent third parties that, as was described above, are able to serve as guardians of trust (Eden et al., 2008; Shapiro, 1987).

While guardians of trust thus solve the problem of the distrust or wary indifference of the consumers, this solution is dependent on their surveillance abilities, and more specifically, as was described above, their ability to set up an impartial, bureaucratic machinery. Their legitimacy and authority will therefore depend on setting up procedural norms and structural constraints, which leaves no or little room for judgement, discretion, experience and innovation from the guardian. An actor's ability to act as a guardian of trust is based on distrust, impartiality and proceduralism, and, as a consequence, the search for transparency and innovation narrows the room for agency in the interaction between guardian and regulatee (Pixley, 1999). Similarly, the notion of independence, which, as we saw, is central to the regulator's ability to gain legitimacy and authority, presupposes a degree of personal and professional distance between auditor and auditee (Dogui et al., 2013). The underlying idea of distrust that pervades the concept of guardian of trust is also apparent from studies of the food industry in the US, which have shown that if consumers can detect deviations from quality assurance systems such as eco-labels, the stringency of these assurance schemes increases, especially if it is a good where producers have individual reputations, rather than the good as a whole (Carriquiry and Babcock, 2007). While this undertone of distrust may be conducive to the role of guardian of trust, and the trustworthiness of the regulatory regime in the eyes of the consumers, the intermediary position of the eco-labels nevertheless makes a tenet of distrust problematic.

The reason for this is that labelling organizations need to make it plausible to producers that they will be able to have a constructive working relationship, not unreasonable or too impersonal and distanced, but something not only the environment but also they will benefit from, and which will deliver consumer trust to them, and will give their products a competitive advantage on the market. In order to form this working relationship, they cannot be too distant – as studies of FSC (Forest Stewardship Council, a private voluntary regulatory regime in forestry) show that global, rationalistic systems of certification and accreditation, the purpose of which is to ensure integrity, quality and legitimacy, in fact counteracted the trust of local producers, and thereby hindered the very development of shared values and commitment to good forestry that the regime was there to support in the first place (McDermott, 2012). In order to be successful in fulfilling their purpose, labelling organizations therefore will have to be everybody's accomplice – the producers' accomplice in convincing sceptical consumers and selling more of their product, and the consumers' accomplice in keeping an eye on untrustworthy producers who only want to increase sales and profits, not necessarily with regard to environmental impact. Obviously, these demands are contradictory, and therefore, the labelling organization needs to be able to meet these conflicting demands, so that they can be the accomplice of both consumer (and organizations acting as guardians of trust for consumers) and producer, while maintaining the impression to both that they have an exclusive relationship, so to speak.

While private voluntary regimes, such as eco-labels, to some extent provide a simple solution to the problem of cognitive and social separation of sites of production and consumption, on closer inspection it would seem that this solution gives rise to new problems, as it means that the relationship between eco-label and producer must harbour seemingly contradictory notions of distrust and trust. The distrust manifests itself in the shape of impersonal control systems, which may affect the trust in the relationship between regulator and regulatee negatively (Costa and Bijlsma-Frankema, 2005; Pixley, 1999; Smets et al., 2013), and is indeed often assumed to do so.

Control, defined as the influencing or steering of actions and events in a reflexive way that fits the interests of the controller (Sydow and Windeler, 2003), might be approached in two main ways: informal, value-based control which is internal, and formal, measure-based control, which focuses on the external (Six, 2013). Informal control uses the regulatory power of norms, values and culture, and where desirable outcomes are encouraged by way of the internalization of goals. Formal control, the form of control that a third-party certification body would be assumed to assert, would be the establishment and application of formal rules and policies, which are then monitored, and sanction and reward mechanisms put in place to ensure compliance with those rules and policies (Costa and Bijlsma-Frankema, 2005). While informal control, and the alignment of values that follows from it, would make the controller perceive the regulatee as compliant and trustworthy, thereby creating trust, the relationship between formal control and trust has been seen as more problematic (Weibel, 2007). The overt monitoring of a formal control system is often interpreted as a sign of distrust, which in turn is likely to lower trust, and thus cause a downward spiral of distrust in the relationship (Vlaar et al., 2006). Trust and control have therefore often been regarded as substitutes, where, if you have one, you do not need the other. Furthermore, they may counteract each other, as trustworthy behaviour in the presence of a control system might be interpreted as a sign of the success of the control system, rather than the inherent trustworthiness of the regulatee (Inkpen and Currall, 2004). Thereby, control may deter regulator trust in the regulatee, and regulate trust in the regulator, effectively hindering the development of trust. Formal control, one might deduce, reduces trust.

However, there is also ample evidence that the relationship between trust and control may be more complex than simple causality, in that they are not substitutes, but parallel concepts, that may counteract but also reinforce each other (Das and Teng, 1998). Strong control systems may increase trust, possibly because they lead to predictability, thereby reducing uncertainty, and enabling trust (Coletti et al., 2005). Trust and control thereby provide two solutions to the same problem, namely how actors may form positive expectations of the behaviour of others, to whom they are vulnerable (Möllering, 2005). Their relation might therefore be seen as one of interrelatedness, rather than substitution. Control may be trust-based in that all interaction requires a measure of trust, and the presence of trust is likely to influence the development of the control system (Sydow and Windeler, 2003). Furthermore, as complete control is costly and impractical, and therefore not realistic when it comes to the auditing process, control systems will build on trust to some extent (Skinner and Spira, 2003; Walgenbach, 2001). A formal control system may also support the development of trust, as the interaction resulting from the monitoring and feedback of a formal control system may end up providing evidence that the regulatee indeed seems compliant and trustworthy (Smets et al., 2013). Furthermore, as a result of the structured personal interaction of a formal control mechanism, informal control may develop as common norms and values develop and are internalized through a process of sensegiving (Fryxell et al., 2002; Gioia and Chittipeddi, 1991). If the regulatee perceives the monitoring and sanction or reward process as a sign of good intentions and benevolence of the regulator, then formal control may lead to trust (Weibel, 2007). Therefore, it is not the actions in and of themselves that determine whether an action builds or hinders trust, but rather the intentions that are perceived to prompt the action. If monitoring is interpreted as a signal of interest and credible concern, then it is also likely to promote trust (Six, 2013; Six and Sorge, 2008). Depending on the level of participation, and the perception of benevolence, formal control might promote or decrease trust levels (Weibel, 2007). In a collaborative setting, control induces cooperation, which positively affects trust, trust which in turn will promote cooperation. It might thus be argued that in the spirals, vicious or virtuous, that trust and distrust tend to develop in, control systems are reinforcers, in that a control system implemented in a trusting relationship is likely to promote trust, while a control system implemented in a distrustful relationship will lead to an escalation of distrust (Coletti et al., 2005; Vlaar et al., 2006).

Compliance, the desired result of control in this context, in and of itself thus has no adverse effect on trust, at least if it is voluntary (Braithwaite and Makkai, 1994). On the contrary, compliance is likely to be the result of trust, and in its turn reinforces trust. When an actor becomes aware that they are being trusted, and that the other has expectations that they will act benevolently to the extent of being willing to make themselves vulnerable, this awareness is likely to cause reciprocity and an unwillingness to disappoint, leading to trustworthy behaviour, as the positive expectations are met (Möllering, 2005). This is of course under the condition that compliance is voluntary, and that the actor has been allowed agency in the choice of honouring the trust bestowed upon them or not (Six, 2013; Weibel, 2007). More coercive ways of attaining compliance are likely to have an adverse effect, decreasing trust (Murphy, 2004).

While the relationship between regulator and regulatee is thus likely to be reasonably close, and denoted by trust rather than distrust if the control system of the certification process is to result in the desired compliance to certification criteria, such closeness is nevertheless problematic from the consumer's perspective, as it undermines the independence and impartial procedural system on which the legitimacy and authority of the regulatory regime is based, as we have seen. The necessity of a close relationship between regulator and regulatee has been seen in other similar auditing contexts, such as ISO and financial auditing. The closeness of the relationship, which may threaten the integrity and thereby the authority of the auditor, is intensified if the auditor, as is often the case in voluntary regulatory regimes, also functions as a business advisor, which may further erode the distance (Dogui et al., 2013). Arguably, in order to have legitimacy and authority, auditors need to be distant, but in order to be effective, they need to be close (Richard, 2006). As it has been shown, in order to solve this dilemma, auditors employ a variety of strategies, including stereotyping, distancing, storytelling, as well as procedural mechanisms. As the production of trust through auditing procedures is proportional to perceptions of auditor impartiality, integrity and absence of conflict of interest, and this production of trust is what caused a demand for guardians of trust and thereby third-party certification as a form of voluntary private regulatory regime in the first place, having such strategies seems a necessity (Dogui et al., 2013; Shapiro, 1987).

To summarize our framework, as we have seen, the authority and legitimacy of intermediaries in the form of private voluntary regulatory regimes depends on a perception of integrity and independence. The demand for these intermediaries is caused by the social and cognitive distancing in the global food industry, which causes a demand for guardians of trust. The ability of guardians of trust to produce trust hinges on their impartial control systems, based on procedures and bureaucratic machinery, and an underlying assumption of distrust towards regulatees (i.e. producers). However, if regulators are to achieve compliance and be effective in their control, they cannot be distant and distrusting, but rather close and trusting. This causes a dilemma for the intermediary, who has to balance trust and distrust, distance and closeness, in the relationship to the regulatee. In the following, we will turn to our empirical context of Swedish eco-labels, where we will seek to further entangle the relationship between regulator and regulatee, that is, analyse how the studied labelling organizations solve the dilemma caused by their intermediary position, and succeed in appearing as everybody's accomplice, so as to gain authority in the eyes of consumers and producers.

METHODOLOGY

The study presented in this chapter forms part of a larger research project[1] about the organization and legitimization of both international and Swedish eco-labels, which means that a larger set of data feeds into the present analysis and contributes to the background picture of the three labelling organizations accounted for (e.g., interviews with transnational labelling organizations, certification firms, accreditation bodies and international membership organizations within the sustainability field, consumers of eco-friendly products, consumer information organizations, stores that specialize in organic foods and household items, and participant observations of certification auditing processes). However, three labelling initiatives were specifically chosen for the analysis made in this chapter.

While there are many different kinds of labels available to consumer goods, such as fair trade or denotations of origin, eco-labels present a common and well-established example of this phenomenon. The three chosen labels are available on the Swedish market for consumer goods: Good Environmental Choice (*Bra Miljöval*) and The Swan (*Svanen*), both used primarily on household chemicals and paper products, and KRAV, used mainly on foods, and guaranteeing not only organic, but also, in the cases of animal production, ethical production. The labels, which share a very high recognition among Swedish consumers (ranging well above 90 per cent for The Swan and KRAV), are interesting to compare as they have diverse origins and owners, which according to the literature review on transnational governance is an organizational dimension that may affect the construction of authority.

Our first case, the label Good Environmental Choice, is regulated and run by the non-governmental organization the Swedish Society for Nature Conservation (SSNC) and started in the late 1980s as a way to assure proper product information on shelves in the store. Thus, the original idea was to make the store managers responsible for labelling the shelves (and not the products) in a correct way (Grettve, 2014). However, due to practical problems of monitoring compliance, in 1992 the label was turned into a product label meaning that the producer was made the party complying with the labelling criteria and responsible for the labelling of approved products (*Ibid.*).

Our second case, The Swan, is the official eco-label in the Nordic countries, founded in 1989 through an intergovernmental eco-labelling initiative. The state-owned non-profit company Svensk Miljömärkning AB (Ecolabelling Sweden) is responsible for the certification of The Swan label in Sweden, and also for the official EU Ecolabel, working on behalf of the government. Good Environmental and The Swan labels overlap to some extent in certain areas, for example in chemical products such as detergents, but differ in the criteria used; Good Environmental Choice usually claims to have somewhat stricter ones, while The Swan takes the quality of the product into account as well as environmental effects (products have to meet minimum requirements in terms of performance as well as environmental aspects).

Our third case, KRAV, is administered by an organization with the same name,[2] initiated in the 1980s by Swedish organic farmers and turned into a multi-stakeholder association that develops organic standards and promotes the KRAV label. The core idea of the standards is for farmers only to use fertilizers that are organic, and not to use chemical pesticides. KRAV is organized as a multi-stakeholder organization with members that are retail companies such as the food store chain ICA, as well as food producers such as Arla, Scan and Organic Farmers (*Ekologiska Lantbrukarna*). There are also civil society organizations among its members, such as the Swedish Society for Nature Conservation and Nature and Youth Sweden.

In the remaining parts of the chapter we will investigate how these organizations, given their diverse ownership, have managed their role as intermediaries and handled the issues of authority and trust. The material used for this analysis is collected in several ways. In addition to analysis of promotional material from websites, standards, and various reports on labelling, certification and accreditation, 19 semi-structured interviews were made for this particular analysis in 2012–2013 with key actors in the studied fields (five officials at the Good Environmental Choice secretariat; one official at the Swedish Society for Nature Conservation (SSNC); two KRAV certification auditors; two officials at KRAV; seven officials at The Swan; one official at a Swedish consumer association; one official at the Swedish accreditation agency (Swedac). The length of the interviews was about one hour and all except for one shorter, email interview, were recorded and transcribed. In accordance with a constructionist approach, questions regarded the organization and conduct of various functions (criteria development, licensing, certification auditing, accreditation, etc.), but also how this organization was decided and justified including changes over time, and dilemmas and tension involved in the work of these functions. The transcribed interviews were then analysed using the software N-vivo, whereby the material was regrouped based on the content of the interviews, and answers to similar questions collected in order to discern patterns and re-occurring answers in the interviews. After broad categories were created, the interviews were then re-read, and re-grouped in an iterative process, until stable categories were attained.

The following account of the empirical material is structured into two analytical sections. In the first section we account for the organization of authority and trust in the three studied cases, with one sub-section on the establishment of *organizational structures* that are visible to the public and have the purpose of providing the labelling organization with credibility. This mainly regards the structures developed for criteria development, monitoring/licensing and voluntary acceptance of complying with various international standards and codes of conduct. In the other sub-section we account for material of a more informal character about the *day-to-day organizing* of labelling activities. Finally, in the second section we account for how the three studied organizations, analysed as intermediaries in need of being everybody's accomplice, reinforce their efforts of creating authority and trust by ways of *storytelling*.

AUTHORITY AND TRUST IN THE MAKING IN AND AROUND THREE ECO-LABELS

Organizational Structures and External Assurance Mechanisms

The work of developing the criteria for Good Environmental Choice is directed and run by a separate secretariat within the Swedish Society for Nature Conservation that controls the budget for the secretariat. This secretariat employs experts in the fields in which the label exist and for this work the international guidelines of the standard ISO 14024 are followed which prescribe dialogue with relevant stakeholders during the development of standards criteria. The staff at the secretariat is still careful to point out that the expert at the secretariat "holds the pen" and decides what comments for stakeholders are to be considered or not.

For many of the traditional product areas of the Good Environmental Choice label, the expert at the secretariat who develops a certain standard is then the one responsible for the licensing process. To approve licences, the experts ask the producers to send content reports of their products which are made by accredited laboratories and if required other data, which is verified by the licensees' own financial auditors, who need to be accredited according to professional codes of conduct, as a way to verify compliance with label criteria. In addition to performing checks of such documents, random checks are also performed if deemed necessary. When it comes to the finances of this labelling program, the organization does not charge any inspection fees. Rather, the costs of monitoring compliance should be covered by fixed licence fees paid once a year. If more thorough checks were to be done, the organization would need to charge higher fees, one interviewee explains, but this was not a desirable development according to this interviewee. The problems linked to charging separately for monitoring activities, rather than as part of the licence fee, is something that the interviewed officials are well aware of and reflect upon. Good Environmental Choice is a member of the Global Ecolabelling Network (GEN), which means that it complies with ISO 14024 and participates in the peer review procedure established by GEN regarding compliance with this standard.

Turning to the case of The Swan, the organizational structures for criteria development, monitoring and compliance with standards are more elaborate. The criteria behind The Swan label for various products are the same within the Nordic countries, but all countries participate in the development of these criteria, a process that follows several steps. Usually a first draft is developed by a small group of experts within the Nordic collaboration. Then the national members, such as Ecolabelling Sweden and the equivalents in the other Nordic countries, undertake a national, multi-stakeholder process with representation from a broad set of stakeholders. The outcome of the national multi-stakeholder processes then is forwarded to the Nordic Ecolabelling Board where the final decision on criteria is made. Ideally, a new set of criteria should mean that 10–30 per cent of the products available in that category can be certified – if more pass, then the criteria are deemed too lenient. If fewer pass, then they are too harsh. Producers should thus not feel that the criteria are unattainable, one interviewee explains, but rather that they are a reasonable strategy in order to increase goodwill and market shares among environmentally aware consumers.

The monitoring and licensing work required to obtain the right to label products are conducted by Ecolabelling Sweden (and its equivalents in the other Nordic countries). There are similar procedures to that of Good Environmental Choice, in that in The Swan, the control is made by scrutinizing documents, rather than by inspectors going on-site and performing tests themselves. In the criteria agreed upon there is also specified what tests must be made, by whom, and what the results should be. The results of these tests are then sent to The Swan and form the basis for the decision whether a product should be licensed or not. Depending on the nature of the tests and the product, these tests must either be performed by specified laboratories, or by the producers themselves, who have to certify that their product does not contain more than a certain amount of substances per dosage. Licensed products must also meet certain performance standards, as the label seeks to counteract consumer perceptions that ecological household products will be less effective. Moreover, the certifier uses a score matrix according to which a product may be approved although it contains a certain chemical, as long as it contains less of another. Products are thus approved based on an overall assessment of the products environmental impact, according to which some aspects are compensated against others, which thus allows for a degree of flexibility, which is not found in the licensing procedures of Good Environmental Choice.

Finally, The Swan complies with a number of international standards and is audited for this compliance by external organizations. First, similarly to Good Environmental Choice, The Swan is a member of the Global Ecolabelling Network (GEN), which as noted above means that it complies with ISO 14024 and participates in the peer review procedure established by GEN regarding compliance with this standard. Second, the annual reports of The Swan that are communicated to the Swedish government and are audited by external auditors. Third, The Swan is complying with the two standards ISO 9001 and ISO 14001 for which The Swan is audited by an accredited certification company.

Examining our third case, KRAV, it is organized as a membership organization that develops organic standards and promotes the KRAV label. KRAV uses a multi-stakeholder process for criteria development building on consensus as a principle for decisions, meaning that interested producers have even greater possibilities to influence criteria development compared with the processes of the two other labels described above. As noted, among the members are retail companies, food producers and civil society organizations. To assure the work of the KRAV organization, it is a member of the international organization International Federation of Organic Agriculture Movements (IFOAM) and follows its principles of organic agriculture.

Unlike Good Environmental Choice and The Swan, both of which have kept the control work in-house, KRAV has organized this function through a separate certification market. More precisely, in order to monitor that a company complies with a KRAV standard, and thereby obtains the right to label its products, a certification auditor must be engaged by the manufacturer to visit the company and go through the policy documents, ask for verifications to verify that the routines are followed in practice, and interview a selection of managers about their work with the management system. A KRAV auditor explains:

> An auditor works basically in the same way as with a management system audit. The auditor performs a risk assessment and has a structured approach to see if

the farmer follows the KRAV criteria. [. . .] Should the auditor note there are deviations in the farming practice, the consequences depend on the seriousness of the deviation. It may lead to partial or full withdrawal of the certificate. [. . .] Some [checks] are of the yes/no nature, others are more about the auditor's assessment. In the carrot case, for example, the auditor checks that the farmer has bought certified seeds and fertilizers in order to grow the carrots. (Interview with KRAV auditor, November 2012)

Another part of the organizational structure around the KRAV label is that only certification companies with an approved accreditation made by a state-run accreditation body – such as Swedac in Sweden, Cofrac in France, BSI in Britain, or DakkS in Germany – are allowed to conduct KRAV certifications. Moreover, according to the regulatory framework that KRAV complies with, it is also required that the accreditation body must be a member of the meta-organization European Accreditation (EA) that conducts peer reviews of its members. EA must in turn be a member of the international equivalent organization International Accreditation Forum (IAF).

Comparing the accounts of the three studied organizations with the literature on transnational governance referred to earlier, we may conclude that only one labelling organization, KRAV, has chosen to fully separate the criteria development work from the control work that is conducted by separate certification companies. In fact, during the past decade there has been an institutionalization of the norm of separating these functions organizationally, which is also the legitimate way of organizing standardization within the EU framework The New Approach that is developed to instil credibility and authority into standards and certification as a regulatory regime. As seen in the KRAV case, The New Approach includes yet more rules about accreditation, which is the procedure used to monitor and assure the quality of certification as a monitoring activity as well as about meta-accreditation in terms of membership in EA and IAF (Bartley, 2007; Bernstein and Cashore, 2007; Boström and Tamm Hallström, 2010; Gustafsson and Tamm Hallström, 2013; Loconto and Busch, 2010).

Still, although both Good Environmental Choice and The Swan have chosen not to comply with The New Approach, they have chosen another type of accreditation through membership in GEN. Moreover, as discussed in the following section, there are other organizational practices contributing to the construction of authority and trust of all three labelling organizations, even though these practices are not made visible to the same extent as the structures discussed in this section.

Organizing in the Day-to-Day Practice

Looking closer at the work practices within The Swan organization, it becomes clear there are elaborate internal organizational structures with specified roles to separate the functions of: marketing/sales towards clients; checking documents submitted by clients wishing to obtain The Swan licence for their products; and evaluating and making final decisions about licences. The purpose of this structure, an interviewee explains, is to handle the dilemma between economic dependency that exists between a labelling organization and its clients – the manufacturers – and independence regarding the audits that is crucial for their trustworthiness as third-party actors and guardians of trust. At the same time, The Swan engages in educational and management consultancy activities towards their clients, the producers, about how to work with The Swan label and runs an organized network for purchasing staff for educational activities and information exchanges.

On the contrary, Good Environmental Choice has no such networks or educational services regarding its own label. However, the secretariat runs a website with information towards consumers about eco-labels in general and other ways for consumers to act in an environmentally friendly way. Moreover, the direct link between the Good Environmental Choice secretariat and the parent organization the Swedish Society for Nature Conservation creates some tension that may explain the resistance of the secretariat to engage too much in activities with producers. One official at the secretariat describes tension arising due to the more ideologically driven members of the parent organization.

> We are constantly handling the balance between being sharp enough to function as a label, that is to be accepted by the ones complying with the labelling criteria, but also credible enough in the eyes of the most ideologically driven stakeholders, so they feel they can support what we do. (Interview with official at the Good Environmental Choice secretariat, February 2013)

Finally, when it comes to KRAV, which is specialized in standard setting only and has outsourced the control work to certification companies, the connection between the labelling organization and producers is obvious, as KRAV is organized as a multi-stakeholder organization and many of the members in this organization are producers themselves.

To conclude so far, as we have seen, all three eco-labels essentially make the same promise of control and expertise to the consumers, in terms of being able to set the right criteria that ensure that products cause minimum harm to the environment, and then being able to monitor that producers follow these criteria, and ensure their compliance to them. However, the way in which this is organized differs. First, KRAV is the only organization that has completely separated the certification function from the organization developing the standard behind the label. In the other two cases – Good Environmental Choice and The Swan – it is the same organization that sets standards and is responsible for the control work. However, in both cases, controls are to a large extent not actually made on the production sites, neither are products tested by the labelling organization itself. Rather, producers are required to make it plausible with the proper documentation that their product does indeed fulfil the criteria. Thus, the monitoring is not performed in close interaction, and furthermore contains an element of trust, as producers are trusted not to change their recipe after the requested tests have been performed, and of course also to do the tests by themselves, without tampering with the samples or results. Thereby, the labelling organization itself strongly reduces its involvement in the monitoring process, and is able to use it to signal trust rather than distrust. In the case of KRAV, this distinction is made even more explicit, as the monitoring is performed by a separate certification company, unconnected to KRAV itself.

The direct interaction between producers and labelling organization evokes trust much more than distrust, firstly in the development of criteria, where all labels employ a fashion of inclusiveness, whereby producers are invited at an early stage to make sure that the criteria are reasonable, and can be met without sacrificing profitability. Secondly, since the monitoring process is never performed in direct interaction, and even may be allocated to other, independent organizations, negative influences on trust may to a large degree be avoided, partly by allowing the producers a degree of agency, and thus displaying trust in them which is expected to be reciprocated, and partly by outsourcing the monitoring to other organizations. Thereby, it becomes possible to develop trust between producer and labelling organization, and consequently compliance, as the labelling organizations appear more helpers in the struggle for market shares, than pernickety regulators. The formal control process thus entails all the elements of collaboration and good intentions that we saw earlier are conducive to compliance and the development of trust (Six, 2013; Weibel, 2007).

This organization is, however, not made overt to the consumers, as all three labelling organizations provide comparatively sparse information about the exact process of criteria setting and control. In communication with the consumers, such as websites and advertising, emphasis is, if anything, put on the content of the criteria, not the process through which they are reached, and even less how they are monitored. The aim for the consumer, Good Environmental Choice explains, is to make the consumer "feel safe when they see the falcon [label]", and moreover that they just need to know that if they choose something with an eco-label, they are safe, as the founder of KRAV puts it: "As long as it is non-toxic, it is good, and then nobody thinks about the details in the rules". Detailed knowledge about the control system would likely be detrimental to trust in the regulatory system, and therefore, the eco-labels have little reason to elaborate on the details of the control system to consumers (Walgenbach, 2001).

Storylines of Trust and Distrust

The organization of authority and trust described above is further supported by separate storylines. In all three labelling organizations, three separate storylines may be discerned, which serve to support the organizational structure, and enable the labelling organization to construct independence in the eyes of the consumers whilst not alienating their clients, the producers (Dogui et al., 2013). These storylines enable and support a dual perception of the regulatory system as at once an impartial, impersonal system of integrity and independence, which puts so little trust in the regulatees that it is not really susceptible to deceit, and an arena for collaborative interaction with a common goal of goodwill for the producers, and consequently trust in the regulatory system based on both these perceptions by producers and consumers.

The *first* storyline deals directly with independence, by highlighting the integrity and importance of values of sustainability for the labelling organizations. As we saw earlier in the theoretical framework, in order for an actor to be able to act as mediator and build trust, it helps if they are able to show a measure of integrity, and that their primary concern is not just getting the parties to cooperate, but moreover serve the issue at stake – in this case, the environment (Kydd, 2006). This was very evident in all three organizations, as they saw as their primary aim not to increase market shares or become more profitable, but rather to make sure "that there are good and sustainable and less environmentally taxing products on the market". One interviewee at Good Environmental Choice accounts for the attitude among its employees that "all have such respect for what we're doing here, that it's the environment, in the end, that's what we're thinking of". This sentiment is re-echoed by the CEO of The Swan, who explains how they want others to perceive their label.

> [We want to be the label] that the consumers can trust, the one that works the best, that the producers can live with, the standard that makes it possible to

make a product which is environmentally friendly at a reasonable cost, so that we can see that we are really able to shift the market. (Interview with the CEO at The Swan, March 2014)

As noted earlier, Good Environmental Choice is part of, and governed by, a larger organization – the Swedish Society for Nature Conservation – that engages in a broad range of environmental activities and which has, during a century, built up a position as an independent, trustworthy organization that is active in the public debate and does not refrain from taking proper actions. One example mentioned during interviews with officials at Good Environmental Choice is when the Swedish Society for Nature Conservation decided to exit the collaboration with another eco-labelling initiative, the Swedish Forest Stewardship Council (FSC), as their actions in regard to non-compliance with their own eco-label FSC were perceived to be too weak.

In the case of The Swan, the state ownership plays a similar role; several of the interviewees talk about the importance of communicating, towards consumers, that The Swan acts on behalf of the Swedish government. Another argument used, by both Good Environmental Choice and The Swan, to reinforce the impression of true independence, is the labelling of themselves as "third party organizations", or type I environmental labelling in accordance with the GEN framework that builds on the ISO 14024 standard. KRAV, on the other hand, rather communicates its independence through the way it organizes the specific act of monitoring and deciding about the right to become licensed to use the label on products, which in this case is organized through "third-party certification". Third-party certification in this case means that it is not the labelling organization performing the actual monitoring, but separate and specialized certification bodies that are competing on a certification market. Thus, KRAV decides and publishes the standards behind the label, but other organizations take care of the control work, which is meant to assure the independence of the label.

Thus, even if the three labelling organizations studied are all financially dependent on the producers, their purity of intent, so to speak, could possibly explain how they are able to convince consumers of their integrity, and ability to let their concern for the environment take precedence over wishes for profitability which might otherwise corrupt this integrity. This storyline distances the labelling organizations from the producers, thereby enabling consumer trust in the legitimacy and authority of the label.

The *second* storyline concerns the relationship to the producer, and supports the development of trust and compliance. This storyline is not conveyed in public information channels such as advertising campaigns or on the homepage, but moreover in interaction with the producers, in meetings and other interactions. The CEO from The Swan explains how.

The first thing that we tell them when they get here is that "We want you to make money on an environmentally friendly product, that's our main aim with this relationship. That you should meet our criteria, and that you should make money!" And they're like "Jesus, is that what you want? That's great!" We don't want to punish them or be moralistic, or hand them over to the press, we just want them to succeed, given that they develop an environmentally sound product, and we're going to do all we can to help them succeed. (Interview with the CEO at The Swan, March 2014)

The storyline also appears in descriptions of the criteria development work in all three organizations as they invite producers to comment and participate in this process. One of the officials at The Swan explains how the multi-stakeholder, inclusive approach to criteria development is crucial for their credibility.

When it comes to criteria development, we have highly elaborated procedures [. . .] It's extremely important to our credibility of course [. . .] It's really not us deciding about the criteria, but all other organizations being part of the national committee [coming up with national proposal and comments on drafts] and then the Nordic committee [making the final decisions]. (Interview with official at The Swan, May 2014)

However, as another official at The Swan points out, the producers are allowed to have a large impact in these committees.

Most of the contact with stakeholders during the criteria development work is really with our customers [the producers]. More so than we have with state agencies. It's really the producers who are most interested in engaging in the rounds for comments, for example. These standards affect them directly so they engage with more resources on this, compared to what state agencies do. (Interview with official at The Swan, June 2014)

On a similar note, interviewees from KRAV and Kiwa Aranea (one of the certification companies working with KRAV standards in Sweden) explain how monitoring in practice is not so "black-and-white", but much more a grey area, where you give the producers advice, allow them to correct minor mistakes, and generally seek to help them improve, rather than just trying to find faults. In this storyline, the labelling organizations are there to help, to provide guidance so as to enable the producers to become more environmentally friendly. This storyline clearly supports the trust development between the labelling organization and the producers, stressing aspects of collaboration, good will and common goals, which is likely to promote compliance in the regulatory regime.

The *third* and last storyline is aimed primarily at the consumers and other stakeholders that are not direct clients of the eco-labelling organizations.

It is a story about control. Here, the labelling organizations are much more of an environmental police, using the development of criteria to push producers, and thereby the market, to become more environmentally friendly. And the control mechanisms are rigorous and objective. One official at The Swan describes the internal organization of the control, to explain how the dilemma between economic dependency and independent control is handled.

> The classical conflict of interest is when the eco-labelling organization both has a responsibility towards the customer and administrates the licence of the eco-label. Of course we want to be service-oriented, customer-oriented and provide good service, which means that we develop a relationship with the companies we work with. Then we have other people who are more sales-oriented, when it comes to attracting new customers. Sure, there can be a conflict of interest there; as an administrator you want "your" companies to obtain their licence. But on the other hand, we have the [two] control functions: we have one control manager and one auditor. It's never the person with the relationship to the customer who approves the licence. (Interview with official at The Swan, June 2014)

Thus, this is a story of surveillance and monitoring and how it is organized, either internally as is the case within Good Environmental Choice and The Swan, or externally as is the case of KRAV. However, it is also about the elaborate system of verifications and certifications that will allow the labelling organizations to be certain as far as possible that products that bear their label are environmentally friendly. In this storyline, there are more actors: the accreditations and the international collaborations that allow Swedish labelling organizations to certify cotton and coffee grown on other continents, and make sure that the production process adheres to environmental standards. One official at The Swan describes the elaborate control structures around this eco-label.

> There is this global organization GEN – Global Ecolabelling Network. There we have a peer review procedure among the members. We who are members state that we comply with the ISO 14024, the standard for ecolabelling systems. Then we have had an audit, I think it was a company from Taiwan, or some other organization, that came to audit how our system was built up and its function. They checked our quality systems. So there is another control. And finally, we are certified for ISO 9001 and ISO 14001, which means that we have auditors here every year to check on our work procedures. So we really do have excessive control structures. (Interview with official at The Swan, May 2014)

It is a storyline that to a large degree seems to be able to produce legitimacy, partly in the eyes of the consumer, but also in the eyes of other labelling organizations and stakeholders – accreditations make it possible to trust international counterparts and collaborate with them. Here, there are fewer grey areas, but more hard criteria and sharp evaluations, as explained by an interviewee at KRAV when talking about how they have chosen to outsource certification to another organization. "It makes for legitimacy. And then, the kind of certification they make, it's a little bit easier to evaluate than our regulations, since they work with quantifiable parameters to such a large extent" (interview with official at KRAV, June 2012).

Here, the attitude towards the producers is much more vigilant, not exactly distrusting them, but certainly making an independent, professional assessment, unclouded by any personal relationships, which the consumers can trust. However, it should also be noted that this storyline is quite devoid of details as to the actual practicalities of the control system. For example, the way Good Environmental Choice is performing and financing monitoring activities is not an issue communicated or discussed with consumers. As with the other two labels, the requirements of the criteria behind the labels are the focus of attention in such communication, as illustrated in the statement below, accessed from the labelling organization's website. "In order for a product to carry our label it must meet the requirements of our criteria. The requirements are tough but not impossible to achieve. Rather, the requirements must be constantly sharpened to become less harmful to the environment".[3]

The complex organization of the KRAV label, described above, is also not communicated towards the consumers. As seen in the cases of the two other eco-labels – Good Environmental Choice and The Swan – KRAV is, on the one hand, careful to point out towards consumers that there is a serious inspection behind a labelled product. The details about the elaborated control apparatus that actually is behind this label are, on the other hand, not specifically accounted for. On their website the following statement is made, to signal that inspection is a fundamental part of the labelling scheme. "Foods that carry the KRAV-label have been produced in an environmentally friendly and ethical manner. Consumers can rest assured that the production of a product with the KRAV-label has been inspected" (www.krav.se 2014-02-12).

Moreover, there are yet other types of arguments articulated towards consumers, for example comparing the producers to a family with the common goal to make the world more environmentally friendly, as illustrated by the quote below from the KRAV website. "All farmers, food producers, fishermen, retailers and restaurants that work according to the KRAV standards are members of a global family. It's a family that together with all conscious consumers promotes increased production and consumption of organic food worldwide – a family that is part of the solution" (www.krav.se 2014-02-12).

The use of the family metaphor can be interpreted as a further way to downplay the economic relationship between the eco-labelling organization and its clients, but rather put the emphasis on the value affinity.

Similar to the other two labelling organizations, The Swan does not communicate any details about the organization of its monitoring mechanism to consumers. Rather, the quality and work behind the setting criteria is emphasized, similarly as could be seen in the case of Good Environmental Choice. The following statement found on the website of The Swan illustrates this:

> Our consumption of products and services affects the environment. If you wish to live a more environmentally-friendly life, knowledgeable choices must be made. Lifestyles must be altered. A Nordic Ecolabelled [Swan labelled] or EU Ecolabelled product or service has fulfilled stringent criteria and are less detrimental to the environment and climate. [. . .] Our climate and environmental criteria comprise the entire life-cycle of a product, from source to waste. The Nordic Ecolabel [The Swan] and EU Ecolabel criteria contain level requirements for chemicals, air, water and ground emissions, energy usage, packaging and waste management. There are also criteria for quality and functionality. A product that works and has a long life span is also better for the environment. These criteria also are continually revised and improved, making these criteria among the toughest in the world. (www.svanen.se 2014-02-12)

Thus, although this storyline emphasizes the impartiality, integrity and robustness of the control systems, in an almost perfect example of the abstract trust systems Giddens and Luhmann envisioned, the less clean cut and more complex practice of these systems is not included in the account – now, this may partly be because consumers are not interested, as research on consumer use and attitudes of organic labels suggests (Eden et al., 2008; Näslund and Tamm Hallström, 2014). But the reason they are not may well be that such a system only seems impartial, exhaustive and distanced if viewed from a distance (Hedgecoe, 2012; Walgenbach, 2001). What you do not know does not hurt you, one might surmise.

These three storylines provide a framework for the interpretation of the actions of the organizations, allowing for trust and distrust, monitoring and compliance to co-exist. It should be noted that they are not all equally visible: the first and last are told in public sources, the second mainly in interaction with the client. As the consumer is not made aware of the second storyline, the other two are not contradictory. Producers on the other hand will be aware of the third storyline, used to earn the trust of consumers, and thereby, the monitoring may be interpreted in a different light, not as caused by distrust, but moreover as a signal of openness and mutual cooperation: "We are working on this together, but I cannot help you if we're not open with each other". It is a sentiment akin to "If you've done nothing wrong you've got nothing to fear. If you've something to hide you shouldn't even be here". Thus, by reframing monitoring not as a sign of distrust, but as a sign of mutual openness, the way you would be open to a doctor or a consultant, thereby, you can combine monitoring and compliance, and both of these with trust (Six, 2013).

BECOMING EVERYBODY'S ACCOMPLICE

Earlier in this chapter, we showed how the intermediary guardian of trust position of eco-labels, as an example of voluntary regulatory regimes, causes an insoluble dilemma, as the regulating organization needs to both trust and distrust, at once be distant and close, to the regulatees. As we have seen, this is not just a marketing problem, similar to any other company who needs to find a way to present its product in the most enticing way possible to its buyers, but moreover, it is a problem that reflects a fundamental contradiction of the middle-man position in itself. Being able to solve this dilemma, and thus bridge the social, spatial and cognitive distance between citizens and private organizations that choose to become regulatees, is thus, in management terms, not a case of finding the right marketing strategy, it is their core business. The strategies used to solve this dilemma, therefore govern the organization and the stories used by the labelling organizations. Regarding them both as regulatory regimes, which have to combine control, trust and compliance, and as guardians of trust, providing abstract systems of control and assurance with authority and legitimacy, provides the key to understanding them, their organizations, and how they present themselves to whom.

This study shows that third-party certification bodies, such as labelling organizations, use a number of strategies in order to deal with this dilemma, which show some similarity but are not identical to what was found in the case of ISO-auditors (Dogui et al., 2013, 2014), suggesting that the choice or availability of strategies is circumscribed by the social and cultural context of the market, which further research into regulatory regimes in other contexts may be able to investigate in more detail. There seems, nevertheless, to be some context sensitivity to the organization and behaviour of regulatory regimes, which should be taken into account when studying them, although the underlying mechanisms that create the dilemma are similar, and seem less context dependent.

In the case of eco-labels on the food market, we have seen how regulators use organization as a strategy to combine independent control and trusting collaboration by separating and decoupling the different tasks necessary to create an eco-label, namely the writing of criteria, the monitoring and the communication of the worth of the label to consumers and producers. Labels may use a multi-stakeholder process for criteria development building on consensus as a principle for decisions, which offers a space for collaboration between producers and the labelling organization, and thereby functions as an arena to build trust (as in the case of KRAV and The Swan). Others (such as Good Environmental Choice) develop and decide the criteria alone, but invite producers to engage in a dialogue through a referral procedure, which also serves as a trust building activity although the final decision concerning criteria content is taken by the labelling organization. Moreover, the criteria development process is in practice kept separate from the monitoring, which may, as in the case of KRAV, be as far removed as to take place in another organization by the use of certification companies such as Kiwa. If, as we saw in the case of Good Environmental Choice, the same administrator responsible for the criteria development also oversees the monitoring, then this decoupling is instead organized internally in the labelling organization. The study reveals Good Environmental Choice's scope to mainly write criteria for and thus label products for their specific content (as opposed to KRAV and many other labelling initiatives developing management system type of standards) – criteria that can be checked through laboratory reports provided by the producers without the labelling administrator even paying the producer a control visit – which allows for impersonal control to co-exist with interpersonal trust (Sydow and Windeler, 2003). In both examples, compartmentalization and decoupling enable the mediators to practise control without signalling distrust, which would be detrimental to future collaboration and the client relationship (Six, 2013).

As evidenced from earlier studies (Six, 2013; Six and Sorge, 2008; Weibel, 2007), it is not the act of monitoring itself that breeds distrust, but rather the attitude of distrust that the monitoring tends to signal. Therefore, organizational strategies are not sufficient, but need to be combined with sense-giving strategies, described here in terms of storylines. In both the case of KRAV and Good Environmental Choice, the control systems were to a large extent interpreted not as signs of distrust from the labelling organization, but as signs of the distrust of the consumers, as a consequence of the storyline used by the labelling organization to describe their actions. Monitoring and regulation might thus be done in agreement between regulator and regulatee, labelling organization and producer, in order to convince the consumer of the trustworthiness of the products in question. Actions do not automatically cause trust or distrust so much as the meanings that are assigned to them, which underlines the sense-making aspect of trust creation (Adobor, 2005). Thus, if we want to understand under what circumstances control may promote and deter trust, the nature of the control mechanism is perhaps less important than the perceived intention behind it. The same control measure may thus have opposite effects on trust and compliance, depending on the frames of reference that are used to interpret it.

Lastly, the study demonstrates how processes of trust creation may run parallel and separate: the labelling organization is able to entice the trust of the consumers by seemingly siding with them, in controlling and monitoring the untrustworthy producers, while at the same time captivating the trust of the producers, by making a joint effort with them to convince the sceptical consumers of the virtues of the products they both know to be environmentally friendly. Keeping this balance, however, siding with both without losing the trust of either, is no mean feat, and requires legitimizing work, as well as the ability to shield the interaction with one party from the other: consumers are not necessarily aware of the involvement of the producers in criteria writing, nor of the separation of criteria writing and monitoring, or details about exactly how monitoring is conducted, as this would likely undermine their trust in the labelling organization. If they are to be trusted, they cannot be seen to consort with the object of distrust too closely, but must keep this interaction shadowed. Thereby, they are able to gain the trust of both producers and consumers, becoming the accomplice of the consumers in finding the right products and pushing producers towards greener products, as well as the producer's accomplice in the fight for market shares and better sales. Creating trust and ensuring compliance in regulatory regimes thus becomes a matter of storytelling and strategic sense making, as much as of carefully designing control mechanisms and regulatory systems. In order to solve the middle-man dilemma and become effective as guardians of trust, voluntary private regulators need to enlist both organizational and storytelling strategies to keep separate and distinct the different and contradictory demands of their position, and it is the combination of both that holds the key to success.

NOTES

1. We are grateful for the generous financial support in 2012–2014 from the Swedish Retail and Wholesale Development Council (HUR) that made this research possible. We also wish to direct our gratitude to our interviewees, and to research assistants Alexandra Kenne, Bernice Lindqvist, Sofie Grettve and Emelie Adamsson who conducted some of the interviews of the studies accounted for.

2. KRAV is an abbreviation of the original name *Kontrollföreningen för Alternativ Odling*, that is, the control association of alternative farming. In English the word KRAV means "requirement". Throughout this chapter, however, we use the name KRAV.
3. www.naturskyddsforeningen.se/bra–miljoval.se 2014-02-12

REFERENCES

Adobor, H. (2005), 'Trust as sensemaking: the microdynamics of trust in interfirm alliances', *Journal of Business Research*, **58**, 330–337.

Almeida, F., H.F. Pessali, and N. Maciel de Paula (2010), 'Third-party certification in food market chains: Are you being served?', *Journal of Economic Issues*, **XLIV** (2), 479–485.

Bartley, T. (2007), 'Institutional emergence in an era of globalization: The rise of transnational private regulation of labor and environmental conditions', *American Journal of Sociology*, **113** (2), 297–351.

Bartley, T. (2011), 'Certification as a mode of social regulation', in D. Levi-Faur (ed.), *Handbook on the politics of regulation*, Cheltenham, UK and Northampton, MA, USA: Edward Elgar Publishing, pp. 441–452.

Bernstein, S., and B. Cashore (2007), 'Can non-state governance be legitimate? An analytical framework', *Regulation and Governance*, **1** (4), 347–371.

Bijlsma-Frankema, K., and A.C. Costa (2005), 'Understanding the trust–control nexus', *International Sociology*, **20** (3), 259–282.

Boli, J. (1999), 'Conclusion: World authority structures and legitimations', in J. Boli and G. M. Thomas (eds), *Constructing world culture: International non-governmental organizations since 1875*, Stanford, CA: Stanford University Press, pp. 267–300.

Boli, J. (2006), 'The rationalization of virtue and virtuosity in world society', in M.-L. Djelic and K. Sahlin-Andersson (eds.), *Transnational governance. Institutional dynamics of regulation*, Cambridge: Cambridge University Press, pp. 95–118.

Boström, M., and K. Tamm Hallström (2010), *Transnational multi-stakeholder standardization. Organizing fragile non-state authority*, Cheltenham, UK and Northampton, MA, USA: Edward Elgar Publishing.

Braithwaite, J., and T. Makkai (1994), 'Trust and compliance', *Policing and Society: An International Journal of Research and Policy*, **4**, 1–12.

Brunsson, N., and B. Jacobsson (eds) (2000), *A world of standards*, Oxford, UK: Oxford University Press.

Carriquiry, M., and B.A. Babcock (2007), 'Reputations, market structure, and the choice of quality assurance systems in the food industry', *American Journal of Agricultural Economics*, **89** (1), 12–23.

Coletti, A.L., K.L. Sedatole, and K.L. Towry (2005), 'The effect of control systems on trust and cooperation in collaborative environments', *The Accounting Review*, **80** (2), 477–500.

Costa, A.C., and K. Bijlsma-Frankema (2005), 'Trust and control interrelations. New perspectives on the trust-control nexus', *Group and Organizational Management*, **32** (4), 392–406.

Cutler, A.C., V. Haufler, and T. Porter (eds) (1999), *Private authority and international affairs*, Albany: State University of New York Press.

Das, T.K., and B.-S. Teng (1998), 'Between trust and control: Developing confidence in partner cooperation in alliances', *Academy of Management Review*, **23** (3), 491–512.

Djelic, M.-L., and K. Sahlin-Andersson (2006), *Transnational governance: Institutional dynamics of regulation*, Cambridge, UK: Cambridge University Press.

Dogui, K., O. Boiral, and Y. Gendron (2013), 'ISO auditing and the construction of trust in auditor independence', *Accounting, Auditing & Accountability Journal*, **26** (8), 1279–1305.

Dogui, K., O. Boiral, and I. Heras-Saizabitoria (2014), 'Audit fees and auditor independence: The case of ISO 14001 certification', *International Journal of Auditing*, **18** (1), 14–26.

Drori, G.S., and J. Meyer (2006), 'Scientization: Making a world safe for organizing', in M.-L. Djelic and K. Sahlin-Andersson (eds.), *Transnational governance. Institutional dynamics of regulation*, Cambridge: Cambridge University Press, pp. 31–52.

Eden, S., C. Bear, and G. Walker (2008), 'Mucky carrots and other proxies: Problematising the knowledge-fix for sustainable and ethical consumption', *Geoforum*, **39**, 1044–1057.

Elder, S.D., J. Lister, and P. Dauvergne (2014), 'Big retail and sustainable coffee: A new development studies research agenda', *Progress in Development Studies*, **14** (1), 77–90.

Fryxell, G.E., R.S. Dooley, and M. Vryza (2002), 'After the ink dries: The interaction of trust and control in US-based international joint ventures', *Journal of Management Studies*, **39** (6), 865–886.

Fuglsang, L., and S. Jagd (2015), 'Making sense of institutional trust in organizations: Bridging institutional context and trust', *Organization*, **22** (1), 23–39.

Giddens, A. (1990), *The consequences of modernity*, Cambridge: Polity Press.

Gioia, D.A., and K. Chittipeddi (1991), 'Sensegiving and sensemaking in strategic change initiation', *Strategic Management Journal*, **12** (6), 433–448.

Goldman, A., and B. Barlev (1974), 'The auditor–firm conflict of interests: Its implications for independence', *The Accounting Review*, **49** (4), 707–718.

Grettve, S. (2014), 'Bra Miljöval. En fallstudie av ett miljömärkes förtroendearbete', *Score report*, Stockholm: Score.

Gundlach, G.T., and J.P. Cannon (2010), '"Trust but verify"? The performance implications of verification strategies in trusting relationships', *Journal of the Academy of Marketing Science*, **38**, 399–417.

Gustafsson, I., and K. Tamm Hallström (2013), 'The certification paradox: Monitoring as a solution and a problem', in M. Reuter, F. Wijkström, and B. Kristensson Uggla (eds), *Trust and organizations. Confidence across borders*, New York, NY: Palgrave, pp. 91–109.

Hatanaka, M., C. Bain, and L. Busch (2005), 'Third-party certification in the global agrifood system', *Food Policy*, **30**, 354–369.

Hatanaka, M., and L. Busch (2008), 'Third-party certification in the global agrifood system: An objective or socially mediated governance mechanism?', *Sociologica Ruralis*, **48** (1), 73–91.

Hedgecoe, A. (2012), 'Trust and regulatory organizations: The role of local knowledge and facework in research ethics review', *Social Studies of Science*, **42** (5), 662–683.

Hooper, J. (2008), 'Italy embarrassed by counterfeit olive oil scandal', *The Guardian*, 23 April.

Inkpen, A.C., and S.C. Currall (2004), 'The coevolution of trust, control, and learning in joint ventures', *Organization Science*, **15** (5), 586–599.

Jacobsson, B., and K. Sahlin-Andersson (2006), 'Dynamics of soft regulations', in M.-L. Djelic, and K. Sahlin-Andersson (eds.), *Transnational governance. Institutional dynamics of regulation*, Cambridge: Cambridge University Press, pp. 247–265.

Jamal, K., and S. Sunder (2011), 'Is mandated independence necessary for audit quality?', *Accounting, Organizations and Society*, **36**, 284–292.

Kouakou, D., O. Boiral and Y. Gendron (2013), 'ISO auditing and the construction of trust in auditor independence', *Accounting, Auditing & Accountability Journal*, **26** (8), 1279–1305.

Kroeger, F. (2011), 'Trusting organizations: The institutionalization of trust in interorganizational relationships', *Organization*, **19** (6), 743–763.

Kydd, A.H. (2006), 'When can mediators build trust?', *American Political Science Review*, **100** (3), 449–462.

Lang, J.T. (2013), 'Elements of public trust in the American food system: Experts, organizations, and genetically modified food', *Food Policy*, **41**, 144–154.

Loconto, A., and L. Busch (2010), 'Standards, techno-economic networks and playing fields: Performing the global market economy', *Review of International Political Economy*, **17** (3), 507–536.

Loconto, A., and Fouilleux, E. (2014), 'Politics of private regulation: ISEAL and the shaping of transnational sustainability governance', *Regulation & Governance*, **8** (2), 166–185.

Luhmann, N. (1979), *Trust and power*, Chichester: John Wiley & Sons.

McDermott, C.L. (2012), 'Trust, legitimacy and power in forest certification: A case study of the FSC in British Columbia', *Geoforum*, **43**, 634–644.

Meyer, J., and B. Rowan (1977), 'Institutionalized organizations: Formal structure as myth and ceremony', *American Journal of Sociology*, **83**, 340–363.

Murphy, K. (2004), 'The role of trust in nurturing compliance: A study of accused tax avoiders', *Law and Human Behavior*, **28** (2), 187–209.

Möllering, G. (2005), 'The trust/control duality: An integrative perspective on positive expectations of others', *International Sociology*, **20** (3), 283–305.

Neville, S. (2013), 'Horsemeat lasagne scandal leaves Findus reputation in tatters', *The Guardian*, 8 February.

Näslund, L., and K. Tamm Hallström (2014), '"I trust they're checking" – the role of eco-labels in reducing consumer uncertainty', *30th EGOS Colloquium*, Rotterdam, the Netherlands.

Perrini, F., S. Castaldo, N. Misani, and A. Tencati (2010), 'The impact of corporate social responsibility associations on trust in organic products marketed by mainstream retailers: a study of Italian customers', *Business Strategy and the Environment*, **19** (8), 512–526.

Pixley, J. (1999), 'Impersonal trust in global mediating organizations', *Sociological Perspectives*, **42** (4), 647–671.

Polidoro, F. (2013), 'The competitive implications of certifications: The effects of scientific and regulatory certifications on entries into new technical fields', *Academy of Management Journal*, **56** (2), 597–627.

Power, M.K. (2003), 'Auditing and the production of legitimacy', *Accounting, Organizations and Society*, **28**, 379–394.

Power, M.K. (2011), 'Assurance worlds: Consumers, experts and independence', *Accounting, Organizations and Society*, **36**, 324–326.

Reinecke, J., S. Manning, and O. Von Hagen (2012), 'The emergence of a standards market: Multiplicity of sustainability standards in the global coffee industry', *Organization Studies*, **33** (5–6), 791–814.

Richard, C. (2006), 'Why an auditor can't be competent and independent: A French case study', *European Accounting Review*, **15** (2), 153–179.

Sapp, S.G., C. Arnot, J. Fallon, T. Fleck, D. Soorholz, M. Sutton-Vermeulen, and J.J.H. Wilson (2009), 'Consumer trust in the U.S. food system: An examination of the recreancy theorem', *Rural sociology*, **74** (4), 525–545.

Shapiro, S.P. (1987), 'The social control of impersonal trust', *American Journal of Sociology*, **93** (3), 623–658.

Six, F.E. (2013), 'Trust in regulatory relations. How new insights from trust research improve regulation theory', *Public Management Review*, **15** (2), 163–185.

Six, F.E. and A. Sorge (2008), 'Creating a high-trust organization: An exploration into organizational policies that stimulate interpersonal trust building', *Journal of Management Studies*, **45** (5), 857–884.

Skinner, D., and L.F. Spira (2003), 'Trust and control – symbiotic relationship?', *Corporate Governance*, **3** (4), 28–35.

Smets, L.P.M., K.E. van Oorschot, and F. Langerak (2013), 'Don't trust trust: A dynamic approach to controlling supplier involvement in new product development', *Journal of Product Innovation Management*, **30** (6), 1145–1158.

Sydow, J., and A. Windeler (2003), 'Knowledge, trust and control: Managing tensions and contradictions in a regional network of service firms', *International Journal of Management & Organization*, **33** (2), 69–99.

Tamm Hallström, K. (2004), *Organizing international standardization – ISO and the IASC in quest of authority*, Cheltenham, UK and Northampton, MA, USA: Edward Elgar Publishing.

Tamm Hallström, K., and M. Boström (2010), *Transnational multi-stakeholder standardization. Organizing fragile non-state authority*, Cheltenham, UK and Northampton, MA, USA: Edward Elgar Publishing.

Tamm Hallström, K., and I. Gustafsson (2014), 'Value-neutralizing in verification markets: Organizing for independence through accreditation', in S. Alexius and K. Tamm Hallström (eds), *Configuring value conflicts in markets*, Cheltenham, UK and Northampton, MA, USA: Edward Elgar Publishing, pp. 82–99.

Tanner, B. (2000), 'Independent assessment by third-party certification bodies', *Food Control*, **11** (5), 415–417.

Vlaar, P.W.L., F.A.J. Van den Bosch, and H.W. Volberda (2006), *On the evolution of trust, distrust, and formal coordination and control in interorganizational relationships: Towards an integrative framework*, Rotterdam: Erasmus Research Institute of Management.

Walgenbach, P. (2001), 'The production of distrust by means of producing trust', *Organization Studies*, **22** (4), 693–714.

Weber, K., and M.A. Glynn (2006), 'Making sense with institutions: context, thought and action in Karl Weick's theory', *Organization Studies*, **27** (11), 1639–1660.

Weber, M. (1948), *Essays in sociology*, New York: Routledge.

Weibel, A. (2007), 'Formal control and trustworthiness. Shall the twain never meet?', *Group and Organization Management*, **32** (4), 500–517.

Homepages of the Studied Eco-labels

www.krav.se
www.naturskyddsforeningen.se/bra-miljoval
www.svanen.se

7. Trust and cooperation over the public–private divide: an empirical study on trust evolving in co-regulation

Haiko Van der Voort

TRUSTING PARTNERS IN CASE OF CO-REGULATION

Public regulators and inspectorates increasingly involve self-regulation in their regulatory regimes. Well-known features of self-regulation are certification and hallmark systems. Regulation then becomes more and more a mutual public and private coordination effort for compliance. If public and private actors cooperate for typical oversight activities, such as standard setting, information gathering and intervention, I speak of "co-regulation" (see also Bartle and Vass, 2005; Van der Heijden, 2009; Börzel and Risse, 2010).

Co-regulation involves cooperation across the public–private divide. Both public and private actors serve common values (such as safety, quality, sustainability), but with different purposes, methods, and motives. A massive amount of literature on self-regulation describes tensions between motives of public regulators ("government") on the one hand and those of self-regulating industries ("industry") on the other (e.g., Gunningham and Rees, 1997; Hutter, 2006; Potosky and Prakash, 2009). This distinction is a bit crude, of course. "Government" involves, for instance, supranational governments, national parliaments, policy departments and inspectorates and self-regulating industry includes for instance trade organizations, participating companies, scheme managers and certifying organizations. The tensions between government and industry described in the literature are seen as important for government, because it is often seen as ultimately responsible for safeguarding public values (Havinga, 2006; Dorbeck-Jung et al., 2010). Government is often held accountable for incidents – regardless who caused them – and it seems hard for government to shift accountability towards private actors (Garcia Martinez et al., 2013).

According to this reasoning, trust between government and industry may be vital for co-regulation, but the risks for government would make distrust understandable, even rational.[1]

Still – regardless of this rationality of distrust for government – all kinds of co-regulatory initiatives emerge, against all odds. This might imply that this rationality of distrust in some way is neglected or it might even disappear. This brings me to the main question of this contribution: How does trust emerge among government and industry in case of co-regulation?

In the further sections of this chapter, I will specify this question, focusing on the government's perspective. First, I will elaborate on the relation between cooperation and trust. I will conceptualize co-regulation as a process of interaction, wherein trust and cooperation are mutually dependent variables. Second, I will assume that this process doesn't emerge in a vacuum. This process is embedded in both formal and informal institutions. Two case studies will show the complex interaction processes among government and industry in case of co-regulation. The cases involve the regulatory regime for the quality of Dutch eggs and the regime concerning the reliability of Dutch temporary employment agencies. Both case studies start with explicitly expressed trust in co-regulation. In one of these cases trust was retained, but in the other it wasn't. The case studies reveal factors that block or stimulate the emergence of trust in the context of co-regulation.

TRUST AND COOPERATION AS MUTUALLY DEPENDENT VARIABLES, BOUNDED BY INSTITUTIONS

Trust is hard to measure for several reasons. It is a multifaceted concept that caught the interest of researchers from multiple disciplines. Disciplines include psychology, sociology, (institutional) economics, and organizational theory. Trust is being researched and conceptualized among individuals and among organizations. As a result of this, a broad range of definitions can be found. Three aspects of trust are worth highlighting.

First, trust is relational. There is no such a thing as trust in isolation. One actor (either a person or an organization) relies on another actor. Recurring concepts are expectations of each other's behavior, predictability of each other's behavior (Zaheer et al., 1998; Young-Ybarra and Wiersema, 1999), and dependability of each other's behavior (Young-Ybarra and Wiersema, 1999; Gassenheimer and Manolis, 2001). Trust is dedicated to a different actor. This dedication has potential for both "trustors" and "trustees", because it lowers transaction costs considerably. In a trusted relationship, for instance, formal arrangements may be replaced by informal arrangements. The latter are quicker and easier to develop and maintain (Smith Ring and Van de Ven, 1994).

However, trusting someone involves risks too. A second aspect of trust is vulnerability. The reliance on other parties may have a price. If a trusted actor (trustee) does not live up to expectations, the trustor may feel considerable damage. This in essence makes the trustor vulnerable (Newell and Swan, 2000). Trust can therefore be defined as a willingness to be vulnerable to the actions of another party (Norman, 2002; Seppänen et al., 2007).

Third, this vulnerability goes beyond calculation. Möllering (2014) makes an important distinction between trust and "competent calculativeness". The latter refers to risk taking based on rational calculations. Interaction, then, is considered subject to some conscious calculation about possible costs and benefits. The distinction between trust and calculativeness suggests that trust is more than such a rational analysis. Trust is to some extent also a "leap of faith", an act that goes beyond calculation.

Two discussions show that trust is inherently subjective. First, what is expected from the trustee? Some scholars focus on purpose, as being the commitments of the trustee to meet expectations of the trustor (Dyer and Chu, 2011; Seppänen et al., 2007). Others focus on conduct, being the behavior of the trustee that unfolds regardless of its intention (Zaheer et al., 1998). This distinction is quite common, either coined "intentions and conduct" (Nooteboom, 1996) or "commitments and execution" (Smith Ring and Van de Ven, 1994). A second difficult question is to what extent the trustor can determine whether the trustee meets the expectations. If interactions among trustor, trustee, and their environments become more complex, it is harder to determine a causal relationship between commitment or conduct, and even between conduct and consequence. Some scholars focus on commitment, conduct or consequences "as is", while others tend to focus on the perceptions by the trustor. In any case, a lack of information about causality and the inherently subjective nature of trust makes trust subject to perceptions of the trustor (and of scholars, indeed).

This is of vital importance for the relation between trust and cooperation. It is often said that trust fuels cooperation (Zucker, 1986; Zand, 1997; Lane, 1998; Nooteboom, 2002; Six, 2007). However, the foundation of trust is subjective, and made up of assumptions by the trustor. These assumptions are fueled by information about factual conduct and consequences. If the feedback is positive, the foundations will get stronger (Six, 2007). This implies that trust may be built up in the course of time. A process description of trust building may find that cooperation also fuels trust. In case of successful cooperation (either measured by consequences or conduct or commitment), feedback is positive and trust may increase. In case of unsuccessful cooperation feedback is negative and trust may decrease. This makes "trust" and "cooperation" mutually dependent variables in the process of trust building (Newell and Swan, 2000; Smith Ring and Van de Ven, 1994). Trust facilitates cooperation, but at the same time cooperation is an occasion to learn about each other's trustworthiness (Luhmann, 1979; Six, 2007).

So why not just do it? If cooperation and trust may reinforce each other, why not start trusting or start cooperating? According to most institutionalists, getting involved in a trust relationship is not just a matter of decision on the basis of some cost–benefit analysis. Such a rational choice idea is popular among economists, but debated by institutionalists (e.g., Six, 2007). A choice to get involved would be bound by institutions. These institutions may both consciously and unconsciously influence a decision to cooperate. According to Bachmann and Inkpen (2011) institutions play at least three roles in a trust relationship. First, institutions may provide meaning to the circumstances before any relationship is built. Second, institutions influence the patterns of how trustors and trustees interact when they start to actively establish a relationship. Third, a trustor has faith in the institutional arrangements themselves, making them the object of trust.

This distinction suggests that institutions are not only static substitutes of persons or organizations. They also provide direction to behavior of trustors and trustees – either consciously or not – before and during cooperation.

TOWARDS AN EMPIRICAL STUDY: TRUST, COOPERATION, INSTITUTIONAL ARRANGEMENTS

How to find out how trust emerges among government and industry in case of co-regulation? This question implies a study of cooperation processes between government and industry and how these processes are shaped institutionally. In other words, I am looking for institutional arrangements that affect the interplay between trust and cooperation. These arrangements might explain the way the process of emerging trust develops, as depicted in Figure 7.1. I call institutional arrangements "trust-on-paper", as they are highly visible in agreements and policy documents, for instance. The interplay between trust and cooperation is perceived as one variable, coined "trust-in-action". The mutual relation between "trust-on-paper" and "trust-in-action" is my object of study.

The previous sections can be summarized as follows:

● Co-regulation requires mutual trust between government and self-regulating industries, as their cooperation reaches over the public–private divide.

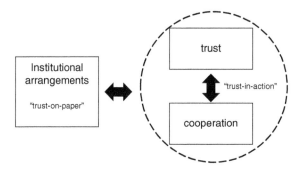

Figure 7.1   Conceptual model

- Trust is the willingness to be vulnerable in interaction, wherein this willingness goes beyond calculation, i.e., it cannot be entirely backed by rational risk analysis.
- Trust and cooperation are mutually dependent variables in a process of interaction between trustor and trustee. The interplay between trust and cooperation can be called "trust-in-action".
- "Trust-in-action" is embedded in institutions. "Trust-on-paper" refers to institutional arrangements wherein trust is reflected.
- The mutual relation between "trust-on-paper" and "trust-in-action" is the object of this study.

I have taken these conceptual ideas to two Dutch case studies about co-regulation. As depicted in Figure 7.1 I focus on the relation between institutional arrangements of co-regulation and the mutual reinforcement process of trust and cooperation.

The cases involve co-regulation on the quality of Dutch eggs and co-regulation concerning the reliability of Dutch temporary employment agencies. Both case studies start with explicitly expressed public and private trust in co-regulation. At least, trust has been announced on paper. In one of the cases the process of trust and cooperation continued, while in the other case trust was decreasing and cooperation has stopped. In other words, in one case "trust-on-paper" did translate into "trust-in-action", but in the other it did not (see Figure 7.1). This provides a good opportunity to find explanations for trust evolving in case of co-regulation.

The institutional arrangements differed among the cases. In the case of the quality of eggs a policy framework on co-regulation and an agreement are developed. The framework is a holistic, hierarchical policy design by the Dutch Ministry of Agriculture of which the agreement is an application to the poultry sector. The agreements included the distribution and frequencies of inspections and responsibilities of both public and private inspectorates. The other case shows the Dutch parliament explicitly announcing its commitment to co-regulation. A parliamentary resolution explicitly provides leeway for self-regulation under threat of a licensing regime. No further institutional arrangements were announced or prepared at that moment.

To determine the interaction process between trust and cooperation ("trust-in-action"), I assumed that co-regulation involves conflicting expectations and assessment criteria, resulting in recurring issues on the agendas of the parties involved. To determine "trust-in-action" I focused on the process of solving those recurring issues. Using the conceptual model (Figure 7.1), I came to the following empirical questions:

- What institutional arrangements can be found that shape the relationship between government and self-regulating industry?
- What issues emerged during the cooperation process?
- How are these issues solved?
- How did the institutional arrangements develop during the cooperation process?

For each case study I will first describe the "starting point", being the trust as announced on paper as a first institutional arrangement. After this I will describe the issues, how they are solved, and how they result in further institutional arrangements. In the seventh section I will summarize the processes in a table. The studies consisted of desk research and 51 semi-structured interviews with parties involved from both categories of actors. Among governments, interviews were conducted with public administrators, policymakers and inspectors. Among regulated industries, interviews were conducted with entrepreneurs, sector executives, sector associations, and certifying bodies. Both studies had a natural "starting point", both in 2005, wherein trust was announced in a policy framework and a parliamentary resolution respectively. Both studies cover a time period of seven years. The interviews took place between May 2009 and July 2012.

TRUST FADING AWAY: TOEZICHT OP CONTROLE[2]

The production of eggs involves many issues that are deemed of public concern. Regulations concern the welfare of the hens and food hygiene (particularly salmonella). Multiple public inspectorates[3] organize inspections in accordance to national food law and European trade norms. Alongside these public inspections a private certification scheme *IKB ei* exists, which includes norms about management systems, production systems and the quality of eggs.

In 2005 the then Dutch Ministry of Agriculture, Nature and Food Safety published a policy framework called *Toezicht op Controle* (TOC).[4] This framework is set up to find efficiencies in cooperation between public and private inspections. Basically it involves the delegation of some public inspections to the private regime. The policy framework defines under what conditions such delegation may take place. The public regulators then supervise the private regulation. This involves supervising the certifying bodies by means of system audits and verification inspections.

One of the public inspectors was in fact a private body that executed mandated tasks. The inspection costs of the latter were paid by the farmers. In the new arrangement these inspections are reduced in favour of audits that would have been performed anyway. This made adopting the system as prescribed in the framework attractive for poultry farmers. They decided to draw up an agreement with the Ministry to apply TOC to the *IKB-ei* system. The coordinator of this system (the *IKB-ei* Foundation; in Dutch *Stichting IKB ei*) would play a pivotal role between public inspectorates, inspectees and certifying bodies.

A working group and steering group that consisted of public inspectorates and industry representatives was founded. The Ministry did not sign the resulting agreement, because it felt that it should not be part of the new system, which would be the industry's responsibility, compliant to the policy framework TOC. *Stichting IKB ei* would take the coordination role. An agreement was signed in 2008.

The starting point is the framework and the agreement. They both announce trust. Getting to an agreement and implementing it, however, proved a challenge. Many issues discussed during the development of the agreement proved to recur in the execution phase. Three issues proved to be dominant here.

Issue: The Number of Unannounced Audits

Coordination among private auditors and public inspectors also means harmonizing inspection strategies and style. An important difference here is the announcements of inspections. Private auditors are used to announcing their visits some weeks before, where public inspectors do not. It is assumed that those participating in a private scheme are eager to learn and announcing visits facilitates dialogue and learning effects. However, public inspectorates would not announce their visits, because of the danger that inspectees prepare for the visits too much, which potentially harms the representativeness of the inspectors' observations.

The Ministry claimed that only announced visits would not comply with the European Directive on Trade Norms.[5] However, the industry was not convinced.[6]

> This approach by the Ministry can be explained by the perceived importance of ruling out risks [. . .] We assume that if the EU doesn't explicitly forbid matters, they are allowed. The Ministry assumes matters to be allowed if the EU explicitly allows them. [. . .] They claim compliance to the Directive. However, the concept "unannounced" isn't defined well in the Directive. This can be either calling a week beforehand, or not calling at all. This suggests room, if the EU would have a problem with calling a week beforehand. Still the Ministry doesn't dare to be flexible in this. [industry]

The agreement involved extra unannounced audits for 50 percent of *IKB-ei* members on top of the regular announced inspections. The extra unannounced audits were to be evaluated after two years. *Stichting IKB ei* would develop auditing criteria and assign the audits to the inspectees. Because the costs would be distributed over the *IKB-ei* members, a part of the potential efficiency gains of TOC would be lost. This resulted in resistance of the members starting to doubt the advantages of TOC. Also, more fundamental objections were raised against unannounced audits. "It cannot be that governments delegate their policing tasks to private actors, and after this move time and again raise demands to the execution of these inspections without providing any financial relief" [industry].

As a result of this resistance, *Stichting IKB ei* was not keen to organize the unannounced visits strictly. In November 2008 it sent the auditing norms to the certifying bodies for that same year. For 2009 they copied the norms of 2008 and sent them in summer, leaving the certifying bodies just a couple of months to carry them out.

Despite the agreement, no evaluation has been initiated after two years. After an exchange of demands between government and the sector, the *Stichting IKB ei* – pressurized by the industry – unilaterally reduced the amount of unannounced audits to 7.5 percent.

Issue: Auditing Certifying Bodies

The Ministry and public inspectorates had doubts about the certification systems, to which public inspections would be delegated. These doubts nurtured their wish to verify how certifying bodies do their jobs. The doubts concerned at least two issues:

1) Certifying bodies operate in a market. Public regulators feared a race to the bottom because of harsh competition among certifying bodies.

> The relation between auditor and auditee must be objective. Don't forget that formerly inspections were done by civil servants that operated under oath. A significant distance existed between auditor and auditee. This now is gone. The auditor visits the client. He gets paid for their visits. [government]

2) The government remains ultimately responsible for the system, as explicitly stated in the TOC framework. Even if this would not be the case in a formal sense, after an accident has happened media and politicians tend to hold public regulators responsible. This makes full trust in private quality systems risky.

> We can only take a step back if we know that these systems are proper. This fits a significant amount of verification audits. [government]

Discussions about these doubts focused on the number of verification audits. The TOC framework already mentioned verification audits to be done by public regulator CPE. These audits are done at poultry farms, with the aim to benchmark the job done by the certifying body. In the agreement a percentage of 15 percent of the poultry farmers was defined. The verification audits would be evaluated after two years, just like the unannounced visits. The costs of the audits would be distributed over the *IKB-ei* members.

The industry had the same objections against the verification audits as to the unannounced visits. The verification audits would imply another reduction of potential efficiency gains.

Next, certifying bodies see the verification audits as a threat. Results of such an audit may be harmful to their market position. Moreover, the verification audits are an additional check on their work, in addition to the regular audits already performed by the Dutch Accreditation Council, responsible for accreditation of the *IKB-ei* scheme and certifying bodies. "If government finds certification a good practice for this sector, then they have to accept the consequences. If the old public supervisors start carrying out considerable checks on our work [. . .] separately from the Dutch Accreditation Council, then I'm not interested in TOC anymore" [standardization industry].

After two years no evaluation was performed. The sector demanded a decrease of the amount of verification audits to 2.5 percent. A solution to the issue was reached after negotiations with the Ministry. The sector would finance the verification audits up to 5 percent. The Ministry would finance a further 2.5 percent.

Issue: Fining by Certifiers

The Ministry found the array of sanctioning instruments too limited. If poultry farmers do not comply, certifiers have the possibility to warn certificate owners or eventually withdraw a certificate. The Minister of Agriculture urged for an increase of sanctioning instruments within TOC. The Ministry and public regulators favored certifying bodies to be able to fine non-compliant farmers. "A fine is the ultimate consequence of taking responsibility [. . .] Until introducing the fine the industry did the easy jobs and the government had to do the difficult jobs, such as sanctioning" [government].

This fine then had to be included in the *IKB-ei* scheme. Both poultry farmers and the certification industry fiercely opposed the fine. Noncompliant farmers would face higher costs, making *IKB-ei* membership again less attractive. The industry started to think government was not withdrawing at all. The standardization industry claimed that the fine would be incompatible with their regulatory system. "As a representative of the poultry farmers I say 'Either you trust us or you do not. And if you do not trust us, then do not continue with this system'" [industry]. "A fundamental rule of accreditation is that we only tell what is. Not more. This cannot be combined with policing tasks. [. . .] Fining is an activity done by an inspector, not by an auditor in a quality system" [standardization industry].

The farmers agreed *contre coeur* to the fine. However, the role of accreditation is significant here. TOC requires accreditation.[7] The Dutch Accreditation Council eventually found the fine "unacceptable" for accreditation. This left the industry a dilemma: comply with the agreement including the fine or comply with TOC and strive for accreditation?

Eventually they chose the latter, because accreditation is important for the reputation and export of "*IKB-ei*" eggs . The industry, with *Stichting IKB ei* as a major spokesman, unilaterally deleted the fine from the scheme.

A Downward Spiral from Trust to Distrust

This case started with trust, expressed in the TOC-policy framework and the agreement that specified the arrangement for the poultry sector. However, the arrangement did not settle. Several issues emerged, but few innovative solutions have been developed. Instead, the issues have been subject to trench warfare. Trust more and more became tied to concrete figures, such as the number of inspections. The issues have been settled mostly by unilateral actions.

All unilateral actions implied a decrease in the number of inspections. The initial agreement would safeguard public values by more frequent inspections dedicated to public rules, accompanied by some extra checks on the work of certifiers. However, each adjustment of the agreement by the industry meant more leniency towards the industry and fewer guarantees for government.

The cooperation eventually has failed. TOC has been abolished in its original form. The promised evaluation was carried out in 2012. After this, the Dutch Ministry of Public Health took over and changed the regime.

TRUST TO LAST? TEMPORARY EMPLOYMENT AGENCIES

Employment agencies range from multinationals such as Randstad to one-man businesses with a laptop and a van. In the Netherlands, the sector has attracted a lot of political attention, because of much wrongdoing, related for example to underpayment and illegality of employees. In order to gain control over the sector, the legislator has introduced what is known as "employers' liability". In the event of wrongdoing being detected, the party that deployed the services of the dubious employment agency is held liable. Prompted by this employer's liability and an effort to improve the image of the sector, the temporary employment sector started a certification regime. The idea is that employers should select certified employment agencies, thereby reducing the risk of being held liable.

This self-regulatory initiative was a response to pressure from the government. This pressure included a threat of introducing a licensing system. The threat, implying major costs for both government and industry, was real. Until 1998 a licensing regime was in operation and a new regime was already under construction. A major lobby of employment agencies, employers and labor unions resulted in a parliamentary resolution in 2005, the *Motie Bruls*.[8] This resolution called for giving self-regulation a chance before implementing a licensing regime. The sector took this opportunity to develop their own scheme of norms called NEN4400 (after the coordinating Dutch standardization organization NEN).

This was a huge effort, because three sector organizations of employment agencies cooperated and the relations among these organizations have been hostile. This was the first time one centralized was developed and one organization was appointed to manage the scheme. This is the foundation SNA (*Stichting Normering Arbeid*).[9] SNA organizes consultations around the development and management of the scheme. It also harmonizes the certifying bodies involved.

The starting point of interaction is the parliamentary resolution (*Motie Bruls*). The following issues have been prominent in the agendas of the involved parties.

Issue: Reinforcing Self-regulation by Government

The reason why employers supported the lobby against the licensing regime was simple: they want indemnity from liability for the agencies' wrongdoing. The main reason for government to implement this liability rule is to provide incentives to employers to choose their employment agencies carefully. There is a practical reason, too. Employment agencies often do not have enough capital to pay possible fines, where employers do.

The sudden cancellation of the licensing regime was both a curse and a blessing for public inspectorates. It has been a curse, because the cancellation meant years of useless preparation. It has been a blessing, because a licensing regime would be very expensive. The alternative – self-regulation – was out of their hands. However, public inspectors have been involved in the development of NEN4400. Both the Tax Agency and the Labor Inspectorate (and the responsible Ministries) have been reluctant. They were keen to keep public and private responsibilities strictly separated. "We have participated, but it stays a private regime. We have told them time and again. Because a hybrid regime is very dangerous" [government].

They took an advisory role to connect NEN4400 to the public regulatory regime. They kept this advisory role after implementation of NEN4400. However, indemnity of employers' liability is a bridge too far at this stage. Instead, the motto was strict separation of public and private responsibilities. Indemnity would blur the line.

> Then [in case of indemnity] you have to make a distinction between certified agencies and the non-certified agencies in terms of quality. But we cannot tell, because then we would refer to the certificate, and we are not responsible for that. [. . .] The major risk is randomness. That we do not take decisions based on uncontested facts. That we are held liable by private parties. That we must tolerate other certificates in the regime. [government]

In theory, multiple norms could co-exist, developed in a market setting. Indemnities because of compliance to a single norm would suggest a public preference for that norm. The public regulators wanted to prevent themselves getting involved in a market of private norms. This is not just a theoretical idea, because relations within the sector have been antagonistic. The different sector organizations were considering developing their own schemes.

Still, over time this strict separation was abandoned step by step. As a first initiative, the Dutch Tax and Customs Administration started providing some services to certified employment agencies. Those services comprised the issue of remittance confirmations and quickening the provision of financial accounts to certified agencies. These are modest incentives for employment agencies to get certified. The services had to be written down in an agreement. An important legal question here is who should be the authors of the agreement. The sector is represented by hostile sector organizations. The SNA manages the common scheme NEN4400, but their legal status is not clear. They are not formal representatives of the industry. However, they seem to be more neutral than a single sector organization, and the sector organizations did not manage to find one common representative. This made the Dutch Tax and Customs Administration decide to develop and sign the agreement with the SNA.

A second initiative in 2011 is a statutory provision developed by the Ministry of Social Affairs and Employment.[10] The provision holds employers liable that do business with non-certified employment agencies. This is a step towards indemnity in two ways. First, employers that do business with certified agencies get indemnity, although to a very limited extent. Second, this is a statutory provision. Still, NEN4400 and the SNA are not mentioned in the law. There is a reference to it in an appendix, which can be changed relatively easy.

After these initiatives, figures about the behavior of employment agencies were still not encouraging. A possible licensing regime is a recurring theme in political debates. This did not discourage public regulators to give room to the new regime.

> This [self-regulation, hv] is quite a complicated construction. There are requirements to the businesses, registration procedures, etc. There is inspection and meta-inspection. [. . .] From a distance it seems to blossom. They are from the good kind, so we must be supportive. So we shouldn't be too hands on. [. . .] You can tear them down, but it is better to get them improving themselves. If you tear them down, you reduce the incentives for employers to do business with certified employment agencies. And we introduced the employers liability to incentify them in the first place. We would not undermine this. [government]

In 2012 a major step towards indemnity was taken. Under constant pressure of the lobby, the Dutch Ministry of Finance took the initiative to organize meetings with sector organizations, employers' organizations, labor unions, Ministries and the SNA foundation. The meetings resulted in an agreement about conditions for indemnity. One important condition – among others – was specifying the criteria for non-conformity to NEN4400. The conditions were serious, and this restricted indemnity is only applicable to tax paying matters (not welfare issues and illegality). Still, this is a breakthrough. At least the Tax Administration left the idea of strict separation between public and private responsibilities. Now certified employment agencies are explicitly favored by a public regulator and NEN4400 is referred to as the standard.

Issue: Information Exchange between the Public and the Private

The Ministry of Finance signed a further agreement with SNA about information exchange. The agreement enables certifying bodies to report wrongdoings by foreign employment agencies. These foreign agencies were conceived as a big problem, because they employed considerable amounts of personnel illegally, while staying largely invisible.

Although the SNA signed the agreement, the industry was not enthusiastic. The SNA is glad to receive information from public regulators to enrich the self-regulatory system. However, reporting to public regulators is a different story, especially in this case. The essence of NEN4400 is the estimation of employers' risks to be held liable for law violations by employment agencies. By reporting information to public regulators they in fact increase those risks. "If an employment agency knows that you are going to exchange information with the government, they will lose interest. This way we are undermining our system" [standardization industry].

In fact, certifying bodies are interested in the risk of employment agencies being fined by public regulators rather than in the violations they would be fined for. Would the public inspectorate fine the employment agency? This way the certifying bodies consider the conduct of public inspectorates in their judgments.

> A client had delay of payment. The Tax Administration and I were auditing there at the same time period. Yes, there was delay, but the client was catching up. In this situation the Tax Administration wouldn't hurt this business by fining it. They would develop an arrangement, without a hurry. If I would withhold certification I would abort his business, so I don't do that. [standardization industry]

A certifying body would rarely report incidents in this "grey area" of employment agency practices, because they have a client–supplier relationship, wherein some trust and discretion is essential. They probably would report practices by a clearly rogue employment agency. However, it is doubtful whether they would accept such an agency as a client in the first place, because of the reputation risks involved.

The agreement was a commitment on paper, but it resulted in very little reporting in practice. There were just too few incentives for certifying bodies to report.

A second effort for information exchange started in 2008 and turned out to be more successful. The Minister of Social Affairs asked the largest sector organization of employment agencies (ABU[11]) to evaluate the self-regulatory efforts after the *Motie Bruls*. Their report also encompassed some recommendations. ABU suggests making employment agencies more visible by obliging them to join a public register. The Minister then asked SNA to approach newly registered agencies for certification and – if the agencies show no interest in certification – to inform the inspectorates. They then can use this information for their risk analysis. This is a major change in the SNA's role, which posed some existential questions to certifying bodies. "If an agency approaches SNA, it indirectly approaches the government. If SNA becomes gatekeeper of government, then what is voluntary about our regulations?" [standardization industry].

These objections have resulted in many discussions. Without getting answers to these existential questions, however, they have agreed upon it. A bill concerning the obligatory registration appeared and has been accepted by parliament in March 2012.[12]

Trust that Seems to Last

This case also started with explicitly expressed trust in self-regulation, as reflected in the *Motie Bruls*. Still, in the first instance the public and private regimes were strictly separated. Over time, however, joint public and private efforts for compliance emerged. The SNA foundation is a central actor here, developing ties towards governments, certifiers and industry and acting as a problem solving intermediary between them. These efforts emerged against the odds. Figures about registered agencies are still not encouraging. The efforts resulted in more institutional arrangements. Some proved effective, others did not. Furthermore, they show public and private responsibilities gradually getting interwoven.

THE EVOLUTION FROM "TRUST-ON-PAPER" TO "TRUST-IN-ACTION"

In the poultry case, a policy framework drawn up by the Ministry of Agriculture was the foundation for an agreement signed by government and industry. The framework described the conditions for inspections, certifiers and industry to cooperate. In the case of employment agencies, the government already had a liability regime for employers and considered a licensing regime. Industry has pushed government to leave the implementation of a licensing regime and trust self-regulation instead. During the development of the self-regulatory regime bilateral agreements among Ministries were drawn up, and the SNA developed as an informal industry representative. Table 7.1 summarizes what happened after trust was announced on paper. The left column represents the empirical questions in the fourth section.

There are two considerable similarities between the cases. First, both cases started with "trust-on-paper". Second, in both cases a couple of tough issues emerged. In both cases such issues have been expected. Third, for both cases there are serious doubts whether public values are safeguarded, at least in the way governments would have liked them to be.

The institutional arrangements differed in many respects. Three differences seem to be of most importance here. First, the arrangement in the poultry sector is developed on a policy level by the former Ministry of Agriculture and later applied to an operational level by means of an agreement. The arrangements in the employment sector were largely developed on an operational level, by covenants between public inspectorates, business representatives, and the SNA. Second, and related, rules for cooperation were already well-defined at the start by TOC, while the starting point for co-regulation with the employment agencies was just an announcement of trust. Further arrangements were developed later on. Third, in the employment agency sector there seem to be natural incentives for the industry to get the process of co-regulation going. Indemnity for liability was a motive for industry to keep in contact with government. This made all institutional arrangements satisfiers. In the poultry sector, such a motive was lacking. Every additional rule by government meant a dissatisfier, at least a reduction of a pre-calculated profit for industry.

Perhaps as a consequence, the stories unfold differently. In the case of employment agencies, governments and industry have negotiated almost continuously, driven by both the current liability regime and the threat of a license regime. The case shows a development from strict separation of governments' and industries' responsibilities towards joint responsibilities. Both government and industry have made concessions. The liability regime has been weakened and the norms for self-regulation substantialized. Information exchange has been facilitated by measures to make employment agencies more visible. In the poultry case the issues have not been solved jointly. Instead, two issues have been "solved" by unilateral action. After the implications of TOC and the agreement became visible, resistance of industry has grown. The rules in the policy framework and the agreement have not been changed. An evaluation was promised, but was delayed. Industry did not wait and felt legitimized to change the rules unilaterally. In other words, while in the employment agencies solutions emerged and became new institutional arrangements, in the poultry sector no innovative solutions were found. Instead, the existing institutional arrangement became subject to resistance.

Table 7.1   Two trust–cooperation processes of co-regulation

	Poultry sector	Employment agencies
Institutional arrangements ("trust-on-paper")	– An agreement between government and industry as an application of a policy framework (TOC) by government – Agreements about the distribution and frequencies of inspections and responsibilities for these inspections – Overall design by government – Separation of execution by private parties and meta-regulation by government	– Parliamentary resolution (*Motie Bruls*) providing leeway for self-regulation under threat of a licensing regime – Multiple, bilateral agreements initiated by the self-regulating industry. Agreements were about information exchange and stimulating self-regulation by governments
Issues emerging	– The number of unannounced audits – Auditing certifying bodies – Fining by certifiers	– Reinforcing self-regulation by government – Information exchange between the public and the private
Problem-solving processes	– Issues mainly solved by unilateral actions by the regulated industry, undermining the arrangement – One issue is solved by a concession by government	– Negotiated agreements driven by industry lobby and political pressure – Private foundation (SNA) catalyzing operational problem-solving process by networking
How did arrangements develop?	– Growing resistance of industry after implementation of arrangements. Arrangements have not been changed – Eventually TOC has been abolished in its original form	– A development from strict separation between government and industry towards joint responsibility – Concessions on both sides: the liability regime has been weakened, the norms for self-regulation substantialized

In one of the cases, trust and cooperation stopped to reinforce each other. This mutual reinforcement process (coined "trust-in-action") continued in the other case, even without indications of the effectiveness of cooperation. In the remainder of this section I look for clues about the relation between the institutional arrangements and the way trust and cooperation provide positive feedback to each other. The temptation is there to attribute the outcomes to the arrangements. This of course should be done with great care, because this contribution involves just two cases and many variables are at stake. Each conclusion will be followed by an agenda for further research.

1. On an operational level, intermediary actors between government and industry play a crucial role in trust and cooperation. Institutional arrangements restricting these actors harm the positive feedback loop between trust and cooperation.
In the poultry case, problem ownership issues emerged. The Ministry of Agriculture developed the framework as a set of conditions for co-regulation, but the Ministry did not want to sign the agreement that applied the framework to the sector. This was to express that the sector and not the Ministry would be responsible. However, when conflicts emerged between actors regarding the framework, no actor felt responsible for conflict resolution. This way TOC became an orphan. In the employment agency sector, cooperation has not been predefined by a framework. There was much ambiguity about questions how to cooperate and about public and private responsibilities. Multiple public regulators were involved, but also industry was fragmented and even antagonistic. Still, or even because of this, an organization started to act as a problem owner. The foundation SNA took a central position, keeping ties to all actors involved, including public regulators, industry associations and certification bodies. Both government and industry had a motive to let this happen, because the SNA provided the necessary coordination to make self-regulation happen. The SNA became an intermediary between government and industry as both "trustors" and "trustees". In the poultry sector the *IKB-ei* Foundation failed to play such an intermediary role. It felt restricted by the institutional arrangements, being a policy framework and an agreement already drawn up. It had few incentives to defend the framework and agreement for several reasons. First, the arrangements did not provide solutions for the problems at hand. Second, the Foundation was not the author. Third, as solutions were not found, the framework and agreement became subject to criticism in the course of time, especially from the industry.

Private intermediaries as operational brokers of trust   Institutional arrangements may restrict actors to act as intermediaries between government and industry. The importance of such intermediaries (or "third parties") has been sparsely acknowledged before. Hallström and Boström (2010: 112–117) observed that the roles of intermediaries for international NGO-driven schemes such as FSC and MSC – they call them "secretariats" – increased in importance over time as the standards and the governance structures became institutionalized. They gradually assumed more decisions, tasks, and responsibilities. For instance, Nooteboom (1999) sketches eight functions of third parties, among them trust building and preventing conflicts to be harmful. The suggestion here is that this potential can be negatively affected by institutional arrangements that fail to provide sufficient leeway to these actors. If leeway is provided, these intermediaries may evolve as crucial elements building trust over the public–private divide. The trust-enhancing potential of these private, intermediary agencies might be crucial for successful co-regulation. Their behavior is understudied and it has huge potential as an object for further research.

2. However, on a policy level co-regulation provides incentives to government to limit leeway to operational parties involved.
Both cases show continuous discussions about tasks and responsibilities. These discussions are sometimes taken up to an existential level. In both cases the separation between the public and the private has been an important issue. Put simply, there is potential to contest almost anything, making cooperation in the context of co-regulation very ambiguous.

Government may be tempted to organize cooperation neatly on a meta-level to avoid accountability issues, as it did for the poultry case. The policy framework TOC was dedicated to define the conditions for self-regulating industries to "take their responsibilities". This happened in a hierarchical framework designed by government. The framework represents a conscious government-driven process, or masterplan. Private parties had to accept their roles as formulated in the framework. The institutional arrangements as designed enabled cooperation on an operational level. However, its definitions and conditions resulted in conflicts. The design proved unable to solve these conflicts, as it represented the perspective of one actor. Over time the designer and the design became subject to criticism and they politicized.

Co-regulation as co-creation　　This invites us to reflect on the concept of co-regulation. Co-regulation is generally presented as an arrangement (Van der Heijden, 2009), a regime (Lodge and Wegrich, 2012: 101) or as delegation (Haufler, 2013; Bamberger, 2006). They present an end state, a fixed moment in time where an agreement between government and self-regulating industry is settled. A strong focus on end states, however, leaves important questions unanswered: who developed the arrangement? And for whom is it an instrument? The employment agency case shows that co-regulation is more than an end state. It shows that "trust-in-action" may emerge during a process of co-creation. This is a time of getting to grips, of trial-and-error, before any arrangement is settled.

If a government treats co-regulation as their arrangement rather than a co-creating process, it will be tempted to prioritize accountability concerns. How can government account for the conduct of industry? Is the self-regulating industry doing well enough, so that government as the ultimate responsible actor may not worry too much? Those questions – logical as they may be – will eventually result in arrangements that can be viewed as an artifact of distrust rather than trust, wherein "trust-in-action" will hardly thrive. Further study may tackle the tradeoffs for government between accountability and more pragmatic advantages (e.g., efficiency) of co-regulation and how government acts upon these tradeoffs over time. Are these tradeoffs hard and predefined by government in an institutional arrangement that should serve as an end state? Or are these tradeoffs more fluid and co-created while the co-regulatory process is running?

3. Urgency on the level of high politics mitigates these incentives.
Then, why did this not happen in the employment agency case? Here there was no preconceived masterplan. Multiple ministries and inspectorates have been involved, all busy with their own definitions of what is a public and what a private responsibility. Indeed, the intention to separate public and private responsibilities was abandoned by government in the course of time.

In fact, the incentives to (over)organize cooperation were in place. The status and potential consequences of the agreements were criticized within the departments and public regulators. They were, however, forced to cooperate by political pressure. A license regime was developed and there were serious questions about the legal status of SNA as a partner for government. The industry lobby, driven by the liability regime, has found fertile ground in the Dutch parliament, which was concerned about lowering the administrative burden of regulation for the Dutch industry. Moreover, there was not one coordinating Ministry involved that could prescribe the rules of the game. The result was a patchwork of agreements that emerged over time, rather than a holistic design by one actor.

Liability regimes as "indirect enforced self-regulation"   Liability regimes have been proposed before (e.g., Parker, 2002: 241). However, the employment agency case shows a special "multi-actor" liability. It is holding a client liable for services carried out by someone else. This facilitated co-regulation, because the service providers had incentives to show their clients that they would not pose liability risks. That said, this liability construction was not purposed to facilitate co-regulation. It was simply impossible to detect and fine the employment agencies themselves. That is why government changed liabilities to the clients of these employment agencies. Further research should be done about liability regimes that may serve as "indirect enforced self-regulation". However an institution of distrust, this arrangement leaves considerable room to regulated industries – in this case, employment agencies – to develop their own regime.

CONCLUSION AND DISCUSSION: TRUST AND DISTRUST ON MULTIPLE LEVELS

Co-regulation is not a new feature and it may not disappear in the future. Government and industry will need each other's knowledge and resources. In this contribution I have asked how trust emerges among government and industry in cases of co-regulation. This requires an interplay between trust and cooperation among public and private actors. What is more, this interplay is embedded in institutions. Institutional arrangements may guide the process of positive feedback between trust and cooperation, or block it. Trust and cooperation may also result in new institutional arrangements.

Two in-depth case studies were performed to identify the interaction between institutional arrangements and the mutual trust-cooperation process. The cases showed large differences between governments cooperating with self-regulating industries. Both case studies start with explicitly expressed public and private trust in co-regulation. In a first case a policy framework on co-regulation and an agreement were developed. The other case shows the Dutch parliament explicitly announcing its commitment to co-regulation. However, in the first case this "trust-on-paper" did not translate into cooperation and trust nurturing each other ("trust-in-action"), while in the other it did.

How does trust emerge among government and industry in case of co-regulation? On an operational level I found a crucial role for intermediaries – in both cases private scheme managers – to keep cooperation and trust nurturing each other. They have ties with all actors of both government and industry. However, they need leeway to improvise and make operational deals. In the first case this leeway was not provided, in the second it was.

Co-regulation provides an ambiguous context for institutional arrangements to develop. What roles and responsibilities belong to whom? Who is accountable for what? Is government either *de jure* or *de facto* ultimately responsible for co-regulatory arrangements? These kinds of questions provide an ambiguous context for institutional arrangements to develop. The ambiguity of co-regulation appeared to provide incentives to government to guide the cooperation process with institutional arrangements that prevent accountability problems. In the first case government was tempted to make a holistic policy design. This, however, encountered too much resistance from industry and provided too little leeway for the intermediaries. In the second case this temptation was resisted. There was no clear policy framework, leaving room to the operational level to solve issues and create institutional arrangements along the way. The explanation why this temptation was resisted can be found on a political level. The incentives of industry lobby and politicians were aligned to keep cooperation going and provide leeway to co-regulation. It suggests that support from a political level is essential to avoid over-organization of cooperation.

Furthermore, I found a willingness of those investing their time in cooperation on an operational level to accept losses in favor of learning effects and problem solving. However, in the first case they had to comply with an institutional design imposed from above. Here policy designers felt incentives to safeguard public values and draw up rules about accountability. A certain amount of trust on this meta-level of institutional design may well be a condition for trust emerging on an operational level of co-regulation. The cases reveal that on an operational level, "trust-in-action" is both an enabler and a result of cooperation. Cooperation and trust are shown to be dependent on the way they are embedded in institutional arrangements of co-regulation as provided by government. These very institutional arrangements, however, may also prove to be artifacts of distrust.

NOTES

1. The same may hold for the self-regulating industry as will be shown later in this chapter. In this contribution, however, I will focus on the government's perspective.
2. More about this case, its regulation and its issues in Van der Voort, 2015a, 2015b.
3. These included the former *Voedsel en Warenautoriteit* (Netherlands Food and Consumer Product Safety Authority; VWA), the *Algemene Inspectiedienst* (AID; a policing service about food and animal welfare) and the former *Controlebureau voor Pluimvee en eieren* (CPE; a private organization that carried out inspections mandated by the Ministry of Public Health).
4. Translates into "Supervising Inspections".
5. EU Commission Regulation 589/2008.
6. All interviews were held in Dutch. The quotes are translations by the author.
7. More specifically: this deals with the norm EN45011 regarding product certification.
8. Dutch Parliamentary Papers 2004/2005, 17050/287.
9. They refer to themselves as "Labour Standards Register".

10. Art. 692 Netherlands Civil Code.
11. They refer to themselves as the "Federation of Private Employment Agencies".
12. Dutch Parliamentary Papers 2011/2012 32872, nr.7.

REFERENCES

Bachmann, R. and A.C. Inkpen (2011), 'Understanding institutional-based trust building processes in inter-organizational relationships', *Organization Studies*, **32** (2), 281–301.

Bamberger, K. (2006), 'Regulation as delegation: Private firms, decisionmaking, and accountability in the administrative state', *Duke Law Journal*, **56** (2), 377–468.

Bartle, I. and P. Vass (2005), 'Self-regulation and the regulatory state; A survey of policy and practice', Research Report 17, Centre for the Study of Regulated Industries (CRI), University of Bath.

Börzel, T.A. and T. Risse (2010), 'Governance without a state: Can it work', *Regulation & Governance*, **4**, 113–134.

Dorbeck-Jung, B.R., M.J. Oude Vrielink, J.F. Gosselt, J.J. Van Hoof and M.D.T. de Jong (2010), 'Contested hybridization of regulation: Failure of the Dutch regulatory system to protect minors from harmful media', *Regulation & Governance*, **4**, 154–174.

Dyer, J. and W. Chu (2011), 'The determinants of trust in supplier–automaker relations in the US, Japan, and Korea: A retrospective', *Journal of International Business Studies*, **42**, 28–34.

Garcia Martinez, M., P. Verbruggen and A. Fearne (2013), 'Risk-based approaches to food safety regulation: What role for co-regulation?', *Journal of Risk Research*, **16** (9), 1101–1121.

Gassenheimer, J.B. and C. Manolis (2001), 'The influence of product customization and supplier selection on future intentions: The mediating effects of salesperson and organizational trust', *Journal of Managerial Issues*, **13** (4), 418–435.

Gunningham, N. and J. Rees (1997), 'Industry self-regulation: An institutional perspective', *Law and Policy*, **19** (4), 363–414.

Hallström, K.T. and M. Boström (2010), *Transnational multi-stakeholder standardization; Organizing fragile non-state authority*, Cheltenham, UK and Northampton, MA, USA: Edward Elgar Publishing.

Haufler, V. (2013), 'New forms of governance: Certification regimes as social regulations of the global market', in E. Meidinger, C. Elliot and G. Oesten (eds), *Social and political dimensions of forest certification*, Remagen-Oberwinter: Forstbuch Verlag, pp. 237–247.

Havinga, T. (2006), 'Private regulation of food safety by supermarkets', *Law & Policy*, **28** (40), 515–533.

Heijden, J. Van der (2009), *Building regulatory enforcement regimes; Comparative analysis of private sector involvement in the enforcement of public building regulations*, Amsterdam: IOS Press.

Hutter, B. (2006), 'The role of non-state actors in regulation', Discussion Paper 37, The Centre for Analysis of Risk and Regulation (CARR), London School of Economics.

Lane, C. (1998), 'Introduction: Theories and issues in the study of trust', in C. Lane and R. Bachman (eds), *Trust within and between organizations, conceptual issues and empirical applications*, Oxford: Oxford University Press, pp. 1–30.

Lodge, M. and K. Wegrich (2012), *Managing regulation; Regulatory analysis, politics and policy*, London: Palgrave MacMillan.

Luhmann, N. (1979), *Trust and power*, Chicester: John Wiley.

Möllering, G. (2014), 'Trust, calculativeness, and relationships: A special issue 20 years after Williamson's warning', *Journal of Trust Research*, **4** (1), 1–21.

Newell. S. and J. Swan (2000), 'Trust and inter-organizational networking', *Human Relations*, **53** (10), 1287–1328.

Nooteboom, B. (1996), 'Trust, opportunism and governance: A process and control model', *Organization Studies*, **17** (6), 985–1010.

Nooteboom, B. (1999), 'The triangle; Roles of the go-between', in R.Th.A.J. Leenders and S.M. Gabbay (eds), *Corporate social capital and liability*, Dordrecht: Kluwer Academic Publishers, pp. 341–355.

Nooteboom, B. (2002), *Trust: Forms, foundations, functions, failures, and figures*, Cheltenham, UK and Northampton, MA, USA: Edward Elgar Publishing.

Norman, P.M. (2002), 'Protecting knowledge in strategic alliances: resource and relational characteristics', *Journal of High Technology Management Research*, **13** (2), 177–202.

Parker, C. (2002), *The open corporation; Effective self-regulation and democracy*, Cambridge: Cambridge University Press.

Potosky, M. and A. Prakash (2009), 'A club theory approach to voluntary programs', in M. Potosky and A. Prakash (eds), *Voluntary programs; A club theory perspective*, Cambridge MA: MIT Press, pp. 17–39.

Seppänen, R., K. Blomqvist and S. Sundqvist (2007), 'Measuring inter-organizational trust – A critical review of the empirical research in 1990–2003', *Industrial Marketing Management*, **36**, 249–265.

Six, F.E. (2007), 'Building interpersonal trust within organizations: A relational signaling perspective', *Journal of Management and Governance*, **11**, 285–309.

Smith Ring, P. and A.H. Van de Ven (1994), 'Developmental processes of cooperative interorganizational relationships', *The Academy of Management Review*, **19** (1), 90–118.

Voort, H. Van der (2015a), 'The meta-governance of co-regulation: Safeguarding the quality of Dutch eggs', in T. Havinga, F. Van Waarden and D. Casey (eds), *The changing landscape of food governance: public and private encounters*, Cheltenham, UK and Northampton, MA, USA: Edward Elgar Publishing, pp. 238–257.

Voort, H. Van der (2015b), 'Co-regulatory failure in the food industry: Explaining regulatory failure by means of two contrasting interpretations of governance', *European Journal of Risk Regulation*, **6** (4), 502–511.

Young-Ybarra, C. and M.F. Wiersema (1999), 'Strategic flexibility in information technology alliances: The influence of transaction cost economics and social exchange theory', *Organization Science*, **10** (4), 439–459.

Zaheer, A., B. McEvily and V. Perrone (1998), 'Does trust matter? Exploring the effects of interorganizational and interpersonal trust on performance', *Organization Science*, **9** (2), 141–159.

Zand, D.E. (1997), *The leadership triad, knowledge, trust and power*, Oxford: Oxford University Press.

Zucker, L.G. (1986), 'Production of trust: Institutional sources of economic structure', *Research in Organizational Behaviour*, **8**, 53–111.

8. Deliberate trust-building by autonomous government agencies: evidence from responses to the 2009 H1N1 swine flu pandemic

Erik Baekkeskov

This chapter shows that autonomous government agencies may act deliberately for the sake of gaining trust from other actors in regulatory systems, rather than relying solely on institutions and other exogenous trust credentials. The analysis conceptualizes trust-building as a sub-set of reputation-seeking activity. It uses direct participant observations of two decision processes within a European public health agency that yielded responses to the 2009 H1N1 swine influenza pandemic. By demonstrating how such a government agency *actually* behaves, the chapter helps to fill a gap in the prevailing literature (Groenleer, 2009, p. 17).

Over the past few decades, in Europe and elsewhere, autonomous government agencies have proliferated and grown increasingly important as specialized advisors to or sources of information for regulators and decision-makers and as formal regulators in themselves. Hence, government agencies' real impact on the regulatory systems in developed democracies has become significant (Groenleer, 2009). How autonomous agencies act, why they do so, and the relationship of their actions to trust, are all worthwhile subjects that this chapter addresses.

The analysis proceeds from the insight that beliefs, like an agency's level of trustworthiness, can be built on actors' own experiences of the agency. Alternatively, agencies may let their trustworthiness depend on credentials beyond their control such as their legally codified mandates or the prestige of their fields of expertise (Bachmann and Inkpen, 2011). This leads to at least two alternative strategies for agencies that wish to appear trustworthy. They can passively let exogenous forces shape the beliefs about their trustworthiness that other actors in state and society have. Or agencies can deliberately engage in trust-building by seeking to manipulate the experiences that other actors have. The analytical questions become: do autonomous agencies *actually* take actions for the sake of shaping other actors' experiences of them? Are such actions directed at establishing or confirming trustworthiness?

Conceptually, trustworthiness can be understood as a specific reputation. As the theory section will detail, reputation and trust use a common conceptual component: an audience's beliefs about an actor. But the concepts operate at different levels. Reputation is the amalgam of beliefs about the agency (i.e., the image) that an audience holds. Trustworthiness is a specific belief about an agency held by an audience. Hence, an agency's trustworthiness can be seen as a part of its reputation. This means that an agency may hope to shape its trustworthiness *vis-à-vis* particular audiences by manipulating audiences' image of the agency, that is, by seeking a particular reputation.

Finding that trust-building can actually motivate agency action is an important advance. If agencies take actions for the sake of audiences' trust, then they may be setting aside priorities like fulfilling agency missions. Conversely, seeking trust may be less insidious or self-serving than motivations attributed to bureaucrats by public choice and bureaucratic politics scholarship. Hence, as a deliberate pursuit of government agencies, trust-building is neither self-evident nor necessarily legitimate.

Linking agency reputation-seeking and regulatory trust theories offers a handle on answering the analytical questions. The literature on government agency reputation-seeking has shown that agencies in different polities *can*, in fact, take action for the sake of constructing their own reputations by way of shaping how outside audiences experience them (Carpenter, 2010; Maor, 2011; Baekkeskov, 2014). The specific research question addressed in this chapter, therefore, is whether an agency known to have deliberately sought to shape its reputation included trustworthiness in the images it disseminated.

As noted, the empirical context is a public health agency located in Europe (EPHA) and responding to the 2009 H1N1 flu pandemic. Earlier analyses have shown that some of this agency's decisions were taken in order to affect its reputation (Baekkeskov 2014). Further, the agency is likely to want the trust of certain audiences because it is not a direct regulator. Rather, it is situated at the international level and can affect health regulation and care indirectly through information it generates. Key audiences for the agency are those that make use of these outputs. One set consists of health regulators and other national and international policymakers in Europe. Another is communities of health professionals and public health scientists. A third is the general public. It is no great leap to believe that EPHA's outputs will tend to impact health care and regulation more if these key audiences trust the agency (which audiences matter more awaits empirical discovery).

This chapter addresses the research question by looking closely at H1N1 response choices taken at EPHA in 2009. The empirical test is whether seeking a reputation for trustworthiness won out over alternative priorities. The data are real-time participant-observations and interviews on two decision processes. Most critically, they show that reputation-seeking related to gaining trust from particular audiences could *decide* response choices, and thus *overrule* rival priorities of the agency. In addition to showing that trust-building can shape agency action, the finding suggests that building trust was regarded by agency leaders as important rather than marginal.

Is there reputation-seeking that is *not* about trustworthiness? Earlier studies have linked reputation-seeking to real autonomy from elected politicians and other superiors in the formal hierarchy of a polity (Carpenter, 2010; Maor, 2010; Roberts, 2006). Real autonomy means the ability to "induce politicians to defer to the wishes of the agency even when they prefer otherwise" (Carpenter, 2001, p. 4). To achieve such autonomy, agencies construct alliances with interests in the state, economy and society (i.e., audiences) based on beliefs about their records (i.e., reputations).

The pursuit of autonomy does not specify contents of agencies' reputations or constraints on reputation-seeking, however. Linking reputation-seeking to trust-building gives a clearer understanding of contents and limitations. Trustworthiness differs from alternative reputations, such as predictability or cooperativeness (Mayer et al., 1995). In addition, the reputation concept illuminates that trust is one audience's belief about an actor, and that the actor can take action to deliberately encourage or discourage this belief. Gaining and maintaining an audience's trust thus requires continual efforts by an agency, which is likely to constrain its repertoire of action and its alternative uses of resources. Becoming trustworthy to powerful audiences may lead to ambiguous outcomes like greater real autonomy; but as suggested, trust may also enable an agency with indirect powers such as EPHA to become more effective as a contributor to social outcomes like public health.

The remaining chapter is organized into sections as follows. The next section reviews the core concepts of reputation-seeking and trustworthiness, and develops empirical expectations based on these. The subsequent section discusses the case selection, data and analyses. The final sections present the analyses and conclusions.

LINKING REPUTATION-SEEKING AND TRUSTWORTHINESS CONCEPTS

Behaviours of government agencies are a key theoretical concern (Baekkeskov, 2014). There is considerable literature on the actual rather than idealized or intuitive motivations for bureaucratic behaviour (Niskanen, 1971; Dunleavy, 1991; Pressman and Wildavsky, 1973; Wilson, 1989). In this tradition, as previously described, explanations have recently been sought for the ability of nominally autonomous executive agencies to gain or maintain real autonomy from elected politicians by way of their reputations among audiences in the state, economy and society (Carpenter, 2000, 2001, 2010; Carpenter and Krause, 2011; Roberts, 2006). The reputational debate confirms that bureau leaders' choices are not only made to fulfil formally legitimated missions. Crucially, this implies that specialized expert agencies cannot be expected simply to offer their expertise as inputs for further regulatory activity.

Agency reputation-seeking is thus linked to the democratic legitimacy of public governance and the effectiveness and efficiency of public organizations. Departmental hierarchies in Europe are frequently fragmented and include formally autonomous agencies (Pollitt and Bouckaert, 2004; Christensen and Lægreid, 2002; Sørensen and Torfing, 2007; Osborne, 2010). Such agencies often have specialized mandates, either as direct regulators or as specialized advisors in policy domains (Groenleer, 2009). Links between formal and real agency autonomy in European contexts have received attention (Yesilkagit, 2004, p. 531; Yesilkagit and Christensen, 2010; Yesilkagit and Van Thiel, 2008; Groenleer, 2009). But despite the intuitive link between expertise and reputation, study of reputation-seeking by specialized government agencies outside of the U.S. is in its infancy (Baekkeskov, 2014). In addition, agencies' reputation-seeking actions have rarely been linked to trust-building in any literature. Thus, there remains a strong need to explain the behaviours of autonomous agencies in Europe, and influence on these actions of reputation and trust in particular.

The reputation of a government agency is defined by Daniel Carpenter as "symbolic beliefs about an organization – its capacities, intentions, history, mission – and these images are embedded in a network of multiple audiences" (Carpenter, 2010, p. 33). Hence, an agency seeking to shape its reputation aims at the dyad of an image and an audience that can believe in that image. In addition, reputation is thus value-neutral, in that images can be liked or disliked by audiences that believe them. Consequently, reputation-*seeking* can be defined as "an intentional effort, however effective, to change or maintain a particular image believed by an identifiable audience or a network of audiences" (Baekkeskov, 2014, p. 4). Empirically, "reputation-seeking can be detected in moments when decision-makers, such as agency leaders, take decisions that are openly justified by likely effects on images of the agency held by specific audiences" (Baekkeskov, 2014, p. 4).

Reputation and trust are related but separate concepts. A commonly accepted definition of trust between entities emphasizes vulnerability contingent on beliefs: "the willingness of a party to be vulnerable to the actions of another party based on the expectation that the other will perform a particular action important to the trustor, irrespective of the ability to monitor or control that other party" (Mayer et al., 1995, p. 712). Like an agency's reputation (see previous discussion), trust in an agency is based on what one or more audiences believe. But in contrast to agency reputation, agency trust is a value in itself rather than being a value-neutral category. In static terms, an audience can trust, not trust or distrust the agency because of its reputation. Dynamically, one actor may grant or withhold its trust from another based on the other's reputation (Bachmann and Inkpen, 2011, p. 284).

The key trust-related reputation for the agency, then, is one that includes trust*worthiness*. The agency that relies on trust for its effectiveness has an instrumental interest in having important audiences believe images of the agency that include trustworthiness. In turn, "perceived trustworthiness" is "a function of the trustee's perceived ability, benevolence, and integrity" (Mayer et al., 1995, pp. 715, 720). Having (high) ability in a field, integrity in its actions and benevolence toward the trustor will equate to being (highly) trustworthy (Mayer et al., 1995, pp. 721–722). Hence, a reputation for trustworthiness turns on an audience's beliefs about the trustee's abilities, integrity and degree of benevolence toward it.

How are reputation-seeking and trust-building related? Given the shared emphasis on beliefs in the two conceptual schemes, perceived trustworthiness *means* having a reputation for trustworthiness. That is, a trustor believes that a trustee has relevant ability, integrity and benevolent intentions. An audience may or may not grant its trust to a trustworthy agency. But it will presumably withhold its trust from an untrustworthy agency. Reputation-seeking can thus be instrumental to gaining trust: by including trustworthiness in the image an agency seeks to project to an audience, it can reasonably hope that the audience will grant it trust.

The previous discussion stated that an agency with indirect powers may depend on others' trust to be effective. The reference is the observation that trustworthiness can affect whether an agency gains relevance in regulation or street-level action. Before direct regulators or actors will turn to inputs from outside, they are likely to have to believe that the inputs will be pertinent. Hence, establishing a reputation for useful or valuable outputs can, for instance, lead an indirect regulator to have actual impact on regulation.

This means that building and sustaining an image as a supplier of outputs that are important to direct regulators or street-level actors is likely to be a condition for effectiveness for government agencies with advisory but no direct regulatory mandates. A faith in important outputs corresponds to trust as defined previously: an expectation that the trustee's actions will be important to the trustor. Hence, seeking a reputation for trustworthiness can be an agency's strategy for actually gaining effect.

There are many paths to becoming trustworthy (Poppo, 2013). Agencies may rely solely on exogenous forces that shape the beliefs of its audiences (trust credentials). For instance, institutions may substitute for an audience's own experience of the agency (Bachmann and Inkpen, 2011). In contrast, reputation-seeking emphasizes an agency's efforts to construct a particular reputation. That is, an agency may deliberately signal competence, integrity and benevolence toward an audience, to give it direct experiences upon which to build its beliefs.

In the agency's decision-making, deliberate trust-building would mean that demonstrating ability, integrity and/or benevolence toward an identifiable audience overrules reasons for taking alternative actions. But what is a clear indication of such ability and intent? One is exogenous trust credentials, as previously discussed. Deliberate trust-building is an alternative. Harkening back to the common definition of trust, a critical indication of trustworthiness is that potential trustees *show* potential trustors that they do important things (see above). In addition, an agency may 'signal' its intent to do so by taking actions that are "too costly for those with untrustworthy quality" to take (Poppo, 2013, p. 137). This yields a set of *empirical expectations: agencies that deliberately seek to show their trustworthiness to specific audiences can demonstrate the credibility of that image to those audiences. This can be done by giving the audience one or more direct experiences that the agency will take actions that matter to the audience, and will do so at significant cost to itself.*

The following section presents methodological considerations related to the selection of cases, the operationalization of the key concepts, and case analyses that test the empirical expectations above.

DECISION CASE SELECTION AND PARTICIPANT OBSERVATION POSSIBILITIES

The case analyses that follow are selected to show whether government agencies can choose trust-building over rival priorities for action. Hence, the argument relies on the demonstrable existence and relative power of such reasons (George and Bennett, 2005; Bennett, 2010), rather than their estimated prevalence among motivations for all agency choices.

The analysed context is the previously described European public health agency (EPHA) as it selected among very different courses of action in response to the 2009 H1N1 influenza pandemic. Pandemic responses call on public health agencies to respond within specific and hectic time-frames and to uncertain situations (Boin, McConnell, and 't Hart, 2008). Pandemics require long-running and sometimes intensive effort. Since agencies must act and do so continually, they are compelled to demonstrate their abilities and intentions to audiences that depend on or can opt to use the outputs. Agencies thus generate direct experiences that can confirm or belie audiences' beliefs about them (Maor, 2010, p. 134). Hence, public health agency reputations for trustworthiness (i.e., perceived high ability, integrity and benevolent intentions) are likely to be particularly malleable while the pandemic lasts.

EPHA has many audiences. As described in the introduction, EPHA is primarily a supplier of information and judgments about public health. Such outputs were shared in many forums during the 2009 pandemic response. These included meetings with national and other international government bodies, conferences with public health scientists and health care providers, and web platforms that health professionals and the general public could access. Hence, the EPHA could encourage several and different audiences to trust it. Conversely, the agency could be forced into choices about which audience's trust was more important.

Two cases have been selected for analysis. Each is a decision process that culminated in a substantive action by the agency and to the exclusion of explicit alternatives. Previously published analyses have shown that EPHA actions in these and other cases were taken for the sake of reputation-seeking rather than direct benefits to public health or employee well-being (Baekkeskov, 2014). From the empirical expectation developed in the previous section, deliberate trust-building is indicated if: *EPHA's decision-makers express that the chosen action is likely to give the favoured audience a direct experience of EPHA doing something important, less "important" alternatives are set aside* and *the chosen action is costly to EPHA*. Hence, three additional case selection criteria were adopted for the present analysis:

1. *Direct evidence*: using direct observations rather than indirect (retrospective) reporting reduces the risk of hindsight and missing information biases. It also enables assessment of the empirical expectation that action was chosen because of its importance to a particular audience, while alternative considerations were set aside.

2. *Substantive cases*: using decisions that demanded substantive EPHA resources reduces the risk that the choices were regarded as trivial or casual. This works to satisfy the empirical expectation that the credibility of signals is strengthened by high cost.

3. *Dissimilar cases and repetition*: using two cases that exemplify different kinds of pandemic response decisions enables assessment of whether trust-building through reputation-seeking was a concern confined to one area of EPHA action.

The analysis benefits from unique participant-observer (PO) data on day-to-day deliberations on such decisions within the agency (a PO record). They include direct and real-time observations of decisions being made within EPHA. Hence, they constitute direct and positive evidence on the expressed motivations and concerns of agency leaders (Bennett, 2010, p. 210). That is, the observations can be sufficient to establish the internal validity of the theory. The presented data and analysis also complement the more common method of using retrospective data to make inferences about agency behaviours.

The data were collected from October to December 2009 by the author of this chapter (the PO). He was present at EPHA every workday in the period. The PO witnessed most formal and informal meetings related to the response effort that occurred during the observation period. He also interviewed most staff involved in the H1N1 response systematically (structured, open-ended interviews), and regularly had casual conversations with them. Interview and conversation notes and experiences were logged after each workday to a private web space limited to the study's participants. The log used a diary format (one entry per workday, with entries for meetings, interviews, conversations and observations). This online diary (PO record) provides the primary data for the empirical examples. The participant-observation at EPHA was a subsection of a multi-site, three-year study of pandemic preparedness and response funded by the U.S. National Science Foundation (the study and its procedures are further described in Keller et al., 2012; Baekkeskov, 2014).

Finally, it should be noted that the identity of EPHA has been deliberately obscured. The PO signed a formal confidentiality agreement with the agency. In addition, a verbal agreement exists between EPHA and the study that gives the agency the right to refuse publication of manuscripts using the PO data. A condition of using PO data for the extant text is anonymization. Definite identifying details of the agency discussed here have been left out to enable plausible deniability.

EPHA AS A TRUSTWORTHY ACTOR

As mentioned in the previous section, the 2009 pandemic was at once a reputational opportunity and threat for EPHA. The pandemic was very likely to give outside audiences direct experiences of its capabilities. Hence, the agency faced a choice between actively shaping those experiences for the sake of seeking to establish a reputation for trustworthiness or leaving its trustworthiness to derive from uncontrolled sources.

EPHA was not compelled to use its scarce resources and the pandemic's threatening circumstances to attract attention. By virtue of its position at the international regulatory level, EPHA had a rare position as an information-generator for all of Europe rather than for domestic settings alone. The agency was also unique as a space that facilitated coordination and exchanges between health authorities in different countries. Hence, health actors in Europe had to rely on the agency for some kinds of information and exchange.

In addition, EPHA entered the pandemic in April 2009 with exogenously generated trust credentials, in the shape of legal and professional institutions that supported trustworthiness. The agency had a formal mandate as an assessor of disease threats and provider of public health-related data and information. In addition, it was led and staffed by highly trained and experienced public health specialists from across Europe. These experts routinely undertook key epidemiological and biomedical scientific tasks such as surveillance of population disease patterns, tracking scientific advances related to specific diseases, intelligence gathering to gain early warnings on outbreaks, and planning for and simulating responses to emergencies. In turn, these outputs were available to multiple audiences.

But EPHA had positive reasons to exploit the pandemic for deliberate trust-building. One was competition. The agency participated alongside national and other international government agencies as a hub of pandemic response information and as a generator of influenza epidemiological updates and analyses. Key audiences such as health policy makers and care takers dealing with the disease could draw upon these every day, if they wished to do so. In this sense, EPHA was one supplier among many vying for clients. High relative trustworthiness could benefit the agency as a way of winning business, and lower trustworthiness could do the opposite.

A second reason for trust-building was that EPHA had a short track record. The pandemic in 2009 was the agency's first opportunity to respond to a global crisis. As noted, EPHA leaders and senior staff were highly trained, experienced and networked public health specialists. But the agency itself had been created in the wake of bioterrorism in 2001 and infectious disease scares between 1997 and 2005. In addition, influenza pandemics are rare events, and few specialists in any agency in 2009 had specific professional experience to draw upon when the novel swine flu arrived (the most recent flu pandemic had been in 1968). EPHA audiences had thus had much to learn about the agency's abilities and intentions.

The following section will analyse whether EPHA leaders were conscious of the opportunity presented by the 2009 pandemic, and whether they *actually* took response actions to signal trustworthiness (in the sense of taking costly actions that were important to particular audiences).

DEMONSTRATING TRUSTWORTHINESS THROUGH PANDEMIC RESPONSES

The following case analyses review evidence on two EPHA pandemic response decisions to explore whether the empirical expectations are fulfilled (summarized in Table 8.1). As previously described, each case discussion uses the PO record of observed debates among agency experts and leaders, including their interactions with representatives of outside stakeholders. This record provides opportunities to note the reasons for acting that were expressed in the decision process and, crucially, how final choices were justified.

Was EPHA motivated by the desire to gain a reputation as trustworthy?

Table 8.1   Two EPHA pandemic response cases and results

Decision process case	Response action	Reputational stakes	Show of trustworthiness
1. Field aid for the Ukraine	Contributed senior expert to int'l field mission in the Ukraine at height of pandemic.	Satisfy stakeholder demands for EPHA action on the Ukraine; show field capacity.	Costly demonstration of capacity and willingness to fill health regulators' needs.
2. Cancelled vaccination communicator meeting	Cancelled participation in a pan-European vaccination communicators' meeting despite promise to health department.	Protect EPHA image of independence from pharmaceutical firms.	Costly demonstration of commitment to health care and scientific professional standards.

Some leaders interviewed by the PO generally acknowledged the importance of the image that they believed outside actors held of the agency. Most explicitly, the agency's most senior influenza expert said that EPHA was viewed by many European national and international government organizations as a "good guy", whereas many other inter- and intragovernment relations were characterized by jealousy and suspicion (PO Record, Nov. 25). In addition, it was stated that "the challenge and the opportunity [for EPHA's response to swine flu pandemic] was to make a difference" (PO Record, Nov. 25). Hence, being thought of as a good guy made it easier to make a difference, and making a difference made it easier to be thought of as a good guy.

Is the image as a good guy the same as a reputation for trustworthiness? Perceived trustworthiness includes perceived ability, integrity and benevolence. The leading expert quoted above thought that being a good guy meant *not* being suspected of insidious motives related to jealousy and suspicion. What might such motives be? An obvious answer, though not necessarily an exhaustive one, is that an agency is suspect if it is thought to be malevolent or lack integrity. By the definition of trustworthiness, the agency would thus be a bad guy if it were not trustworthy. Hence, trustworthiness may be a condition for being a good guy and, by implication, for being able to affect public health (make a difference). The following two cases explore whether this perceived linkage between action and trust had sufficient power to shape the agency's choice of pandemic response actions in 2009.

Case 1: Field Aid for the Ukraine

On 29 October 2009, news of an explosive infectious disease event in the Ukraine became an important topic for analysis and reaction within EPHA (Baekkeskov, 2014, p. 16). The Ukrainian government press release on 27 October broke the news that 6,000 cases of an unknown infectious disease and seven fatalities had been recorded in a western province. By 30 October, the numbers had risen to 38 fatalities, 131 Intensive Care Unit (ICU) cases and 2,300 hospitalizations across the Ukraine (WHO, 2009a). On 3 November 2009, 70 people were reported dead, 235 were in ICUs, and 250,000 had been recorded as ill (WHO, 2009b). In six days, reported cases had multiplied 42 times and fatalities ten times.

In response, public health agencies across Europe and beyond paid close attention from 29 October through early November. The Ukrainian epidemiological data suggested a far more aggressive disease than the H1N1 flu detected elsewhere. On 30 October, Ukrainian authorities requested aid through their embassies in Europe and North America. Ukraine's Ministry of Health simultaneously reported the disease event through the World Health Organization (the WHO International Health Regulation event information system). Simultaneously, EPHA received an aid request from the Ukraine and requests for risk assessments from various European health agencies and departments.

Response action
EPHA quickly analysed the available data on the Ukraine. The agency then seconded one of its most senior epidemic intelligence experts to a nine-member WHO field team. The team was deployed on 31 October 2009 to aid Ukrainian health authorities and to supply epidemic intelligence to health authorities elsewhere.

Reputational stakes
Internally, EPHA experts quickly made sense of the apparent explosiveness of the Ukrainian outbreak as an artefact of Ukraine's reporting infrastructure rather than an accurate epidemiological picture. Deliberators also observed that the high level of attention to the outbreak from the country's authorities could be linked to a particularly contentious presidential election occurring a short time later. Hence, EPHA's direct involvement was not a given on epidemiological grounds.

During the day of Friday 30 October, the agency nevertheless offered staff to WHO's European office (WHO Euro) for the Ukraine field team. WHO Euro declined. During the evening, the PO recorded from a meeting that "the Director wants a person on the ground" (PO Record, Oct. 30). Informants told the PO that the evening meeting was followed by phone calls to network contacts. The EPHA senior expert had joined the field team by the time that it landed in Kiev the next day. Hence, EPHA had used its connections to gain membership of the WHO field team.

The PO record indicates that EPHA leaders expected that visibility on the field team would strengthen EPHA's reputation. According to a senior manager, "it was 'good' for EPHA to be in the Ukraine because it was the first time that the agency had been asked to do a 'needs assessment'" (PO Record, Nov. 3; Baekkeskov, 2014, p. 17). The deployment fulfilled an explicit request from the national health agency of a major country in Western Europe. During the first days of the crisis, that agency had expressed concern about the evolving situation and prodded EPHA to act. An involved senior expert reported to the PO that insertion in the field team had been an opportunity to prove to the national agency that EPHA could and would respond to its needs. This view was echoed in meetings on 2 and 3 November 2009. Some leading experts expressed that the field deployment raised the profile of the agency by showing that it would go out of its way to satisfy health department needs.

Hence, EPHA leaders and senior staff saw the expert secondment as an opportunity to demonstrate abilities and intentions. That is, the agency saw an opportunity to shape the beliefs of other health authorities. This meant that reputation-seeking was a driving motivation for the field placement (Baekkeskov, 2014). But was this deliberate demonstration simultaneously about trust-building?

Costs of acting

EPHA leaders' dedication of network and staff resources to a mission with tenuous links to public health occasioned open discussions that the PO could observe. In the aforementioned meetings on 2 and 3 November, staff experts expressed that the secondment would give them inside information that they might not otherwise have been privy to. That is, it could give them real epidemic intelligence. In contrast, other expert staff expressed reservations about the use of resources.

In a meeting on 3 November, the organization's day-to-day H1N1 crisis manager questioned whether EPHA should actually be in the Ukraine. Precedent was a key issue: if other governments in Europe had events like the one in the Ukraine (i.e., a highly politicized outbreak), and if scarce agency manpower were exhausted from other field missions, what could EPHA do? The following day the crisis manager raised the issue again at a meeting of senior management (PO Record, Nov. 4). One senior manager gave support: how thinly should EPHA spread its resources? The agency's Director (i.e., its most senior executive) responded: the agency should be prepared to respond to many requests at one time. The discussion closed.

The cost highlighted by the crisis manager and senior manager was a significant risk. Missing one epidemic intelligence expert in late fall 2009 did not mean that duties went unattended. But the precedent time meant that if the pandemic took more unexpected turns, some duties could be. The pandemic was peaking in the Northern Hemisphere during those weeks, in terms of total number of people affected. But the time was actually relatively calm at EPHA in the sense that H1N1 was following a predicted trajectory. A key priority remained readiness, however. The actual disease (rather than the political situation) could change, in which case the agency would have had to act fast to develop knowledge and assess risks (fulfilling its formal mission). The senior epidemic intelligence experts were particularly crucial in these tasks. Hence, the Ukraine field mission and the precedent it set was a visible demonstration that EPHA would throw aside other concerns to do what was important to a particular audience, in this case national health authorities of certain major countries.

Trust-building?
By taking visible action in the Ukraine, EPHA leaders could give national
health authorities a direct experience of EPHA's abilities and intentions.
EPHA leaders explicitly disregarded the marginal epidemiological value
of the mission. They acted to satisfy direct demands from European and
Ukrainian health agencies, for information and aid, respectively. Hence,
EPHA was taking action that was evidently important to the trustor. In
addition, the mission also incurred substantial costs. The choice to participate in the Ukraine field mission was thus consistent with the empirical
expectation of trust-building, that is, EPHA gave a particular audience
a direct experience of relevant ability, integrity and benevolent intent by
taking important and costly action.

Case 2: Cancelled Vaccination Communicator Meeting

EPHA had scheduled its participation in an international conference
for health communicators in London in the week of 19 October 2009
(Baekkeskov, 2014). A major European health department had organized
the conference to discuss ways to handle mass media and related relations
for the pandemic vaccination campaigns in the winter of 2009–10.

Response action
The EPHA's Director cancelled the agency's participation a few days
before it began. The organizing department expressed surprise and dis-
pleasure at the agency's absence.

Reputational stakes
A related teleconference call between EPHA and the department was
witnessed by the PO on the morning of Thursday 29 October 2009 (i.e.,
after the London conference). Several senior EPHA executives exchanged
words before the call. EPHA's head of communications had learned that
vaccine producers would participate in the meeting and had informed
the Director. EPHA had then "withdrawn because the head of communications and the Director agreed that the [EPHA's] scientific neutrality
was put at risk by participation of the pharma-industry" (PO Record,
Oct. 29).

The teleconference itself was a discussion between EPHA and the
department. The department's representative quickly raised the London
meeting. He "directly stated that what they wanted to understand and
discuss was why [EPHA] had withdrawn from the health communicators'
meeting" (PO Record, Oct. 29). The London conference had been called at
the behest of the political leadership rather than just the department. The

department accepted that the agency had the formal authority to make the choice; but it was unfortunate.

EPHA's head of communications explained the withdrawal. The agency had been surprised when it learned that vaccine producers were invited. He stated that "the Director [. . .] did not want [EPHA]-industry collaboration that could be construed as compromising [EPHA's] scientific independence" (PO Record, 29 Oct.). In addition, the setting mattered; public health professionals were the crucial actors in a public health emergency. If the agency mingled with industry there would be a perception issue. Indeed, public health and industry communicators should be separated by a firewall. Finally, the general public debate showed huge opposition to vaccination.

The withdrawal was thus trading-off one image and audience for another. The image of the agency as server of needs (here, attending a meeting) of certain health departments challenged the image of the agency as a useful and reliable source to the health professionals and scientists. By taking drastic action, the agency's senior leaders showed that they would deliberately seek to shape the EPHA's reputation (Baekkeskov, 2014). Was this also trust-building?

Costs of acting

Most obviously, the cost incurred by EPHA in this case was the quality of its relationship with the department and with the political leadership. Almost certainly, the health department now had less faith in the image of EPHA as a reliable agency. In addition, the health department was probably less likely to trust the agency to perform important actions in the future. Hence, by cancelling its participation and with little warning, the EPHA probably changed its reputation and reduced the trust of at least one important health department.

In addition, the European health department representative argued that the agency's withdrawal could damage the general effort in pandemic response. It presented a missed opportunity to review scenarios, and a real life public health emergency would involve pharmaceutical producers (PO Record, 29 Oct.). That is, the department was suggesting that the European regulatory system was now less well prepared than it could have been to handle its primary pharmaceutical intervention against the 2009 H1N1 influenza. By withdrawing, the EPHA might thus have increased the risk of response failure.

Trust-building?

As described, EPHA leaders explicitly based their action on the perceptions of public health professionals. By avoiding association with vaccine producers, they hoped to protect their perceived scientific independence. By implication, EPHA's participation in the London meeting would have given health scientific and care professionals a direct experience of the agency as *un*trustworthy. The mass media context underscores this. As the agency's head of communications suggested, damning reports on industry–regulator ties were beginning to appear as mass vaccinations began in late October 2009. In some, the WHO (another international public health agency) emerged as particularly suspect. Hence, EPHA leaders were aware that the perceived scientific integrity of public health agencies was in public question.

Considering the background adds importance to the decision about the London conference. EPHA was not simply making a choice between two audiences. The issue was whether the agency could, in an environment of suspicion and uncertainty, afford any association with "big pharma" if it wished to supply information on H1N1 vaccines to health care providers and their patients. Integrity was thus at stake: to be used as a source of accurate and reliable disease and treatment information, EPHA's image should not include association with pharmaceutical producers. Going ahead with the meeting could well have amounted to a public demonstration of *un*trustworthiness. The cancellation was thus a demonstration of EPHA's commitment to integrity, and to its ability to serve the needs of health professionals and the general public. Avoiding a demonstration of untrustworthiness thus constituted deliberate trust-building, that is, it was costly action to preserve the agency's ability to take future actions of importance to particular audiences.

CONCLUSION

Reputation-seeking and trust-building can usefully be linked to demonstrate empirically that government agencies can act deliberately for the sake of gaining trust from audiences in political systems and societies. In the Ukraine case, EPHA leaders ignored the essentially political construction of the situation in favour of explicitly giving certain other health authorities direct experiences that the agency could and would satisfy their expressed needs. In the communicators' meeting case, EPHA's most senior leaders explicitly acted to protect the agency's perceived scientific integrity. Hence, the two cases show that deliberate trust-building actually *can* shape government agency action. In addition, they show that trust-building can be relatively important to agency leaders, who can be willing to set aside other priorities for the sake of taking actions that demonstrate trustworthiness.

This conclusion is given validity by the substantial character of the cases. Trust could have had a hard time winning the day in contests with rival concerns during a crisis response, such as mitigating the crisis or conserving scarce resources. But the EPHA leaders were willing to risk future agency response effectiveness to show ability and intent to satisfy demands of certain national health agencies, and to protect the agency's scientific trustworthiness by jeopardizing the trust of a major health department and its political leaders. In the face of priorities pushing for different decisions, deliberate trust-building was able to shape EPHA choices.

The validity is further strengthened by the presence of the trust-building priority in different areas of agency activity during a time of crisis. Had a concern for trust been a marginal factor in EPHA's 2009 pandemic response, cases where trust-building had clear influence might have been difficult to find. But as shown, EPHA at least twice sought to boost its image as trustworthy to selected audiences during two months where the ongoing pandemic offered it attention from governments, health care and science professionals and the general public across Europe.

Why an agency such as EPHA would dedicate some of its actions to the pursuit of trust from key audiences should be reiterated. This chapter has noted that EPHA has indirect impact on regulation and health care in the sense that it only has a mandate to produce information. Hence, trustworthiness can be a prerequisite for an agency's ability to affect public health through actions of health regulators, professionals or the general public. As previously described, the PO record shows that at least one senior expert at the centre of EPHA's pandemic response believed in this link: being "a good guy" was necessary for "making a difference".

Finally, the reputation-seeking perspective highlights a fragmentation in trust-building that is rarely emphasized in the literature on trust between government organizations. Reputation is conceptualized as a dyad: an *image* held by an *audience*. This means that one agency can have many reputations, corresponding to the existing image–audience dyads. It also means that the agency can target some audiences and ignore others, much as can any organization that seeks to promote its outputs. For instance, EPHA evidently cared a great deal about what other health agencies believed about it, and perhaps more about what health and science professionals believed. Since trustworthiness is a part of a reputation, different actors in state and society may trust, not trust or distrust the same agency. More subtly, different actors may trust the agency for different things. Hence, an agency is likely to project different images to different audiences, and its trustworthiness is likely to vary by audience.

The presented analysis is neither generalizable to all agency contexts, nor does it show whether all EPHA actions were or are controlled by a drive for trust-building. The analyses above have demonstrated that trust-building *can* be a powerful motivation for agency behaviour. EPHA may have been particularly motivated by its relative newness and the competition in the marketplace for ideas. In addition, its mandate limited it to indirect influence on public health. To the extent that its leaders and staff hoped to shape public health, they needed to persuade direct regulators and health care providers that the agency's outputs were valuable. Finally, the pandemic was a rare opportunity to exploit the attention of many audiences. These conditions are thus evident limitations on the generalizability of the findings above. Hence, at least two avenues for future research are offered by this chapter's conclusions. First, how likely is trust-building to dominate other motives in general among agencies that face one or more of the evident conditions above? Second, how likely is trust-building to dominate other motives among agencies and departments in general? Answers to these questions would provide valuable contributions to the literature on bureaucratic behaviour and regulatory trust.

REFERENCES

Bachmann, R., and A.C. Inkpen (2011), 'Understanding institutional-based trust building processes in inter-organizational relationships', *Organization Studies*, **32**(2), 281–301.

Baekkeskov, E. (2014), 'Reputation-seeking by a government agency in Europe: Direct evidence from responses to the 2009 H1N1 "Swine" influenza pandemic', *Administration & Society*, doi: 10.1177/0095399714528177.

Bennett, A. (2010), 'Process tracing for causal inference', in H. Brady and D. Collier (eds), *Rethinking social inquiry: Diverse tools, shared standards* (2nd ed.), Plymouth: Rowman & Littlefield Publishers, pp. 207–219.

Boin, A., A. McConnell, and P. 't Hart (eds.) (2008), *Governing after crisis: The politics of investigation, accountability, and learning*, New York: Cambridge University Press.

Carpenter, D. (2000), 'State building through reputation building: Coalitions of esteem and program innovation in the national postal system, 1883–1913', *Studies in American Political Development*, **14**, 121–155.

Carpenter, D. (2001), *The forging of bureaucratic autonomy: Reputation, networks, and policy innovation in executive agencies, 1862–1928*, Princeton: Princeton University Press.

Carpenter, D. (2010), *Reputation and power: Organizational image and pharmaceutical regulation at the FDA*, Princeton: Princeton University Press.

Carpenter, D., and G.A. Krause (2011), 'Reputation and public administration', *Public Administration Review*, **72**(1), 26–32.

Christensen, T., and P. Lægreid (2002), *New public management: The transformation of ideas and practice*, Aldershot: Ashgate.

Dunleavy, P. (1991), *Democracy, bureaucracy and public choice*, London: Pearson.

George, A.L., and A. Bennett (2005), *Case studies and theory development in the social sciences*, Cambridge and London: MIT Press.

Groenleer, M. (2009), *The autonomy of European Union agencies: A comparative study of institutional development*, Delft: Uitgeverij Eburon.

Keller, A.C., C.K. Ansell, A.L. Reingold, M. Bourrier, M.D. Hunter, S. Burrowes, and T. MacPhail (2012), 'Improving pandemic response: A sensemaking perspective on the spring 2009 H1N1 pandemic', *Risks, Hazards & Crisis in Public Policy*, **3**(2), 1–37.

Maor, M. (2010), 'Organizational reputation and jurisdictional claims: The case of the U.S. Food and Drug Administration', *Governance*, **23**(1), 133–159.

Maor, M. (2011), 'Organizational reputations and the observability of public warnings in 10 pharmaceutical markets', *Governance*, **24**(3), 557–582.

Mayer, R.C., J.H. Davis, and F.D. Schoorman (1995), 'An integrative model of organizational trust', *The Academy of Management Review*, **20**(3), 709–734.

Niskanen, W.A. (1971), *Bureaucracy and representative government*, Chicago: Aldine, Atherton.

Osborne, S.P. (2010), *The new public governance? Emerging perspectives on the theory and practice of public governance*, Oxon: Routledge.

PO Record (2009), 'Record for the [European Public Health Agency (EPHA)], Oct–Dec 2009', *2009 H1N1 "Swine" Influenza Pandemic Response Participant-Observer (PO) Diaries*. Private collection.

Pollitt, C., and G. Bouckaert (2004), *Public management reform: A comparative analysis* (2nd ed.), Oxford: Oxford University Press.

Poppo, L. (2013), 'Origins of inter-organizational trust: A review and query for further research', in R. Bachmann and A. Zaheer (eds.), *Handbook of advances in trust research*, Cheltenham, UK and Northampton, MA, USA: Edward Elgar Publishing, pp. 125–145.

Pressman, J.L., and A. Wildavsky (1973), *Implementation: How great expectations in Washington are dashed in Oakland,* Berkeley: University of California Press.

Roberts, P.S. (2006), 'FEMA and the prospects for reputation-based autonomy', *Studies in American Political Development* **20**(1), 57–87.

Sørensen, E., and J. Torfing (2007), 'Theoretical approaches to governance network dynamics', in E. Sørensen and J. Torfing (eds), *Theories of democratic network governance*, Houndsmills: Palgrave Macmillan, pp. 25–42.

WHO (2009a), *Pandemic (H1N1) 2009, Ukraine*, Geneva: World Health Organization.

WHO (2009b), *Pandemic (H1N1) 2009, Ukraine – update 1*, Geneva: World Health Organization.

Wilson, J.Q. (1989), *Bureaucracy: What government agencies do and why they do it*, New York: Basic Books.

Yesilkagit, K. (2004), 'Bureaucratic autonomy, organizational culture, and habituation: Politicians and independent administrative bodies in the Netherlands', *Administration and Society*, **36**(5), 528–552.

Yesilkagit, K., and J.G. Christensen (2010), 'Institutional design and formal autonomy: Political versus historical and cultural explanations', *Journal of Public Administration Research and Theory*, **20**(1), 53–74.

Yesilkagit, K., and S. Van Thiel (2008), 'Political influence and bureaucratic autonomy', *Public Organzational Review*, **2008**(8), 137–153.

9. An agenda for further research into the role of trust in regulatory regimes

Frédérique Six and Koen Verhoest

The chapters in this edited volume all address one or more of the gaps in our knowledge identified in the literature review presented in the introductory chapter. In this final chapter we take stock of what we now know about the role of trust in regulatory regimes and present an agenda for further research. This agenda follows the five themes identified in the introductory chapter: 1) there are outstanding issues for most trust relations within regulatory regimes that need further research; 2) the interactional dynamics between the different trust relationships within regulatory regimes needs more systematic research; 3) the dynamics of processes of trust building and repair within regulatory relationships are understudied; 4) there are still unresolved conceptual issues around trust and related concepts that need further study; and 5) the field is ready to move to more theory building and hypothesis testing research.

UNDERSTUDIED RELATIONS

After the literature review performed in the introductory chapter (Six and Verhoest, this volume), we conclude that several relations are under studied, most in particular to relation 7, the relation between public regulator and public regulated organization (Figure 9.1). The chapters in this book cover many of the relations in Figure 9.1 with two chapters focusing on relation 7. We also identify outstanding issues that require further research.

Relations 1 and 2: Citizen Trust in Regulated (Private and Public) Organizations

In our conceptualization of the role of trust in regulatory regimes, as depicted in the regulatory trust triangle, regulation starts with a need to

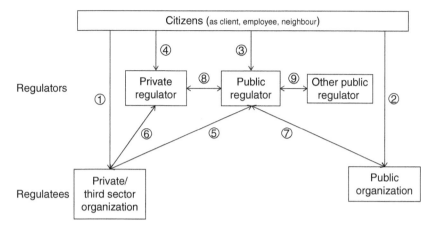

Figure 9.1   Role of trust in different relationships within regulatory regimes

reduce the vulnerabilities of citizens as they, as customers, employees, neighbours or otherwise stakeholders, interact with organizations in society. And regulation, effectuated in more or less complex regulatory regimes, aims to reduce those vulnerabilities and thus increase trust in this citizen-regulated organization relationship. The quality of interaction within all the other relationships and the effectiveness of each relationship, in which trust and distrust play a role, determines the overall effect of the regulatory regime on the vulnerabilities experienced by citizens in their relation with regulated organizations. Undoubtedly, for many sectors there are studies into the trust citizens, as customers or employees, have in a particular sector and its organizations, and possibly also into the risks, uncertainties and vulnerabilities that citizens experience in their interactions with the organizations. Our interest for relations 1 and 2 in Figure 9.1 lies in the impact of regulation and the wider regulatory regime on citizen trust in regulated organizations. So not surprisingly, studies purely focusing on trust in citizen-regulated organization relationship did not appear in our search, given our combined search terms – trust *and* regulation and derivatives of these words. In the studies that we found stakeholder interests are often formulated without direct research being conducted among individuals (e.g., Abbot, 2012), although sometimes focus groups are organized (e.g., Brown and Kuzma, 2013), or stakeholder activist groups are involved in research (e.g., Gouldson, 2004; Holm and Halkier, 2009). Two chapters in this volume touch on citizen trust in regulated organizations, Carter's study into trust in regulated luxury wine markets and Näslund and Tamm Hallström's chapter on private ecolabels, but neither actually measure citizen trust; they interview regulators, regulated businesses and experts. Research that measures both citizen trust in regulated organizations and the way trust in the regulator or regulatory regime influences this trust is needed as it would help further theory building. Future research should focus more on which aspects of a regulatory regime are important for impacting upon citizen trust in the regulated organization.

Relation 3 and 4: Citizen Trust in Public and Private Regulators

In our semi-systematic literature review in Chapter 1 we find only a few empirical studies into citizen trust in public regulators. Regulatory agencies tend to be relatively unknown to the general public, especially when things go well within the sector. These agencies only get media attention when they get into enforcing actions or are accused of having failed to act in time, for example during the Global Financial Crisis of 2008. When trust in these regulatory agencies is measured after such a crisis, it is not surprising that low scores are obtained. But when all is well and the agency is unknown to many, what do scores for citizen trust in these organizations actually measure? Do they then not rather reflect general trust in government? We do not know. In many ways that might be the tragedy of regulatory enforcement agencies: when all is well, they are unknown and unacknowledged and when things go wrong they get at least part of the blame. More research is needed into citizen trust in regulators and regulatory regimes. For public regulators this trust needs to be related to trust in government more generally. When one knows little about the object of trust, one may rely more on one's generalized trust in the broader category that the object belongs to. So when one knows little about the regulator apart from that it is part of government, one's trust may be more strongly derived from one's trust in government more generally.

Within public administration research the common assumption around public trust in government has been, in line with the New Public Management discourse, that when public service delivery is improved in terms of outcomes for citizens, then citizen trust in public organizations will increase. This, however, is not found in empirical research (Van de Walle and Bouckaert, 2003). In their interactions with government, citizens value process, similar to procedural justice, at least as much if not more than outcome (Van Ryzin, 2011). It would be interesting to see whether a similar dynamic exists for citizen trust in public regulators. Tyler (2006) shows that procedural justice is most important for citizens when they are regulatees confronted by a regulator, but what is important for citizens when they are the actor on whose behalf the regulator inspects and enforces rules?

There is probably more research into customer trust in private labels and certificates, because these labels need to earn customer trust to be viable. However, this research is more difficult to find as it often is published without using the concept of regulation. It would be interesting to systematically compare the degree of trust in public and private regulation and discover whether what makes a public regulator trusted by citizens is different from what makes a private regulator trusted, or whether it is similar. This may help evidence-based decisions about how to design regulatory regimes and to assign roles for public and private regulators (co-regulation). It is also interesting to study whether public or private regulators use different regulatory enforcement styles in order to earn that trust of citizens. A recent study by Carter (2016) only finds limited variation in regulatory approaches by public, private and non-profit third-party organizations charged with administering US organic food regulations, but future studies should seek whether these results hold in other regulatory fields and administrative contexts and whether the (non-)variation in regulatory approaches affects the level of citizens' trust in these regulators differently or not.

Relations 5–7: Trust in the Regulator–Regulatee Relation

Relation 5, referring to a public regulator inspecting a private regulatee, and relation 6, referring to a private regulator inspecting a private regulatee, are relatively well researched. However, relation 7, in which the regulated organization is a public organization, is not. The chapters by Six and Van Ees, and by Oomsels and Bouckaert (this volume), are examples of studies into the latter relation. Further research is needed to examine whether the relation between a public regulator and a public regulatee is different in a meaningful way from public regulators inspecting private or third sector organizations. Six and Van Ees suggest that such a difference exists in case the two public organizations also interact in different contexts. In their study the local authorities and water boards also collaborated as equal partners in policy-making networks for spatial planning. The question is whether this context interferes in substantive ways with the regulatory relation between these actors and the trust within that relation. We do not as yet know enough about this.

Trust depends on perceptions of trustworthiness the trustor has of the trustee. Intentions and competence are two important dimensions of trustworthiness. Is the regulatee willing and able to comply with the regulations? If yes, then the regulator is more likely to be able to trust the regulatee. Do intentions and competence vary substantially across sectors? Do public or third sector organizations generally have better intentions to comply with regulation and reduce citizen vulnerabilities better than private, profit-oriented organizations? Do they act differently when the regulator is a public or private actor? Or can we not generalize along the dimension of degree of publicness (Bozeman, 2013)? How about regulatee abilities to comply, do these vary by sector or other factors, such as size? If there are differences, what are the implications for regulatory strategies?

Relation 8: Trust between Public and Private Regulator(s)

Our literature review concludes that the jury is still out on whether the basic idea of co-regulation is flawed, because interests vary too widely; or whether it is just very difficult to get the collaboration to work effectively and we have not yet figured out how to achieve this. As Van de Voort's chapter (this volume) shows, it may make a difference to the success of co-regulated regimes whether government provides blue-prints or whether it allows negotiated regimes to emerge over time. In Van der Voort's study, trust was able to grow over time in the negotiated regime and not in the blue-print regime. Further research is needed to better understand the dynamics of co-regulation. Further research is also needed into the role of mediating actors that may help build trust between public regulators, private regulators and the regulated organizations.

Relation 9: Trust between Collaborating Public Regulators

Only a few studies study explicitly this relation (Rommel, 2012). Baekkeskov's chapter in this volume addresses the relation. There is a rapidly increasing volume of research into the role of trust between collaborating public organizations, (see e.g., O'Leary and Vij, 2012) and the question is whether there are substantive differences when these organizations are regulatory enforcement agencies. Further research may investigate this. If there are no substantive differences then the field may learn from the existing broader research, but if there are substantive differences we need to know where these lie.

As we said in the introductory chapter (Six and Verhoest, this volume), organizations are often regulated by more than one public regulator (e.g., tax, food safety, labour conditions, smoking ban, fire safety for restaurants and bars and general competition) leading to calls for these regulatory enforcement agencies to collaborate in order to reduce the administrative burden for the regulated organizations (see e.g., Aubin and Verhoest, 2014; Dabbah, 2011; Freeman and Rossi, 2012). These regulatory agencies often have very different cultures, base their mandate on very different regula-tions and face privacy issues if they want to exchange information. Also, sometimes these agencies report to different levels of government with dif-ferent accountability regimes. These factors may hamper processes of trust building and maintenance. Furthermore, regulators in different geographic regions need to collaborate when organizations cross jurisdictions, either in developing regulatory norms and practices (e.g., through regulatory networks, see Levi-Faur, 2011; Maggetti and Gilardi, 2014) or in effective enforcement (Boin et al., 2014; Busuioc, 2016). Examples are tax, food safety, fisheries or shipping (see Temby et al., 2015). Different national and administrative cultures, legal regimes, again privacy issues surrounding information exchange, but also reputational issues (see Busuioc, 2016) may hamper processes of trust building and maintenance. Are these contextual factors substantially different from the public collaborations studied so far?

A specific relation that has received quite some attention in regulatory studies is the relation between regulatory agencies and their parent minis-ter or ministry. This relation could be also understood in some ways as a regulator–regulator interaction, especially in those fields where ministers and their ministry still hold considerable regulatory enforcement powers. An interesting element in this literature is the extent to which the trust between the regulatory agency and its minister is enhanced by the extent to which the regulatory agency cooperates with other regulators within or across country borders (see Bach and Ruffing, 2013; Verhoest et al., 2015). It would be worthwhile in future research to dig more deeply into this issue: how collaborative relations with other regulatory bodies enhance the reputation and trustworthiness of public regulators for other regulators, and by extension politicians, regulatees and citizens?

Role of Public Interest Groups in Regulatory Regimes

In the introduction we identify the role of organizations that represent citizen concerns and interest; Ayres and Braithwaite (1992) call these PIGs, Public Interest Groups. In their concept of tripartite regulation (see Six and Verhoest, this volume) these PIGs act as guardians to the regulatory arrangement between public regulator and regulated organization. Since we found no studies explicitly on the trust between PIGs and other actors in the regulatory regime as well as on the role of PIGs in trust building in regulatory systems in our semi-systematic search, we excluded them in our literature review. They are, however, important non-state actors in regulatory regimes, as the abundant research on interest group-agency relations in general and on regulatory capture in particular shows (Braun, 2012; Dal Bo, 2006; Levine and Forrence, 1990). However, further research is needed into their role in helping build citizen trust and reduce citizen vulnerabilities.

DYNAMICS BETWEEN RELATIONS: INTERACTIONS OF TRUST IN DIFFERENT RELATIONS

Our literature review concludes that systematic research into the dynamics between different trust relations is scarce, but we find several studies starting to investigate this interaction. Not surprisingly, the focal point for studying the interaction of trust relations is the regulatory trust triangle. In this volume, several chapters (Carter, Näslund and Tamm Hallström and Van der Voort) also address the interaction between different trust relations within the regulatory regime.

Regulatory Trust Triangle

In the introductory chapter (Six and Verhoest, this volume) we introduce the regulatory trust triangle and positioned the regulatory agency as the third party that facilitates citizen trust in the regulated organization so that the interaction between the two may materialize and/or improve. Regulatory agencies are thus facilitators of trust; or guardians of trust (Shapiro, 1987). This mechanism works as follows: the citizen is not in a position to assess the trustworthiness of an organization but trusts the regulator that regulates the involved organization. Hence, the citizen will follow the regulator's judgement of the regulated organization (cf Nooteboom, 1999). So if the regulator trusts the (private or public) regulated organization then the citizen will also trust the regulated organization, but if the regulator distrusts this organization, then the citizen will also distrust it. Näslund and Tamm Hallström in their chapter on private regulation (this volume) argue that in situations of impersonal trust, like is the case with citizen trust in a private regulatory regime, this mechanism works differently. They argue that the citizen does not yet trust the private regulator, so the private regulator needs to earn the citizens' trust first. The private regulator shows its trustworthiness best by showing that it does not trust the regulated organization. It may even have to show that it distrusts the regulated organization to gain citizen trust. But does this affect the regulatory approach chosen by the regulator?

Nooteboom (1999) did not specify the third party actor and seemed to refer to all types of trust relations, which would include regulators. Also, Nooteboom referred to a third party that the trustor already trusts, not one that first needs to earn its trust. Näslund and Tamm Halströmm studied the position of a new private voluntary regulatory regime that had to gain a substantial market share to be viable. To what degree, if at all, does this create other dynamics compared with those in public regulatory regimes where regulatory agencies are often well-established and when newly established are part of the larger public administration? Is it relevant whether regulation is voluntary, as it often is with private regulation, or obligatory, as is the case with public regulation? Or does Näslund and Tamm Hallström's argument – regulators need to earn citizens' trust by not trusting the regulated organizations – apply to all regulators, because the trust involved is impersonal? This has consequences for the regulatory trust triangle. Further research is needed to come to better insight and possibly solve this puzzle. If publicness is relevant, what are the implications for mixed regimes, for example public regulatory systems with (partly) private auditors/inspectors? Or is it not publicness that is relevant, but rather whether the regulation is voluntary or obligatory?

Studies into the role of regulatory agencies within the regulatory trust triangle not only need to measure citizen trust in both regulated organization and regulator, but also the risks, uncertainties and vulnerabilities that citizens are concerned about in their interactions with the regulated organization/sector. Furthermore, such studies should assess how the regulator and its regulatory approach may help reduce these risks, uncertainties and vulnerabilities; and how successful the regulator is in reducing them. Only then can we gain a better insight into what the level of trust that citizens have in regulated organizations/sectors as well as the regulator actually means. This research is not only needed within a sector or domain, but comparative research across sectors and domains may provide more insight into the mechanisms of how regulators perform their role within regulatory regimes.

Multiple Audiences

Especially Näslund and Tamm Halström's chapter, but also Baekkeskov's chapter, address the challenge that regulators face in dealing with multiple audiences. Citizens have different expectations from the regulator from regulated organizations and maybe politicians have yet other expectations. And within larger, more complicated regulatory regimes a regulatory agency may face multiple audiences among the different actors involved. And to complicate things even further, citizens as clients of regulated organizations may have different expectations from citizens who are only involved as tax payers, paying for the regulation. How do regulators deal with the conflicts and dilemmas that they inevitably face when these multiple audiences make contradictory demands? This mirrors to a high extent the dilemmas that organizations face in enhancing and maintaining their organizational reputation (as an important dimension or predictor of organizational trustworthiness) vis-à-vis their different audiences (see Baekkeskov, this volume; Carpenter and Krause, 2012; Luoma-aho, 2008; Rousseau et al., 1998; Verhoest et al., 2015). How do regulatory organizations manage these different demands? Näslund and Tamm Halströmm conclude that the private label organizations that they study can only make this work because citizens are kept in the dark about the relationship between private regulator and regulated organizations. We question though, how sustainable such secrecy is and can private regulation only work with this secrecy? Or are there alternatives where everything is in the open? Perhaps Ayres and Braithwaite's (1992) concept of tripartism may help here – where public interest groups may contest the performance of the regulator as the primary guardian (see Six and Verhoest, this volume)?

Regulatory Capture

The third-party trust role for regulators works as long as citizens trust regulators. When regulators are "captured" by the regulated sector or organization, they may not be trusted by citizens (Levine and Forrence, 1990). This may happen if the regulator's norms and values and its underlying assumptions are more in line with the sector that it regulates than with the citizens on whose behalf it regulates (see e.g., McPhilemy, 2013 with his reference to regulatory groupthink), as Mills and Reiss (this volume) show happened in the Southwest airline case. It may also happen when the sector has the power to avoid (serious) sanctions when they violate regulations, by threatening with the economic repercussions like taking their business elsewhere, thus reducing employment.

The challenge for regulators is tough: they need to gain the trust of regulatees to get access to the information they need and ultimately have trust in the regulatee without getting captured by the regulatee. Mills and Reiss (this volume) propose that the way out of what they call "cultural capture" is to acknowledge the role each has to play in ensuring both safety and economic viability. Clear, steady role performance is thus key, which requires competencies beyond the purely technical. These include also interpersonal and reflexive competencies as Six and Van Ees (this volume) showed.

DYNAMICS WITHIN RELATIONS: PROCESSES OF TRUST BUILDING AND REPAIR

Based on their literature review, Six and Verhoest (this volume) identify as a gap that processes of trust building and repair are under studied in the context of regulation and regulatory regimes. Six and Van Ees, and Oomsels and Bouckaert (both this volume) study processes of trust building (and repair). In the trust literature several models have been proposed for understanding processes of trust building. Most of these models focus on interpersonal trust and most also are still contested; there is little consensus (e.g., Lewicki and Bunker, 1996; Six, 2005). The same holds for processes of trust repair (e.g., Dirks et al., 2011; Kim et al., 2013; Six and Skinner, 2010). The understanding of processes of organizational trust building and repair is even more limited (Gillespie and Dietz, 2009), let alone how interorganizational trust may be rebuilt. And within regulatory regimes the actual interactions between the different organizations, be they the regulator and the regulated organization or different regulators, is usually even less frequent and intense than between collaborating business organizations. We distinguish between the interpersonal level in interorganizational trust and the organizational level dynamics to identify avenues for further research (cf Six and Verhoest, this volume).

Interpersonal Level in Interorganizational Trust

As already mentioned in the introductory chapter, Responsive Regulation Theory (RRT; Ayres and Braithwaite, 1992) emphasizes the importance of trust in a dynamic regulatory strategy as inspectors interact with inspected organizations and their representatives during inspections. We observe that they, however, underplay the importance of processes of trust building and repair with the implication that important concepts are currently absent or underplayed in RRT. For trust to be built effectively and trust repair to have a chance – after (perceived) trust violations – interpersonal and reflexive competencies for both regulator and regulatee are important (Six and Sorge, 2008; Six and Van Ees, this volume). RRT appears to assume that the regulator has the interpersonal and reflexive competencies to choose the appropriate strategies within the pyramid and communicate clearly with regulatees. Mascini and Van Wijk (2009) show that these assumptions do not always hold empirically, as do Six and Van Ees (this volume). In terms of regulatee competencies, attention is paid to the compliance related competencies (Winter and May, 2001), but not to interpersonal and reflexive competencies. Again, Mascini and Van Wijk's research showed the relevance of these competencies. Furthermore, motivational postures and general propensity to trust the other actors are important in trust building. For regulatees, this is acknowledged in Valerie Braithwaite's motivational postures (2009) with disengagement resembling generalized distrust of government. For regulators, however, this is not problematized. RRT assumes no influence of regulator generalized trust or distrust towards regulatees. Van der Voort's study (this volume) shows how a government that imposed a blue-print for co-regulation based on distrust affected the success of the co-regulation initiative in a negative way. Mills and Reiss's study (this volume) shows how the FAA's realization of the sector's distrust in it led to the FAA asking NASA to be a neutral, trusted intermediary in one of the voluntary disclosure programmes. Van der Voort (this volume) also highlights the importance of the trust building process, taking it one step at a time.

Further research is needed to study, at least, four aspects of trust processes within the context of regulatory regimes: the general dynamics of building and maintaining trust; the role of generalized trust and distrust; how to deal with the inevitable disruptions of trust; and the role of procedural justice. Or is a special model needed for a proper understanding of the particularities of regulatory regimes?

General dynamics of trust processes
Which of the models already existing in the trust literature are appropriate for better understanding the dynamics of trust building processes between organizations within regulatory regimes (Dirks et al., 2011; Gillespie and Dietz, 2009; Kim et al., 2013; Lewicki and Bunker, 1996; Six, 2005; Six and Skinner, 2010)?

Generalized trust and distrust
An important driver of trust building is the general propensity to trust others (Mayer et al., 1995; see also Oomsels and Bouckaert, this volume). In regulatory relations, a regulator's generalized trust, or distrust, in regulatees is relevant, as is a regulatee's generalized trust, or distrust, in regulators and government. In political science and public management research, much attention is paid to citizens' trust in government and Braithwaite's research into motivational postures includes the disengagement posture which resembles high generalized distrust of regulators (Braithwaite, 2009).

In regulation research, as is also the case in political science or public management research, hardly any attention is paid to regulators' generalized trust, or distrust, in regulatees. If measured at all, it is not called trust. Mascini and Van Wijk (2009, p. 33) found that 47 per cent of inspectors believed "there are more bad companies than good companies", i.e., showed generalized distrust towards regulatees, while only 31 per cent believed the opposite, showing generalized trust. What is the influence of inspector generalized trust versus distrust towards regulatees on the regulatory interaction and regulatee compliance? And equally what is the influence of regulatee generalized trust versus distrust towards regulators on the regulatory interaction and regulatee compliance?

Dealing with disruptions of trust

Trust research also shows that to build trust attention must not only be paid to the task at hand, but also to the relationship itself. Giving positive feedback and praise is among the most important relational behaviours that help build trust (e.g., Six and Sorge, 2008). The crux in repairing trust after a (perceived) trust violation is making clear that the person is okay, but the problem is with the behaviour (e.g., Makkai and Braithwaite, 1994; Six and Skinner, 2010). Reintegrative shaming disapproves of the behaviour while accepting the person, and disintegrative shaming disapproves of both behaviour and person. The former led to much better compliance in later interactions (Makkai and Braithwaite, 1994). Six and Van Ees (this volume) also show the importance of paying attention to the relationship as well as paying attention to the task at hand.

How may trust be repaired between organizations in a regulatory regime after a disruption? How and where, if at all, is this different from trust repair between collaborating business corporations or individuals?

Procedural justice

Several regulatory studies showed the importance of procedural justice (e.g., Haines and Gurney, 2003; Murphy et al., 2009; Tyler, 2006). But most of these studies are with individuals as regulatees, not organizations. It is likely, however, that procedural justice will also be important in regulatory relations with regulated organizations, but we do not know. What is the role of (perceived) procedural justice when the regulatees are organizations?

Organizational Level in Interorganizational Trust

Apart from the critique on RRT about underplaying the importance of actual processes of trust building and repair at the interpersonal level during inspections, RRT largely ignores the organizational dimension, for example that the next inspection may be performed by other inspectors and that for large regulated organizations the relations may be at different levels, both operational and strategic. Previous research also understudies this. Many chapters in this volume, however, contribute insight into the institutional framework in processes of trust building and repair.

Oomsels and Bouckaert (this volume) study the impact of macro-level factors more systematically in their multi-method study of interactions between public regulator and public regulatee in the Flanders public administration. They conclude that formal and informal institutional frameworks are important to interorganizational interactions as they facilitate trust building processes. Clear informal routines, values identification and knowledge about the other party's motivations were all examples of factors at this level that impacted trust building.

Näslund and Tamm Hallström (this volume) and Six and Van Ees (this volume) both focus on the consequences within the organizations. Näslund and Tamm Hallström (this volume) see a structural solution to the impossible "middle man position" by separating and decoupling the different tasks: setting standards, monitoring and communicating the judgement. Six and Van Ees (this volume) show the importance of being able to escalate between levels (operational, managerial, executive) when trouble occurred at the operational level. They propose that the more both parties create opportunities for constructive escalation and hold regular meetings aimed at improving relations, the more likely it is that trouble may be resolved and trust is repaired.

Other chapters identify the importance of neutral intermediaries to take away distrust, thus going beyond the organizational level within the two organizations involved in the trust relation and creating third parties. Mills and Reiss (this volume) observe that the federal regulator acknowledged the need for a neutral third party for voluntary disclosure programs to work, in their case NASA, to take away regulatee distrust and allow trust to be built. Van der Voort (this volume) stresses the crucial role that intermediaries play in building trust across the public–private divide in co-regulation.

Finally, Carter (this volume) shows how the effectiveness of a regulatory regime is very context-dependent. Copying a regulatory regime from one country (France) to another (Italy), without the same administrative heritage or degree of trust within the supply chain, is likely to fail. This may be important to remember as more and more regulation is agreed in international institutions, such as the European Union (see also some of the international comparative studies discussed in the introductory chapter, Six and Verhoest, this volume).

All these findings need to be tested and integrated into a coherent theory in further research.

RESOLVING CONCEPTUAL ISSUES

There are still several outstanding conceptual issues and the chapters in this volume have shed light on most of these outstanding issues, but have not been able to resolve them. This is not surprising given how long running these contestations are. We take stock of where we stand now in these debates. We identify three main outstanding conceptual issues: trust and distrust, trust and confidence, and trust and control that still need to be addressed in general but also in the context of regulation and regulatory regimes in particular.

Trust and Distrust

We realize that we may have a bias towards seeing the positive role that trust has to play in regulation, however complex it is to get it right in practice. Maybe, actually distrust is the better approach in regulation? Oomsels et al. (2016) showed, in line with Luhmann's (1979) argument, how both trust and distrust can be functional and dysfunctional, depending on the context. Is distrust more functional in regulatory contexts? If so, we need to better understand why in regulation this might be the case, while it is not in the rest of society. More research is needed to directly investigate the role of trust and distrust, and which works better when. And, most importantly, what impact each, trust and distrust, have on the core relation, the trust that citizens may have in the regulated organization. In other words, the degree to which trust or distrust within the different relations in the regulatory regime, help to reduce the vulnerability and uncertainty that citizens have, in whatever role, as employees, customers or neighbours, towards the regulated organization.

How exactly are trust and distrust related in the context of regulatory interactions? Are they at opposite ends of one continuum or are they independent concepts, like Lewicki et al. (1998) suggest, or even in a truncated form as Oomsels (2016) finds? Or is Lindenberg's (2000) concept of legitimate distrust situations a fruitful avenue, in which we first need to take away distrust before we can begin to build trust? Further research is needed for regulatory relations that are largely driven by impersonal trust.

Trust and Confidence

In the introduction Six and Verhoest (this volume) discuss the Trust, Confidence and Cooperation (TCC) model that is often used in risk management and is therefore relevant for research into the role of trust in regulatory regimes (Earle et al., 2007). They observe that there is currently conceptual confusion over the distinction between trust and confidence as some prominent trust researchers seem to have moved towards calling everything trust (e.g., Bachmann, 2011; Dietz, 2011; Kroeger, 2012), while others have moved towards sharpening the divide (most notably Earle et al., 2007) and attaching more meaning to confidence than Luhmann (1988) did originally. This is another topic of contestation. In several languages this distinction is even impossible because both confidence and trust translate into the same word (e.g., in Dutch both translate into *vertrouwen*). Further empirical *and* conceptual research is needed especially in the context of regulatory relations, together with researchers being more explicit about how they use the two concepts. We need to examine in detail whether the explanations provided are largely similar, just using different terminology; or whether there are fundamental differences. If the latter, further research is needed to examine which model has the better explanatory power, possibly distinguishing in which context.

Trust and Control

Related to the two previous conceptual issues is the issue of the relation between trust and control. There are two perspectives of the relationship between trust and control. In the dominant perspective, trust and control are substitutes, either you trust and do not control, or you control and do not trust. This perspective seems to also be dominant in regulation literature. In the other perspective trust and control may complement each other, provided certain conditions are met. Six (2013) showed that it is very plausible that the conditions under which trust and control actually strengthen each other, as found in manager–subordinate relations, also apply to regulatory relations. Six, however, does not problematize the difference between trust between individuals, as is the case in the manager–subordinate relation – and trust between organizations, as is the case in most regulatory relations. Several of the chapters in this volume suggest further empirical support (e.g., Mills and Reiss) for Six's (2013) model, however, a direct empirical test has yet to be performed and further conceptual work is needed to account for the organizational context.

Further research is needed to specify in more detail how exactly these three conceptual issues – trust or distrust, trust or confidence and trust–control relationship – interact in general and in regulatory interactions in particular.

TOWARDS BUILDING THEORY FOR TRUST IN REGULATORY REGIMES

In this volume we brought together the current state of knowledge on the role of trust in regulatory regimes. Overall, the conclusion is that there is a fair amount of mainly exploratory research into many different relationships and different issues related to this topic. The chapters in this volume contribute to this body of knowledge. We argue that the field is now ready to move towards more systematic theory building and more consistency in the use of the different concepts involved (trust, distrust, confidence, regulation, control). Ideally the field should move towards consensus on this, but that is probably out of reach. So in the meantime all researchers need to be explicit about the assumptions and conceptualizations in their studies, so that when comparative research is done, or meta-analyses performed, apples and apples are compared where possible.

Methodologically, we believe that the field is ready to move beyond exploratory research to more systematic theory building and testing, using a wider range of methods, including quantitative methods, regression analyses and structural equation modelling, and qualitative comparative analysis (for small and larger N-studies). At the same time, interpretive methods are also necessary to deepen our understanding of the sense making processes involved in processes of trust building and repair. Participant observer studies, like Baekkeskov's (this volume) may be difficult to realize, due to the difficulty of gaining access, but are very valuable especially for longitudinally investigating regulatory processes. Nested Mixed-Method Research Designs, as used by Oomsels and Bouckaert (this volume), seek to combine the advantages of quantitative and qualitative methods by selecting small-N qualitative cases on the basis of quantitative large-N research results. Such approaches may be key to strengthening the external validity and generalizability of deep, qualitative insights into the causal mechanisms of trust building and repair.

It is our hope that this volume and its chapters provide inspiration and enthusiasm to researchers to design and conduct future studies on the role and dynamics of trust in regulatory systems.

REFERENCES

Abbot, C. (2012), 'Bridging the gap – non-state actors and the challenges of regulating new technology', *Journal of Law and Society*, **39**(3), 329–358.
Aubin, D. and K. Verhoest (eds) (2014), *Multilevel regulation in telecommunications:*

Adaptive regulatory arrangements in Belgium, Ireland, the Netherlands, and Switzerland, Basingstoke: Palgrave Macmillan.

Ayres, I. and J. Braithwaite (1992), *Responsive regulation: Transcending the deregulation debate*, New York: Oxford University Press.

Bach, T. and E. Ruffing (2013), 'Networking for autonomy? National agencies in European networks', *Public Administration*, **91**, 712–726.

Bachmann, R. (2011), 'At the crossroads: future directions in trust research', *Journal of Trust Research*, **1**(2), 203–213.

Boin, A., M. Busuioc and M. Groenleer (2014), 'Building European Union capacity to manage transboundary crises: Network or lead-agency model?', *Regulation & Governance*, **8**, 418–436.

Bozeman, B. (2013), 'What organization theorists and public policy researchers can learn from one another: Publicness theory as a case-in-point', *Organization Studies*, **34**(2), 169–188.

Braithwaite, V. (2009), *Defiance in taxation and governance: Resisting and dismissing authority in a democracy*, Cheltenham, UK and Northampton, MA, USA: Edward Elgar Publishing.

Braun, C. (2012), 'The captive or the broker? Explaining public agency-interest group interactions', *Governance*, **25**(2), 291–314.

Brown, J. and J. Kuzma (2013), 'Hungry for information: Public attitudes toward food nanotechnology and labeling', *Review of Policy Research*, **30**(5), 512–548.

Busuioc, E.M. (2016), 'Friend or foe? Inter-agency cooperation, organizational reputation, and turf', *Public Administration*, **94**, 40–56.

Carpenter, D.P. and G.A. Krause (2012), 'Reputation and public administration', *Public Administration Review*, **72**, 26–32.

Carter, D.P. (2016), 'Public, nonprofit, and for-profit sector regulatory approaches in third-party regulatory administration', *Journal of Public Administration Research and Theory*, first published online April 16, 2016.

Dabbah, M.M. (2011), 'The relationship between competition authorities and sector regulators', *The Cambridge Law Journal*, **70**, 113–143.

Dal Bo, E. (2006), 'Regulatory capture: A review', *Oxford Review of Economic Policy*, **22** (2), 203–225.

Dietz, G. (2011), 'Going back to the source: Why do people trust each other?', *Journal of Trust Research*, **1**(2), 215–222.

Dirks, K.T., P.H. Kim, D.L. Ferrin and C.D. Cooper (2011), 'Understanding the effects of substantive responses on trust following a transgression', *Organizational Behavior and Human Decision Processes*, **114**(2), 87–103.

Earle, T.C., M. Siegristand H. Gutscher (2007), 'Trust, risk perception, and the TCC model of cooperation', in M. Siegrist, T.C. Earle and H. Gutscher (eds), *Trust in cooperative risk management*, London: Earthscan, pp. 1–49.

Freeman, J. and J. Rossi (2012), 'Agency coordination in shared regulatory space', *Harvard Law Review*, **125**(5), 1131–1209.

Gillespie, N. and G. Dietz (2009), 'Trust repair after an organization-level failure', *Academy of Management Review*, **34**(1), 127–145.

Gouldson, A. (2004), 'Cooperation and the capacity for control: Regulatory styles and the evolving influence of environmental regulations in the UK', *Environment and Planning C-Government and Policy*, **22**(4), 583–603.

Haines, F. and D. Gurney (2003), 'The shadows of the law: Contemporary approaches to regulation and the problem of regulatory conflict', *Law & Policy*, **25**(4), 353–380.

Holm, L. and B. Halkier (2009), 'EU food safety policy, localising contested governance', *European Societies*, **11**(4), 473–493.

Kim, P.H., C.D. Cooper, K.T. Dirks and D.L. Ferrin (2013), 'Repairing trust with individuals vs groups', *Organizational Behavior and Human Decision Processes*, **120**(1), 1–14.

Kroeger, F. (2012), 'Trusting organizations: The institutionalization of trust in interorganizational relationships', *Organization*, **19**(6), 743–763.

Levi-Faur, D. (2011), 'Regulatory networks and regulatory agencification: Towards a Single European Regulatory Space', *Journal of European Public Policy*, **18**(6), 810–829.

Levine, M.E. and J.L. Forrence (1990), 'Regulatory capture, public interest, and the public agenda. Toward a synthesis', *Journal of Law Economics & Organization*, **6**, 167–198.

Lewicki, R.J. and B.B. Bunker (1996), 'Developing and maintaining trust in work relationships', in R.M. Kramer and T.R. Tyler (eds), *Trust in organizations: Frontiers of theory and research*, Thousand Oaks: Sage Publications, pp. 114–139.

Lewicki, R.J., D.J. McAllister and R.J. Bies (1998), 'Trust and distrust: New relationships and realities', *Academy of Management Review*, **23**(3), 438–458.

Lindenberg, S. (2000), 'It takes both trust and lack of mistrust: The workings of cooperation and relational signaling in contractual relationships', *Journal of Management and Governance*, **4**, 11–33.

Luhmann, N. (1979), *Trust and power*, Chicester: John Wiley & Sons.

Luhmann, N. (1988), 'Familiarity, confidence and trust: Problems and alternatives', in D.Gambetta (ed.), *Trust: Making and breaking cooperative relations*, New York, NY: Basil Blackwell, pp. 94–108.

Luoma-aho, V. (2008), 'Sector reputation and public organisations', *International Journal of Public Sector Management*, **21**(5), 446–467.

Maggetti, M. and F. Gilardi (2014), 'Network governance and the domestic adoption of soft rules', *Journal of European Public Policy*, **21**(9), 1293–1310.

Makkai, T. and J. Braithwaite (1994), 'Reintegrative shaming and compliance with regulatory standards', *Criminology*, **32**, 361–385.

Mascini, P. and E. Van Wijk (2009), 'Responsive regulation at the Dutch food and consumer product safety authority: An empirical assessment of assumptions underlying the theory', *Regulation & Governance*, **3**, 27–47.

Mayer, R.C., J.H. Davis and F.D. Schoorman (1995), 'An integrative model of organizational trust', *Academy of Management Review*, **20**(3), 703–734.

McPhilemy, S. (2013), 'Formal rules versus informal relationships: Prudential banking supervision at the FSA before the crash', *New Political Economy*, **18**(5), 748–767.

Murphy, K., T.R. Tyler and A. Curtis (2009), 'Nurturing regulatory compliance: Is procedural justice effective when people question the legitimacy of the law?', *Regulation & Governance*, **3**(1), 1–26.

Nooteboom, B. (1999), 'The triangle: Roles of the go-between', in R.T.A.J. Leenders and S.M. Gabbay (eds), *Corporate social capital and liability*, Boston: Kluwer Academic Publishers, pp. 341–355.

O'Leary, R. and N. Vij (2012), 'Collaborative public management: Where have we been and where are we going?', *The American Review of Public Administration*, **42**(5), 507–522.

Oomsels, P. (2016), *Administrational trust: An empirical examination of interorganisational trust and distrust in the Flemish administration*, Leuven: KU Leuven.

Oomsels, P., M. Callens, J. Vanschoenwinkel and G. Bouckaert (2016), 'Functions and dysfunctions of interorganizational trust and distrust in the public sector', *Administration & Society*, prepublished September 8.

Rommel, J. (2012), *Organisation and management of regulation, autonomy and coordination in a multi-actor setting*, Leuven: Katholieke Universiteit Leuven.

Rousseau, D.M., S.B. Sitkin, R.S. Burt and C. Camerer (1998), 'Not so different after all. A cross-discipline view of trust', *Academy of Management Review*, **23**, 393–404.

Shapiro, S.P. (1987), 'The social control of impersonal trust', *American Journal of Sociology*, **93**(3), 623–658.

Six, F.E. (2005), *The trouble with trust: The dynamics of interpersonal trust building*, Cheltenham, UK and Northampton, MA, USA: Edward Elgar Publishing.

Six, F.E. (2013), 'Trust in regulatory relations: How new insights from trust research improve regulation theory', *Public Management Review*, **15**(2), 163–185

Six, F.E. and D. Skinner (2010), 'Managing trust and trouble in interpersonal work relationships: Evidence from two Dutch organizations', *International Journal of Human Resource Management*, **21**(1), 109–124.

Six, F. E. and A. Sorge (2008), 'Creating a high-trust organization: An exploration into organizational policies that stimulate interpersonal trust building', *Journal of Management Studies*, **45**(5), 857–884.

Temby, O., A. Rastogi, J. Sandall, R. Cooksey and G.M. Hickey (2015), 'Interagency trust and communication in the transboundary governance of Pacific salmon fisheries', *Review of Policy Research*, **32**, 79–99.

Tyler, T.R. (2006), *Why people obey the law* (2nd ed.), Princeton: Princeton University Press.

Van de Walle, S. and G. Bouckaert (2003), 'Public service performance and trust in government: The problem of causality', *International Journal of Public Administration*, **26**(8 and 9), 891–913.

Van Ryzin, G.G. (2011), 'Outcomes, process, and trust of civil servants', *Journal of Public Administration Research and Theory*, **21**(4), 745–760.

Verhoest, K., J. Rommel and J. Boon (2015), 'How organizational reputation and trust may affect autonomy of independent regulators? The case of the Flemish energy regulator', in A. Waeraas and M. Maor (eds), *Organizational reputation in the public sector*, London: Routledge, pp. 118–138.

Winter, S. and P.J. May (2001), 'Motivation for compliance with environmental regulations', *Journal of Policy Analysis and Management*, **20**(4), 675–698.

Index